"Since the medieval period, Christians and Muslims have been dialoguing about the nature of God. Carefully working through the thought of medieval Arab Christians, Sherene Khouri shows how they articulated and defended the Trinity in their contexts. This study offers wisdom for Christians today discussing God's relationality with Muslim friends."

Edward Smither, dean of the College of Intercultural Studies, Columbia International University

"Most Western Christians are unaware that Christianity predates Islam on the Arabian peninsula, that Christians interacted intellectually with Arabs in the centuries after the rise of Islam, that much of this interaction consisted of discussions about the Trinity, and that Christians in the region even adopted Arabic as their spoken and written language. For modern Christians interacting with Muslims today, the history of the early interchanges between the two faiths is crucially important. Furthermore, modern Christians who seek to articulate the doctrine of the Trinity in a world that regards it as nonsense would do well to draw on the riches of early Arab Christian writing on this most central doctrine of our faith, in response to their neighbors who also thought this doctrine was illogical. For both sets of modern readers, this book provides a great service as it describes the Christian understanding of God, who is intrinsically and eternally relational, in contrast to the Muslim conception of Allah as merely contingently relational."

Donald Fairbairn, Robert E. Cooley Professor of Early Christianity at Gordon-Conwell Theological Seminary and author of *Life in the Trinity*

"Sherene's insights on the Trinity were gained through a combination of God's providential hand in her life and her personal thirst for the truth of God. We are all privileged to have the result of God's grace and Sherene's diligence as expressed in this fine work. I share with Sherene in prayer and in hope that this work will accelerate the necessary dialogue between Christians, Muslims, and all who seek to know God better."

Gaylen P. Leverett, professor and faculty chaplain at Liberty University

"*Triune Relationality* shares with readers the riches of Eastern Christian theological tradition. As Christians today reflect on dialogue with Islam, they will benefit immensely from Khouri's thoughtful presentation of three Christian theological masters who lived under early Muslim rule and defended not only the coherence but also the beauty of Christian doctrine on the Trinity and the incarnation."

Gabriel Said Reynolds, Crowley Professor of Islamic Studies and Theology at the University of Notre Dame

"This book on the oneness of God links the past and the present. It adds to the recent trend of drawing attention to Eastern writers of the past who can speak to Western and other readers in the present. Khouri introduces us to sometimes complex terrain, yet we emerge not only with ideas clarified but with a renewed sense of the importance of the topic."

Martin Whittingham, academic dean at the Centre for Muslim-Christian Studies Oxford

"Dr. Khouri launches her book with a much-needed survey of the literature covering the logical, historical, and apologetic treatment of Islam's objection to the Trinity during the zenith of Islamic scholarship in the Abbasid caliphate. This leads to an investigation of the trinitarian apologetics of John of Damascus, Theodore Abū Qurrah, and Yahyā Ibn ʿAdī. The book climactically endorses the conclusion espoused by recent Arab theologians that the true God cannot be perfect unless he is relational in himself, so that the Trinity is not a problem to be solved but rather a beauty to be discovered."

Imad N. Shehadeh, president and professor of theology at Jordan Evangelical Theological Seminary

NEW EXPLORATIONS IN THEOLOGY

TRIUNE RELATIONALITY

A TRINITARIAN RESPONSE TO ISLAMIC MONOTHEISM

SHERENE NICHOLAS KHOURI

Foreword by Gary R. Habermas

IVP Academic
An imprint of InterVarsity Press
Downers Grove, Illinois

InterVarsity Press
P.O. Box 1400 | Downers Grove, IL 60515-1426
ivpress.com | email@ivpress.com

InterVarsity Press® is the publishing division of InterVarsity Christian Fellowship/USA®. For more information, visit intervarsity.org.

Cover design: David Fassett
Interior design: Daniel van Loon
Image: © Germán Vogel / Moment / Getty Images

ISBN 978-1-5140-0884-3 (print) | ISBN 978-1-5140-0885-0 (digital)

Printed in the United States of America ♾

Library of Congress Cataloging-in-Publication Data
A catalog record for this book is available from the Library of Congress.

31 30 29 28 27 26 25 24 | 12 11 10 9 8 7 6 5 4 3 2 1

To the soul of my father, Elias,

my mother, Laila, and my husband, Daniel

Contents

Foreword by Gary R. Habermas ix

Acknowledgments xi

Introduction 1

1 The Rise of the Abbasids and the Golden Age of Islam 25

2 The Iconoclastic Effect of the Qur'anic Perception of the Trinity 53

3 The Christian Explanation of the Trinity in the Eighth, Ninth, and Tenth Centuries 81

4 Western Contemporary Explanations of the Trinity 120

5 A Contemporary Christian Answer to Islamic Objections Against the Trinity 153

Conclusion 181

Bibliography 195

General Index 207

Scripture Index 209

Foreword

Gary R. Habermas

There are a number of reasons why Christian logical, theological, historical, and other apologetic treatments of Islam are crucial in the world today. That Islam is usually counted as having the second largest religious following of all the world religions alone makes this topic important. Further, fewer publications on this subject are available as compared to many other key apologetic topics, some of which may be thought to be overly saturated. In fact, even with Christians who publish on world religious apologetics, Islam may not be the most plentiful pursuit focus. Moreover, it appears that this is a very difficult area in Christian missions, especially with a number of closed Islamic nations. But persons involved in this ministry presumably need strong materials to digest and utilize. Further, fewer of these treatments are written by authors who were raised in the Middle East, which helps to facilitate vital subjects such as language, theological and social understandings of the culture, and how doctrinal discussions transpire.

Last, the Trinity is the most frequent objection to Christianity raised by Muslims, and few volumes treat this theological subject in relation to the Islamic objections. Other factors could be raised, as well, but these are sufficient to make Sherene Khouri's treatment in *Triune Relationality* a crucial one on the current scene.

Khouri's work developed from her PhD dissertation, which is still another important angle. Her critiques throughout concern the four areas mentioned above, namely, logic, theology, history, and providing still other apologetic inroads. As reflected in the title of the volume, her treatment of the differences between the orthodox theologies of the respective views of God in the Christian understanding of the Trinity and the Islamic denial of this position forms the crux of this work. But these other subjects above all work together throughout, both as relevant considerations within the main topic and as separate critiques and discussion points in themselves. The upshot of these focal points joins together at many relevant angles that contribute to the whole, including the Islamic understanding of the Trinity as involving Mary the mother of Jesus (Isa), semantic differentiations concerning members of the Trinity, and logical questions, such as how can three persons still be considered as one God, as monotheism requires.

Two major purposes are addressed and accented throughout this text. One major theme is to defend and advance the understanding of the trinitarian nature of God. The other chief idea is to provide answers to strict monotheistic (absolute oneness) worldviews that reject the Trinity due to many common misunderstandings of what orthodox Christian theologians actually teach on this doctrine.

Khouri's work can be a challenging read for those who are not as versed as she is in matters such as the original Arabic terms, as well as other areas. Yet traversing these waters can provide an overview of the relevant charges, countercharges, and explanations and defenses for those who desire more depth on these subjects. Those with these interests have much to gain from reading Khouri's publication.

Acknowledgments

FIRST AND FOREMOST, I thank God for helping me immensely during this journey by bringing many special people into my life. The whole project is done to glorify and honor his name.

This book is dedicated to my husband, Daniel Khouri. You have been my source of inspiration and support through this long journey. Your enduring love, patience, and encouragement helped me make this project a reality. I am truly blessed to be your wife and partner in life.

To the soul of my father, Elias Nicholas, who is unfortunately not with us to see and celebrate this accomplishment. He was my supporter right from the beginning, and I am so blessed to be his daughter. Without him, I could not have had the discipline to achieve this accomplishment. My father played a major role in my life because of his highly disciplined personality. He taught me how important it is to be diligent in everything I do and how vital it is to inspire others and leave a legacy.

To my mother Laila and my siblings, Iyad, Ihab, and Nisrine. Despite the distance, you were a great source of help. I could not survive without my mother's prayers and encouragement. Thank you Nisrine for the endless conversations that we had, in which you opened my eyes to many facts. I am so blessed to have you in my life as my twin sister and my best friend.

This work is also the result of the immense help and encouragement of my second mother, Margie Zacharias, which was encouraging me since my first day in higher education.

I want to thank my PhD committee and Dr. Gaylen Leverett, who has been alongside me since the beginning of my writing journey. I would like to thank Dr. Gary Habermas for his encouragement during classes and for the wealth of knowledge that he has poured into his students. I'm so grateful for his foreword to this book, which prayerfully will help me reach a wider audience. Special thanks go to Ki Won Seo and Ruth Buchanan for their great support. I will always be in debt to the people whom God placed in my life. Without them, this book would have never seen the light.

Introduction

FROM HUMANKIND'S EARLIEST HISTORY, philosophers and theologians have pondered the nature of God. Is God a mystery, or can he be known? If he can be known, what are his nature, attributes, and characteristics? What is his relationship to creation, and how is he supposed to be worshiped? Several religions came up with different answers to these questions and diverging understandings of the nature of the deity.

The Christian understanding of the divine nature is trinitarian (Mt 28:18-20; Mk 14:62; Jn 1:1; 20:28; Rom 9:5; 1 Cor 8:6; Phil 2:6-9; Titus 2:13; Heb 1:1-3; Rev 1:5-9; 22:13). God lives forever in intrarelationship, never alone because he is one God living in an eternal coinhering community of equals. Christians settled their debates about the trinitarian nature of God in the Nicene Creed in AD 325 and 381 and about the nature of Jesus in the council of Chalcedon in AD 451. However, when Muslims expanded beyond the Arabian Peninsula and invaded the Levant (contemporary Syria, Palestine, Lebanon, and Jordan), Arabophone Christian theologians and philosophers found themselves obligated to defend the Trinity against *tawḥid* (the absolute oneness of Allah)—the Islamic understanding of the divine.[1] Allah is alone—without a partner, rival, or equal.

In the West, scholars were not in touch with Muslims in the same capacity, but they wanted to preserve the orthodox belief of the Trinity by following the Nicene Creed. Therefore, they strived to show that the Trinity is not a contradiction. During the Enlightenment, many wrote about it to refute liberal scholars, such as Kant and his infamous pronouncement that the doctrine of the Trinity, taken literally, has no practical relevance to the

[1]Surah Muminoon 23:84-89; Surah az-Zukhruf 43:9; Surah az-Zukhruf 43:87; Surah al-Ankaboot 29:63; Surah az-Zumar 39:3; Surah Yunus 10:18; Surah al-Kafiroon 109:2-5; Surah Sad 38:5; Surah al-Mumtahinah 60:24; Surah al-Fath 48:6.

Christian consciousness. Today, scholars see a great relevance and high importance of this doctrine and consider it the foundation of other doctrines, especially the morality of God. As Thomas R. Thompson says, the doctrine of the Trinity is "a veritable treasure trove of ethical and practical riches, not least of which is its redolence for human social form and function."[2]

In the Middle East, in around AD 750, the Abbasids overthrew the Umayyad caliphate and reigned until they were destroyed by the Mongols in AD 1258. This period is known as the Golden Age of Islamic scholarship because of the translation movements that took place. This movement began with the Arabization of the administration of the empire by the Umayyad caliph ʿAbd al-Malik ibn Marwan (AD 646–705) in the seventh century. This movement made Arabic the Muslim lingua franca. Up to this point, Christian communities had preserved Greek learning in their libraries and monasteries in Alexandria, Antioch, and Edessa. They also taught and wrote their theological works in Greek; therefore, they were able to contribute to this translation movement by translating many philosophical, medical, and religious books from Greek to Arabic and participate in the dialogue between Christians and Muslims.

This era witnessed many conversations and discussions between Muslims and Christians about the nature of the deity in each religion. This dialogue served as an instrument by which authors would intellectually verify and defend their positions while critiquing their opponent's worldview. During this period, many Christian theologians and philosophers left written documents explaining the differences of the nature of Allah (both were calling God *Allah* in Arabic) and defending the Trinity. This study will focus primarily on two Christian theologians—John of Damascus (died in AD 749) and Theodore Abū Qurrah (died in AD 820)—as well as one Christian philosopher—Yaḥyā Ibn ᶜAdī (died AD 974).[3] These three Christian scholars came from different backgrounds and defended the Trinity in three dissimilar constructions.

The history of Christian-Muslim relations, especially in the Abbasid era, sheds great light on the interreligious dialogue between Christians and

---

[2]Thomas R. Thompson, "Trinitarianism Today: Doctrinal Renaissance, Ethical Relevance, Social Redolence," *Calvin Theological Journal* 32 (1997): 10.

[3]John of Damascus is also known as John Damascene. I will refer to him as John.

Muslims. It provides contemporary Christians with many insights for interacting fruitfully and effectively with Muslims without compromising the nature of the Christian gospel. Today's Christians might not realize that early Arab Christians faced several objections to the Trinity when Islam expanded to the Levant. This study, therefore, aims to prevent contemporary Christians from reinventing the wheel and missing the positive contributions of early Christian-Muslim history.

After considering these early Arab scholars, I will explore themes in contemporary trinitarian arguments in the West. Several scholars who are immersed in philosophy, especially metaphysics, came out with many models that help explain the Trinity in a logical and philosophical way. The book will focus on three different models to help readers compare the Arabic and Western explanations of the doctrine of the Trinity: social trinitarianism, Latin trinitarianism, and the relative identity theory. This study will present the theory that the orthodox doctrine of the Trinity has never changed throughout history. Christians have never stopped believing or defending it.

Rationale and Need

This study relates to the philosophy of religion, to theology, and to medieval Christian history. The book will cover the times between the end of the Umayyad and early Abbasid dynasties. The period between the eighth and the tenth centuries, known as the Golden Age of Islam, is considered an illustrious period of Muslim-Christian interaction. As mentioned above, the early centuries of the Abbasid era were a period when Muslims became increasingly eager to validate their beliefs in light of the challenges confronting them by more educated Christians. The doctrine of the Trinity is one of these challenges, and it is inevitably discussed in terms of the *sifat Allah* (the beautiful names of God) found in the Qur'an. During that time, the Arabic church produced several theologians and philosophers eager to answer the trinitarian theological objection, and thus their works deserve to be known in the West.

The academy needs Eastern Christian scholars; their expertise would be especially beneficial because research in this area is still in its infancy. Unfortunately, few academics write on John of Damascus, Theodore Abū Qurrah, and Yaḥyā Ibn ᶜAdī; the ones who do are mostly Arabs, and many of their studies are not translated to English. Few Western scholars have attempted to introduce and translate their works and they are still, in my opinion, underrepresented in Western scholarship. This study therefore attempts to bridge the gap between the East and the West by shedding light on the Islamic context of Arab scholars and how they were able to defend their Christian faith.

Despite the primary and secondary resources available on John of Damascus, Theodore Abū Qurrah, and Yaḥyā Ibn ᶜAdī, there are not many academic works written on their arguments for the Trinity, especially when compared to those of early, medieval, and Reformed theologians, such as Augustine, Aquinas, and Calvin. A small number of monographs were written on the life and the work of each of these scholars, but few focused on their methodology in examining and explaining the Trinity in their Islamic surroundings. To my knowledge, no scholars have used or developed the arguments of these three Arab scholars to defend the Trinity.

In addition to reporting the historical data that is collected from Arabic and non-Arabic resources of John of Damascus, Theodore Abū Qurrah, and Yaḥyā Ibn ᶜAdī, this book will seek to trace the sources of the Islamic Trinity in the Qur'an, especially the idea of including Mary in the Trinity.[4] This investigation is needed because a few studies have stated that Mohammad derived his information from cultic Christianity that was spreading in the Arabian Peninsula at that time. Although this hypothesis might be true, there might be another influence on Mohammad's belief, one related to the veneration of icons in the church. Therefore, this study shall investigate the possible influence of the *Theotokos* icons and how their presence in cathedrals came to influence Muslim understanding of the veneration of Mary and their eventual inclusion of her in the Trinity. To my knowledge, no other studies have investigated this influence.

The value of this study is to bring Eastern and Western scholarship together by shedding light on an area of history that is ambiguous and not very well known. The book will also be beneficial for those who want to compare and contrast the Arabic and Western scholarships on the doctrine of the Trinity. I hope that this study becomes a great aid for scholars of history,

[4]The Trinity as it is understood in the Qur'an.

theology, and apologetics as they seek to develop their arguments about the Trinity. Even laymen would benefit greatly from understanding the history behind the current defense of the Trinity and learn how to defend the Trinity themselves in Islamic context.

Research Problem, Sub-questions, Limitations, and Terms

The main question this book is asking is this: "Does the Trinity make sense?" Christians and Muslims agree that human beings will never fully perceive God in their minds. For both, God is an unlimited, infinite, divine being, and they are limited, finite, human beings. However, while Muslims think that God should make sense in order for human beings to believe in him, Christians believe that human beings are capable of perceiving limited aspects of God—the ones that he has revealed to them. Founding their belief on the biblical data, the early church perceived God as trinitarian in nature. Today, Christians still accept the Nicene and the Chalcedonian definitions of God as a Trinity and consider them logical. They believe that the Trinity makes perfect sense based on the relational aspect of God's nature. To address whether the Trinity makes sense, sub-questions should be asked further: How do Muslims and Christians perceive the Trinity? How do the Arab medieval fathers, such as John of Damascus, Theodore Abū Qurrah, and Yaḥyā Ibn ᶜAdī, understand and explain the Trinity to Muslims? How do they differ and agree with the Nicene and the Chalcedonian creeds? Do their perceptions of the Trinity vary among each other? How do contemporary scholars explain the Trinity? How can contemporary scholars benefit from the Arabic explanations of the Trinity?

This study does not seek to criticize the Islamic belief in *tawḥīd* as much as it attempts to further the dialogue between the two religions. It does not intend to investigate whether Christians and Muslims believe in the same God. However, since this topic is related to the book, it will appear in the conclusion. The principal aim is to inform the reader of the historical contexts of John of Damascus, Theodore Abū Qurrah, and Yaḥyā Ibn ᶜAdī. The study will examine how they defended the Trinity in their medieval Islamic surroundings and will build on their arguments to further the conversation with contemporary Muslims. Furthermore, the study does not seek to redefine the historical understanding of Trinitarian orthodoxy or come up with a new perception. The book will adhere to the Nicene and the Chalcedonian definitions of the apostolic faith, which are based on the Bible.

Since the book does not aim to compare *tawḥīd* and the Trinity, the use of polemic language against Islamic theology and its understanding of *tawḥīd* will be minimized, except for language used by the three chosen scholars in their arguments. The Western trinitarian arguments do not mention Islamic belief. They focus primarily on philosophical understanding of the doctrine. In the final section of the study, the relational aspect of the nature of God will be emphasized. This emphasis might be perceived by some as a criticism of *tawḥīd*.

In these discussions, the book will use Greek, Arabic, and English terms related to the topic of the Trinity: Greek terms such as *Theotokos, hypostasis, ousia*, and *perichoresis*; and Arabic terms such as *Uqnūm* (singular) / *Aqanīm* (plural) اقنوم/أقانيم and *Asma' Allah al-Ḥusna* [the beautiful names of Allah] أسماء الله الحسنى.

According to the *Oxford Dictionary of the Christian Church*, *Theotokos* means "the 'one who gave birth to God.' . . . The word was used of the Virgin by the Greek Fathers (perhaps by Origen and possibly even by Hippolytus) and increasingly became a popular term of devotion)."[5] This word will appear in the section in which the investigation about the Islamic Trinity is made.

According to the *Evangelical Dictionary of Theology*, the literal meaning of the Greek word *hypostasis* is "'substance,' 'nature,' 'essence' (from *hyphistasthai*, 'stand under,' 'subsist,' which is from *hypo*, 'under,' and *histanai* 'cause to stand'), and denotes a real personal subsistence or person."[6] The word developed theologically to describe any one of the three distinct subsistences/persons of God. Later on in history, it is used more to refer to the hypostatic union of the two natures of Christ (human and divine).

In the Council of Nicaea, *hypostasis* is taken as a synonym of *ousia* (substance). However, after Nicaea,

> The Cappadocians established a clear distinction between ousia as the name for what is common to the Persons of the Trinity, and hypostasis as the

---

[5]F. L. Cross and Elizabeth A. Livingstone, eds., *The Oxford Dictionary of the Christian Church* (Oxford: Oxford University Press, 2005), 1619.

[6]W. E. Ward, s.v. "Hypostasis," in *Evangelical Dictionary of Theology*, ed. Walter A. Elwell (Grand Rapids, MI: Baker Books, 2013). Accessed through Credo Reference online.

> name for their distinctness: each Person is a hypostasis precisely to the extent that it is characterized by specific individuating characteristics (or idiomata). The Son, for example, is everything that the Father is (i.e., with respect to ousia) except that the Son is begotten and the Father the one who begets (the particular characteristics of their respective hypostases).[7]

This is the meaning the author will follow in this study. The formula of one *ousia*/three *hypostases* was translated into Latin as "*una essential/substantia, tres personae*" or "one essence/substance in three persons."[8]

Perichoresis is a theological term that describe the relational aspect of the Trinity. As Randall Otto puts it, it is "the necessary being-in-one-another or circumincession of the three divine Persons of the Trinity because of the single divine essence."[9] It is the intertwining, inexistence, and immanence of the divine Persons. According to Thomas H. McCall, "The divine hypostases are genuinely distinct, and they are related to one another in the interpersonal *perichōrēsis* of holy love."[10] The divine persons are three fully personal and fully divine entities who know and love one another. While this concept existed in patristic thought, the term *perichoresis* was popularized in the eighth century by John of Damascus. Some modern theologians, such as Jürgen Moltmann, have used this term in a different sense that denies its basis in the one divine nature; however, this book will use it in the historical sense used by the patristic fathers.

Ousia or essence denotes the "whatness" of a thing. It designates the real being of God. According to Francis Turretin, the essence is "often met with in Scripture, not only in the concrete when God is cladded on (Ex 3:14; Rev 1:4), but also in the abstract when deity (*theotēs*, Col 2:9), nature (*physis*, Gal 4:8), divine nature (*theia physis*, 2 Pet 1:4) is attributed to God."[11]

Uqnūm/*Aqanīm* (singular/plural) is attributed to the three persons of the Trinity. Instead of using the word "person/s" in Arabic or Syriac, Arab and

---

[7]Mike Higton, s.v. "Hypostasis" in *Cambridge Dictionary of Christian Theology*, ed. Ian A. McFarland et al. (Cambridge: Cambridge University Press, 2011). Accessed through Credo Reference online.

[8]Ward, "Hypostasis."

[9]Otto, Randall E., "The Use and Abuse of Perichoresis in Recent Theology," *Scottish Journal of Theology* 54, no. 3 (2001): 366-84.

[10]Thomas H. McCall, "Relational Trinity: Creedal Perspective," in *Two Views on The Doctrine of the Trinity* (Grand Rapids, MI: Zondervan, 2014), 129.

[11]James T. Dennison Jr., ed., *Francis Turretin Institutes of Elenctic Theology*, trans. George Musgrave Giger, vol. 1 (Phillipsburg, NJ: P&R, 1992), 253.

Syriac theologians created a new word, *Uqnūm/Aqanīm*, and dedicated it to the persons of the Trinity. *Uqnūm/Aqanīm* is a word early Arab fathers used in the defense of the Trinity that they took from their fellow Syriac theologians to express the difference in meaning between the human person and the divine person. James Sweetman mentions that the Syriac word ܩܢܘܡܐ *uqnūm* was accepted and widely used without causing any debate or quarrel because of its use in the Syriac translation of John 5:26.[12] This is important to establish because the word *Uqnūm/Aqanīm* will be used repeatedly in this study.

Arab-Syriac apologists believe that it is hard for Muslims to understand the concept of the Trinity in a metaphysical sense as opposed to a simple numerical one. Therefore, they decided to create a new word to convey the idea of divine person and illuminate the similarities with the concept of a human person as they understood it. According to Imad Shehadeh, a leading contemporary scholar on the subject of the Trinity in Jordan, "The only benefit from using this word [*uqnūm*] in Arabic language is to distance the word 'person' from God and substitute it with a foreign and an unknown word that conveys its meaning."[13] In other words, dedicating a special terminology to divine person indicates a special meaning and illustrates the confusion Muslims faced regarding the human/physical meaning of the word *person*. Furthermore, Awad Sim'an, who is a leading Arab Christian scholar on the subject of the Trinity in Egypt, defines *Aqanīm* in the following way:

> The word *Aqanīm* differs totally from the word "persons," the one that is used in Arabic language and its synonyms in other languages, in two ways: a) "persons" have separate essences from each other. Whereas, *Aqanīm* means one essence, which is the essence of God who does not have associates, or anyone like him. b) Even if persons participate in one nature, none of them has the same qualities, attributes, or characteristics of the others. Whereas regarding the *Aqanīm*, despite the fact that they are distinct from each other regarding the person, they are one in essence with all its qualities, attributes, and characteristics of the other because they are the essence of the one God.[14]

---

[12]James W. Sweetman, *Islam and Christian Theology: A Study of the Interpretation of Theological Ideas in the Two Religions*, vol. 2 (London: Lutterworth Press, 1945), 225-26.

[13]Imad Shehadeh, *al-Aab wa al-Ibn was al-Roḥ al-Qudus ilah waḥid, amin: Daroret al-Ta'adudiya fi al-Wiḥdaniya al-ilahiya* [The Father and the Son and the Holy Spirit On God Amin: the Necessity of the Multiplicity in the Divine Oneness], (al-Matin, Lebanon: Dar al-Manhal, 2009), 31.

[14]Awad Sim'an, *Allah fi al-Masiḥiya* [God in Christianity] (Cairo: Qassir Ad-Dubara Church, 2004), 16.

This definition is needed to avoid the modern concept of a person as merely an individual will and consciousness, an understanding that would inevitably lead to tritheism. The divine *Aqanīm* (persons) are three in a way that does not apply to human persons and cannot be understood from human experience apart from divine revelation.

Asmā' Allah al-Husnā means "the beautiful names of Allah" (Surah 7:180; 17:110). These names are understood to refer to the divine essence and act. Therefore, understanding the names of Allah is foundational to Islamic theology, especially to an inquiry into the nature and characteristics of the deity. The attributes that Muslims impute to Allah reflect who he is and how he acts.[15]

The book will talk about three different groups of Christians that were active before the Islamic conquer into Levant, Mesopotamia, and Egypt. The first group is called the Chalcedonian/Melkite. This group (both Eastern and Western) affirmed the Chalcedonian Definition.

The second group is called the Oriental Orthodox/Jacobite (pejoratively and incorrectly called Monophysite). This group separated from the Chalcedonians in the sixth century because they believed (incorrectly) that the Chalcedonian Definition was Nestorian. The Oriental Orthodox and Chalcedonians were certainly consistent in their Christologies, as modern ecumenical dialogues have demonstrated.

The third group is called the Church of the East (pejoratively and incorrectly called Nestorian). This group separated from the churches in the Roman Empire in the early fifth century. Contrary to popular opinion, they separated as an organizational matter, not because of Christology. Nestorius had not arisen on the scene yet in 424 when the separation happened! It is possible, although not agreed, that their Christology was not actually Nestorian and was in fact consistent with the rest of the church.

Literature Review

To demonstrate the unique contribution of this present work, I will survey the relevant literature in order of importance and relevance to the stated

---

[15]As for the transliteration from Arabic to English, I am using Billie Jean Collins, Bob Buller, and John F. Kutsko, *The SBL Handbook of Style: For Biblical Studies and Related Disciplines*, 2nd ed. (Atlanta: SBL Press, 2014).

thesis. In addition to the primary resources of the written works of John of Damascus, Theodore Abū Qurrah, and Yaḥyā Ibn ᶜAdī, secondary works on their writings are beneficial. Despite the fact that there is not a plethora of secondary resources on these three theologians, there are plenty of studies available on the history of their contexts, which will be included in this study. This is not to say that other works on the Trinity should be overlooked. On the contrary, contemporary research on the Trinity will be used as well because it forms the foundation for the present inquiry.

As for secondary resources on John of Damascus, Daniel Janosik has written an excellent monograph about his life and his Islamic context.[16] He calls John the first apologist to the Muslims and includes several theological arguments that were circulating among other sects of Muslims, such as Ash'arites and Mu'tazilites. Moreover, Charles C. Twombly has written a book called *Perichoresis and Personhood: God, Christ, and Salvation in John of Damascus*.[17] This book focuses on the *Perichoretic* concept of the Trinity that John explains. Both of these books offer great insights into John's trinitarian theology.

Andrew Louth has written extensively on John in his book *St John Damascene: Tradition and Originality in Byzantine Theology*.[18] In addition to informing his readers of John's life and context, he offers a chapter on John's position in defending the veneration of icons against the iconoclasm initiated by Emperor Leo III in AD 726. Furthermore, Peter Schadler has written *John of Damascus and Islam: Christian Heresiology and the Intellectual Background to Earliest Christian-Muslim Relations*. In this book, Schadler focuses on the idea that John considered Islam not a new religion but a heresy. In his opinion, the main reason for this classification is to establish a church's institutional and social power under the Melkites' foundation. Defining what is orthodoxy helped the faith community build a refutation of all alternatives, including Islam.[19]

[16]Daniel J. Janosik, *John of Damascus: The First Apologist to the Muslims* (Eugene, OR: Pickwick, 2016).

[17]Charles C. Twombly and Myk. Habets, *Perichoresis and Personhood : God, Christ, and Salvation in John of Damascus* (Eugene, OR: Wipf and Stock, 2015).

[18]Andrew Louth, *St John Damascene: Tradition and Originality in Byzantine Theology* (Oxford: Oxford University Press, 2002).

[19]Peter Schadler, *John of Damascus and Islam: Christian Heresiology and the Intellectual Background to Earliest Christian-Muslim Relations* (Boston: Brill, 2017).

The second theologian this book focuses on is Theodore Abū Qurrah, who was a Melkite.[20] He left several tracts (called *Mayāmer*), one of which is on the Trinity. Sara Leila Husseini, who wrote her doctoral work on this period, included in her sources Abū Qurrah and two other Arab Christian theologians from the ninth century: 'Ammar al-Baṣrī and Abū Rā'ita Al-Takrītī.[21] These men were Nestorians (the church of the East) and Jacobites, respectively.[22] Husseini focuses on their historical, social, linguistic, and religious contexts under the Islam rule to determine how their explanation of the Trinity was affected by their Christian tradition. While she gives great attention to Abū Qurrah, she only briefly mentions John and Yaḥyā Ibn ᶜAdī.

Wafik Nasry contributed a major work on Abū Qurrah and paid special attention to his book *Al-Mujādalah*. In his book, Nasry provides arguments both for and against the authenticity of *Al-Mujādalah* book as well as discussing whether Abū Qurrah actually wrote it or not. Since this study is not focusing on Abū Qurrah's writings in general, our concentration will be given to his argument for the Trinity, which Nasry discusses thoroughly.[23] Recently, Najib Awad published a large monograph on Abū Qurrah's life and writings. In it, dedicates a whole chapter to Abū Qurrah's trinitarian theology. He even makes a comparison of Qurrah's trinitarian argument and other theologians contemporary with him, such as John and Maximus the Confessor.[24] Awad describes Abū Qurrah as not just a mere witness or testifier to patristic orthodoxy but also a protector and defender of it. In Awad's opinion, Abū Qurrah does more than simply preserve and protect Christian orthodoxy against the heresies: he also defends it against Islamic monotheism.

---

[20]Melkites are Orthodox Christians who follow the Chalcedonian definition.

[21]Sara Leila Husseini, *Early Christian-Muslim Debate on the Unity of God: Three Christian Scholars and Their Engagement with Islamic Thought (9th Century C.E.)* (Leiden, Netherlands: Brill, 2014).

[22]This study will call Nestorians "The church of the East." This appellation was attributed to the Eastern Syriac-speaking region in the eighth and ninth centuries. For further information, see Sidney H. Griffith, *The Church in the Shadow of the Mosque: Christians and Muslims in the World of Islam* (Princeton, NJ: Princeton University Press, 2008), 110; and Dietmar W. Winkler, "The Age of the Sassanians" *in The Church of the East: A Concise History*, ed. Wilhelm Baum and Dietmar W. Winkler (New York: Routledge, Taylor & Francis Group, 2003), 7.

[23]Wafik Nasry, *The Caliph and the Bishop: A 9th Century Muslim-Christian Debate: Al-Ma'mūn and Abū Qurrah* (Beirut: CEDRAC Université Saint Joseph, 2008).

[24]Najib George Awad, *Orthodoxy in Arabic Terms: A Study of Theodore Abu Qurrah's Theology in Its Islamic Context* (Boston: De Gruyter, 2015).

In addition to these works, Abū Qurrah has also been the subject of several scholarly papers. In one, John Lamoreaux revises Abū Qurrah's earlier biography. In a paper titled, "The Biography of Theodore Abi Qurrah Revisited," Lamoreaux defends the idea that Abū Qurrah was a member of Mar Saba's monastery in Palestine. He also mentions that Abū Qurrah is the first Syriac scholar to write in the Arabic language, acknowledging him as a significant defender in the history of the iconoclast controversy, especially in its non-Byzantine form.[25] Moreover, Nestor Kavvadas contributed a paper called "Theodore Abu Qurrah and Byzantine Orthodox Iconoclasts in the Early Abbasid Society," in which he examines the reason why Abū Qurrah defended the veneration of the icons.[26] This paper relates both to our investigation of Mary and the Trinity and to whether the veneration of the icons has anything to do with the Muslim understanding of her inclusion in it.

The third thinker that this study seeks to examine is Yaḥyā Ibn ᶜAdī. His original writings were lost for some time but were found in Tehran Codex. This study will examine the article "The Life of Yahya Ibn 'Adi: A Famous Christian Philosopher of Baghdad" by Mohd. Nasir Omar.[27] This article is important because it not only sheds light on Ibn ᶜAdī's life, education, and career as a philosopher, but it also records the Islamic scholars and resources that mention him, for Ibn ᶜAdī was a famous philosopher who had Christian and Muslim pupils. Moreover, Father Samir Khalil al-Yasu'i analyzes, commentates, and interacts thoroughly with Ibn ᶜAdī's *Essay in Monotheism* in his book *Al-Turāth al-'Arabī al-Masiḥī* (the Arabic Christian Heritage).[28] Al-Yasu'i contrasts and compares Ibn ᶜAdī's answers to the Trinity and the nature of God with 'Abd al-Masīḥ al-Kindī's apologetics against Islam. This work is written in Arabic, and it will expand the horizon of this research by shedding great light on Ibn ᶜAdī's sources. Finally, Nadine Abbas has written

---

[25]John C. Lamoreaux, "The Biography of Theodore Abi Qurrah Revisited," *Dumbarton Oaks Papers* 56 (2002): 25-40.

[26]Nestor Kavvadas, "Icon Veneration as a Stumbling Block: Theodore Abu Qurrah and Byzantine Orthodox Iconoclasts in the Early Abbasid Society," *Journal of Eastern Christian Studies* 72 (1-2) (2020): 71-82.

[27]Mohd. Nasir Omar, "The Life of Yahya Ibn 'Adi: A Famous Christian Philosopher of Baghdad," *Mediterranean Journal of Social Sciences MCSER* 6 no. 2 S5 (2015): 308-14.

[28]Samir Khalil al-Yasu'ī, "'Maqala fi al-Tawhid [An Article in Divine Oneness]" in *al-Turath al-Arabi al-Masiḥi* [the Arabic Christian Heritage] (Jounieh, Lebanon: Al-Maktaba al-Boulissiah, 1980).

several articles as well as her doctoral dissertation on Ibn ᶜAdī in Lebanon. Her book is published in Arabic, but it is not available in the United States. Her articles in Arabic summarize her thoughts on Ibn ᶜAdī. The first article is called "Al-Falsafa wa al-Lāhūt 'nd Yaḥyā" (The Philosophy and the Theology of Yaḥyā), in which she lists Ibn ᶜAdī's essays and traces the weight of logic in defining and explaining his theology.[29] The second article is called "Mafhūm al-'lūhiya 'ind Yaḥyā Ibn ᶜAdī fi Kītāb 'al-Rad 'ala al-Warrāq' wa Maqālah fi al-Mawjūdāt" (The Concept of Divinity for Yaḥyā Ibn ᶜAdī in the Book "The Reply to al-Warrāq" and "A Tract in Things that are Existing"), in which she reviews the terminologies that 'Adi used in his explanation of the meaning of the divine.[30]

As for Muslim-Christian relations in the eighth, ninth, and tenth centuries, David Thomas has written and edited several books on this topic. In *Routledge Handbook on Christian-Muslim Relations*, the writers walk the readers through the history of Christian-Muslim relations from the beginning, through the Middle Ages, and to early modern and modern periods.[31] Thomas reports the situation of Christians in the Middle Ages under Islamic rule. He starts by explaining the Pact of 'Umar and how it affected the liberties of Christians by opening the doors for mistreatment. During that time, many Islamic officials treated Christians as lesser citizens by asking them to dress in a certain way, to show respect to Muslims and give up their seats for them, and possibly not to teach the Qur'an to their children. Additionally, in the same volume, Sandra Toenies Keating discusses in her article "The First Arabic-Speaking Christian Theologians" the situation that forced the Christians who knew Greek and spoke Aramaic and Syriac to see a great need to shift to the Arabic language. By the late eighth century, deeper differences were introduced that necessitated creative responses to the emerging religion of Islam. The situation further escalated with the accession of the Abbasids dynasty and their intentional

[29]Nadine Abbas,"al-Falsafa wa al-Lahoot was al-Akhlaq 'ind Yaḥya ibn ᶜAdī [The Philosophy, Theology, and Ethics of Yaḥya ibn ᶜAdī]," *Tafahum Magazine* (2015): 138-68. Retrieved from https://tafahom.mara.gov.om/storage/al-tafahom/ar/2015/048/pdf/07.pdf.

[30]Nadine Abbas, Mafhoom al-Ulohiya 'ind Yaḥya ibn Adi in the Book of Maqala fi al Mawjoodat [Yaḥya's concept of divinity in the book 'the Reply to al-Waraq and the Article of the Findings']," *Dar Al-Machreq Magazine* 87, no. 1 (2013): Kindle.

[31]David Thomas, ed., *Routledge Handbook on Christian-Muslim Relations* (New York: Routledge, Taylor & Francis, 2018).

program of Arabization and Islamization. Consequently, the early ninth century saw an intensified effort on the part of all Christians to provide theological responses to the questions of both common people and elite Muslims. Moreover, I. Mark Beaumont briefly surveys the earliest written Christian references to Islam in his article "Early Muslim Attitudes Towards the Bible." None of the articles included in this book, however, carefully examine the early argument for the Trinity.

Daniel King provides another edited work titled *The Syriac World of the East,* which includes great information about the status of the church during the early invasion of Islam and the Abbasid period.[32] In this source, David Wilmshurst includes a chapter about "The Church of the East in the ʿAbbasid Era." By this time, the church's losses were too many. After the loss of the patriarchates of Rome and Constantinople, nine metropolitan provinces of the patriarchate of Alexandria were placed under the Arab Islamic conquest of Egypt, and three metropolitan provinces in the patriarchate of Jerusalem and twelve metropolitan provinces in the patriarchate of Antioch were placed under Islamic rulers. The time between the reigns of the Caliphs al-Mahdī AD 775–785 and al-Mutawakkil AD 847–861 was marked by a religious debate, enabling few scholars (such as the ones this study is focusing on) to introduce their defense for the Trinity and other topics.

Regarding the divine images and icons in the church, this study shall investigate several resources. As mentioned earlier, the three above scholars had their own teachings on the icons of the church. John and Abū Qurrah argued for the veneration of the icons, and Ibn ᶜAdī was against it.

In a book published for the J. Paul Getty Museum, Alfredo Tradigo explains the different types of icons that churches used throughout history.[33] Many of them were used in the Byzantine era, especially in the cathedrals of Constantinople. During the struggle of the iconoclasts in the seventh century, the use of The Virgin Nursing icon spread widely in Egypt, Constantinople, and Jerusalem. Pope Gregory, while writing to his adversary Emperor Leo III, mentioned that The Virgin Nursing icon should be

[32]Daniel King, ed., *The Syriac World of the East* (New York: Routledge, Taylor & Francis Group, 2019).

[33]Alfredo Tradigo, *Icons and Saints of the Eastern Orthodox Church,* trans. Stephen Sartarelli (Los Angeles: The J. Paul Getty Museum, 2004).

worshiped. He also referenced the Three-Handed Virgin Icon that healed John's hand when the Islamic emperor amputated it. This source is necessary to learn what type of icons were circulating among cathedrals during that period.

In the book *The Virgin Goddess: Studies in the Pagan and Christian Roots of Mariology*, Stephen Benko proposes that there is a direct line between the goddess-cults of the ancients to the reverence paid to the Virgin Mary.[34] One cult he mentions is the Collyridians (Kollyridians), who worshiped Mary in Arabia. Many scholars related this cult to the misunderstanding of the Islamic Trinity. While this idea is not impossible, it is not known how or when this cult developed in Arabia. There is also no record in Islamic literature that Mohammad was in contact with such a cult. While Benko's book does not give a definite answer to our question about the Islamic Trinity, it sheds light on several Marian cults and how they affected the development of Mariology within the church.

Imad Shehadeh wrote a two-volume work titled *God With Us and Without Us*, in which he makes a comparison between Trinity and *Tawḥid*.[35] In the first volume, subtitled *Oneness in Trinity versus Absolute Oneness*, he examines the historical struggle over absolute oneness between two Islamic schools in the eighth century. At the end of this volume, he attempts to harmonize the nature of the doctrine of the Trinity with logic by explaining that the eternal existence of God is in harmony with the eternal activity of his attributes. In order for God's attributes to be part of him, they must exist eternally with him. In other words, they need to be eternally functional and active with him in order for him to be the highest conceived divine being. In volume two, Shehadeh deals with several topics related to the Trinity, such as the difference between Old Testament oneness and absolute oneness. One such difference is that the oneness of the OT shows God's desire to be known. This idea is clear "in God's revelation of his attributes, in his promise of knowing him, and in the use of anthropomorphism to describe him,"[36]

---

[34]Stephen Benko, *The Virgin Goddess: Studies in the Pagan and Christian Roots of Mariology* (Leiden, NY: Brill, 1993).

[35]Imad N. Shehadeh, *God With Us and Without Us, Volumes One and Two: The Beauty and Power of Oneness in Trinity versus Absolute Oneness* (Carlisle, UK: Langham Creative Projects, 2020).

[36]Imad N. Shehadeh, *God With Us and Without Us, Volume Two: The Beauty and Power of Oneness in Trinity* (Carlisle, UK: Langham, 2019), 7.

whereas within absolute oneness, the idea that God desires to be known is completely rejected. There are several covenants in the OT in which God expresses his desire to have a relationship with his people. Moreover, Christ's revelation of the special relationship between the Father and Jesus revealed God's desire to be the Father of all believers by extending the sonship to them. The fatherhood and sonship concepts are absent from the absolute oneness.

Another important work on the subject of the Trinity is written by Miroslav Volf and titled *Allah: A Christian Response*.[37] In it, Volf develops part of his argument in a dialogical manner with Sheikh al-Jifri. Volf, a prominent trinitarian theologian, explains some of the difficulties of explicating the Trinity. For instance, he mentions the tension that the term *begets* sparks in the Muslim's mind and explains that this word does not mean a male and female relationship. Furthermore, Christians are not trying to soothe the troubled conscience of their supposed tritheism by means of a belief in trinitarian monotheism. Volf clarifies that the acts of the Christian God are divided because they belong to three different persons. Volf explains that regarding creation, God is acting "toward the outside"; his acts are undivided and inseparable. Every act of one person of the Trinity is always caused by all three.

William Montgomery Watt's work *Islam and Christianity Today: A Contribution to Dialogue*[38] makes a comparison study on several topics between Islam and Christianity. On the transcendence and the immanence of God, Watt states that the Qur'an shows Allah's immanence; he concedes that immanence is more obvious in the Christian faith than it is in Islam. On the topic of oneness and unicity, he is probably the first scholar to use the word *unicity* to explain the nature of Allah and God. He demonstrates that the problem of the attributes of Allah arises from the fact that in mainstream Islamic thought the Qur'an is not created but is accepted as the speech of God, which makes it eternal with the eternality of God. The opponents of this view do not accept the idea of the eternality of the Qur'an because they could not admit to two Eternals. Although Watt's book does not include a

[37]Miroslav Volf, *Allah: A Christian Response* (New York: HarperCollins, 2011).

[38]W. Montgomery Watt, *Islam and Christianity Today: A Contribution to Dialogue* (London: Routledge & Kegan Paul, 1983).

thorough discussion of the Trinity, it offers good analysis and comparisons over several topics, which in turn are helpful for this study.

Additionally, Gregory A. Boyd has written an article titled "The Self-Sufficient Sociality of God: A Trinitarian Revision of Hartshorne's Metaphysics."[39] In it, he compares classical trinitarianism on one hand, and process trinitarianism and the sociality of God on the other. The former believes that God's essential sociality is defined within Godself. The only important metaphysical relationship that God has is within the Trinity of the divine persons. Any relationship with creation is highly contingent on God's will or choice. The process of trinitarian thought, in contrast, believes that God is essentially social but that his sociality is defined by his relationship with the world—a relationship that lies "beyond the accident of God's Will."[40] The notion that God could exist apart from the world is, within process thought, an unintelligible notion. Boyd's article is important because the thought process seems similar to Islamic belief about the *tawḥidic* nature of Allah. The supposition of a self-sufficient social God who satisfies the a priori requirements of relationality (God-God) when he is alone before the creation is a necessary idea to provide the metaphysical foundation for a coherent understanding of the contingent relationality (God-creation).

Michael J. Chan and Brent A. Strawn have collected several essays by Old Testament theologian Terence E. Fretheim and published them in a book called *What Kind of God? Collected Essays of Terence E. Fretheim*. Fretheim's central theology rests on a God-world relationship.[41] God is and remains transcendent while simultaneously immanent. God has taken initiative and freely entered both into a relationship with his creation and into a covenant with Israel. Having done so, He "has decisively and irrevocably committed himself to be in relationship with the world."[42]

---

[39]Gregory A. Boyd, "The Self-Sufficient Sociality of God: A Trinitarian Revision of Hartshorne's Metaphysics," in *Trinity in Process: A Relational Theology of God*, ed. Joseph A. Bracken and Marjorie Hewitt Suchocki, (London: Bloomsbury Academic, 1997), 73-94.

[40]Boyd, "Self-Sufficient Sociality," 73.

[41]Terence E. Fretheim, Michael J. Chan, and Brent A. Strawn, *What Kind of God? Collected Essays of Terence E. Fretheim* (Winona Lake, Indiana: Eisenbrauns, 2015).

[42]Fretheim, Chan, and Strawn, *What Kind of God?*, 26.

Survey Conclusion

From the content of our literature survey, it is clear that of the several resources written on Christianity under the Abbasid dynasty, few dealt with the Arabic trinitarian apologetics under the Islamic context. However, none whatsoever reflected on John of Damascus's, Theodore Abū Qurrah's, and Yaḥyā Ibn ᶜAdī's arguments of the Trinity/iconoclasm particularly for the purpose of creating contemporary trinitarian apologetics. Many separate studies reported these three thinkers' trinitarian arguments without reflecting on how contemporary readers can benefit from their contributions. Moreover, no literature on record has attempted an abductive/analytical method to show the trinitarian God as the greatest conceived divine being. Once this analysis is properly integrated, the path will be open for adding new insights to the apologetical argument against Islamic objections in our contemporary days.

Statement of Methodology

Because this volume relates to history, theology, and apologetics, it will employ a combination of methodologies. Due to its historical nature, a textual analysis will be done to establish the context the Arabic church in general and the three thinkers, in particular, were facing. Then, an abductive historical investigation will follow, exploring the probable cause behind the Muslim misunderstanding of the orthodox Christian Trinity. The trinitarian arguments of the three thinkers will be textually analyzed and closely defined and compared. Last, a deductive analysis will be applied to reach into an apologetical answer to Islamic objections against the Trinity.

The historical investigation will adopt abductive reasoning, which typically begins with an incomplete set of observations and proceeds to the best explanation for the set. Abductive reasoning does its best with the available information, often incomplete. It relaxes the standard and gives up the search for absolute certainty. While I cannot prove that the *Theotokos* icons are the main reason for Mohammad's misunderstanding of the Trinity, I can at least show that it is probable. My goal in using this method is to provide the best explanation for the Islamic perception of the Trinity.

The abductive reasoning process of inquiry is one of the most widely used ways to examine a perceptual problem that cannot be addressed through immediate observation and background knowledge.[43] Mark Tschaepe calls this step "a guessing procedure," in which the inquirer's starting point is an attempt to resolve a genuine doubt about a certain issue and arrive at a stable belief. Tschaepe explains:

> The more the problem is examined, the further we move from the perceptual judgment and into the procedure of guessing. Perceptual judgment simply declares the problem or question at hand. Guessing is the process that creates a Third by which to understand the problem that was determined by perceptual judgment but for which perceptual judgment could not supply an answer.[44]

At the beginning of the process, the inquirer guesses by defining a new starting point in his examination. This new point serves as an attempt to address the surprising phenomenon that has led to doubt. Next, the inquirer draws a number of elements without ranking them or giving them any priority over each other for the purpose of reaching into the best explanation of the inquiry.

In identifying the starting point, I will review the answers that were provided for the Islamic conception of the Trinity, arguing against their adequacy. Next, I will examine Islamic historical resources that mention the relationship between Christians and Mohammad in the areas where he visited or lived. I will also evaluate the conversations that were widely spread among Christians and Muslims from the seventh century to the tenth century to verify whether they are consistent with the Islamic understanding of the Trinity.

Some previous attempts of the concept of "guessing," which is the starting point of the inquiry, have led to the post hoc *propter hoc* fallacy: the belief that "because event B happened after event A, therefore there must be some causal connection between the two events."[45] Sometimes there is no connection, and in other cases, there might be more complicated reasons and connections than the historians have proposed. To avoid

---

[43]Sami Paavola, "Abduction through Grammar, Critic, and Methodeutic," *Transactions of the Charles S. Peirce Society* 40, no. 2 (2004): 261-62.

[44]Mark Tschaepe, "Guessing and Abduction," *Transactions of The Charles S. Peirce Society* 50, no. 1 (2014): 118.

[45]Carl R. Trueman, *Histories and Fallacies: Problems Faced in the Writing of History* (Wheaton, IL: Crossway, 2010), 102.

such fallacies, this study shall follow the criterion of "the sufficient cause" rather than "the necessary cause." According to Carl Trueman, the necessary cause means, "if phenomenon B is present, then A must be present too; though the presence of A does not necessarily imply that B will occur";[46] whereas, the sufficient cause means, "A necessarily implies the presence of B, but B could be caused by C; thus the presence of B does not mean that A is necessarily present."[47] The misunderstanding of the doctrine of the Trinity necessarily implies a false narration, teachings, or implications of some other beliefs, which are caused by the spread of cults, other religions, or misrepresentation of orthodox Christianity. Thus, the false narration, teachings, or implication of some other beliefs does not mean that the misunderstanding is necessarily present. The presence of the misunderstanding of the doctrine of the Trinity does not mean that the extensive reach of icons is necessarily the cause of this misunderstanding, but it is a sufficient cause, given other circumstances.

While the historical application of this study will adopt abductive reasoning, the philosophical application will require deductive reasoning. Deductive reasoning starts with true premises and ends with a strongly supported conclusion. If the premises are true, then it would be impossible for the conclusion to be false. By employing the deductive method, the study will defend the relational character of God to refute the Islamic objection that the Trinity is a theologically contradictory concept that minimizes the perfection of the divine nature.

The argument goes this way:

P1: One aspect of divine perfection is relationality—the greatest conceived being should be a relational being in order to be perfect (the greatest).

P2: The Trinity shows God as a relational divine being (intrarelational and interrelational).

C: The Trinity is noncontradictory.

If I am successful in defending the first and second premises, then the conclusion should necessarily be true and therefore demonstrate that the Trinity is not a contradiction but instead a necessary attribute of the greatest conceived divine being.

---

46 Trueman, *Histories and Fallacies*, 104.

47 Trueman, *Histories and Fallacies*, 104.

The main question of this study is related to the divine nature, a topic that falls under theology proper. Therefore, the idea of the Anselmian God (as presented by David Baggett and Jerry Walls) shall be both presented and assumed in this study. In their book *Good God: The Theistic Foundations of Morality*, Baggett and Walls identify the Anselmian God "as a being who has no ontological deficiencies, and who is also the proper desire for human beings."[48] I will use the notion of the Anselmian God throughout the study to refer to the highest perceived divine being, and not necessarily the Christian God. On one hand, both Islam and Christianity affirm their belief in the "greatest conceived being," which is monotheistic in nature. They both also deny any type of atheism, agnosticism, or skepticism. Likewise, both believe that God is monotheistic, omnipotent, omniscient, glorious, and worthy; and both deny that the "greatest conceived being" is an impersonal force, chi, or amorphous cosmic power. On the other hand, Christians and Muslims disagree about the nature of the divine. Muslims believe in *tawḥid* and Christians believe in the Trinity. The differences between the two doctrines will be briefly explained to show the general direction. The bulk of attention, however, will be given to trinitarian apologetics.

While recognizing that the interaction between theology and philosophy has been an apologetic necessity in the history of Christian thought, several distinctions should be made at this point to offer more clarity to this argument.

Throughout this book, I will be using the term *apologetics*. Some people think that all apologetical methods are polemic. I admit that the latter term is related to the former, but it has a different meaning. Apologetics is a subset of theology involving the art of providing a defense for one's faith. A person can develop an apologetic that defines her belief in opposition to other people's beliefs and religions. Defined in this way, apologetics is related to polemics. The differences, however, have to deal with the tone, intent, and content. Polemics is a critique of other ideologies and sets of belief. Polemic is less interested in defining one's religion than it is in defining and criticizing others' doctrines and beliefs. The three thinkers examined in this study used a combination of apologetics and polemic. On some occasions,

[48]David Baggett and Jerry Walls, *Good God: The Theistic Foundations of Morality* (Oxford: Oxford University Press, 2011), 54.

they defined the orthodox Christian faith; and at other times, they explained the weaknesses of certain Islamic beliefs and pointed out their illogical and philosophical flaws.

Most encyclopedias of Islam present a classification according to the attributes of essence, such as existence, divine eternity, and divine permanence, and the attributes of action, such as divine power, will, and knowledge.[49] Other scholars have categorized the attributes of Allah in relationship to God's essence, to the universe, to the natural world, and to human beings. This study, however, shall follow two categorizations of essence and action.

This analysis focuses on the nature of the divine and its moral perfection, not moral goodness and rightness. The study is not related to God's commands or actions, but his divine nature and whether it is lacking any attributes that prevent him from being perfect. The study presupposes that being relational is one of the attributes that contribute to God's goodness and perfection. If God is nonrelational, then his nature is missing a major attribute, and therefore is imperfect. Christians believe that God's inherent trinitarian nature and desire for harmonious relationships with his creation demonstrate a profoundly social and relational divine nature. His trinitarian nature shows that He is eternally relational, from eternity to eternity. He is intrarelational before the foundation of the earth through the persons (*aqānīm*) of the Trinity, and He is interrelational with his creation in the Old Testament, New Testament, and through the Holy Spirit in today's church age.

Chapter Breakdown

Following this introductory chapter, chapter one examines the historical, linguistic, and intellectual environment of the Arabic church in the eighth to the tenth centuries. The church lived under the Abbasid dynasty in a period known as the Golden Age of Islam. Special attention was given to science, philosophy, and language during this brief period, and Arabic became the official language of the government after replacing Greek, Hebrew, and Aramaic. Many Christians converted to Islam to avoid heavy taxation and to facilitate entry to government services. This massive

[49]Zaki Saritopark, "Allah," in *The Qur'an: An Encyclopedia*, ed. Oliver Leaman, (London: Taylor & Francis Group, 2005), 38-40.

conversion prompted Christian authors of this period to compose apologetic treatises that reflect Islamic concerns and explain Christian doctrines by using the Arabic language and Islamic concepts. This shift explains the widely recorded Islamic contextual perception of the doctrine of the Trinity.

Chapter two presents the answer to the Qur'anic objections against the Trinity. The writer of the Qur'an thinks that Christians believe in the divinity of Mary and they include her within the Trinity as being God's wife and the mother of Jesus. This chapter summarizes the efforts that have been done to explain the Qur'anic reference of Mary and examines the historical prevalence and the theological beliefs about the *Theotokos* icons in the history of Christianity, seeking to discover a link between these icons and the impression they might have left on Mohammad's understanding of the Trinity.

Chapter three investigates the trinitarian apologetics of John, Theodore Abū Qurrah, and Yaḥyā Ibn ᶜAdī by comparing, contrasting, and defining the essential and the fundamental components and layouts of their apologetics, noting how they used Islamic and Qur'anic concepts in their defense. It is important to discuss their arguments and understand how the Arabic church defended the Trinity against Islamic objections to learn from their apologetical style and to form a modern defense that suits the current Islamic objections in the twenty-first century.

Chapter four explores the historical development of the doctrine of the Trinity in the West after the Nicene Creed with a concentration on contemporary studies. The chapter presents three trinitarians models presented by four Christian contemporary philosophers/theologians in the last thirty years. The three models are Social trinitarianism, Latin Trinitarianism, and the relative identity theory. The purpose of this chapter is to inform the reader about the recent development of this doctrine and give him a chance to compare the Arabic and Western rationalizations of the Trinity.

Chapter five provides trinitarian apologetics against the claim that its doctrine is illogical (*tawḥīd* is unsurpassable) and therefore does not present God as the greatest conceived being. Since the idea of the Anselmian God is a common ground between Christians and Muslims, this chapter argues that the greatest conceived being should be relational. Otherwise, he is not the greatest being because he lacks an essential attribute—the one that makes him merciful and compassionate. For God to be relational, he has to be trinitarian in nature because the Trinity is the only manner in which he reveals himself as a relational divine being—he is intrarelational within himself as a Trinity and interrelational with his creation. In this way, God is not dependent on his creation because there is no time in history when he was alone without a relationship before the creation, and there is no time when he needed the creation in order for his attributes to be functional (such as being a seer, being a hearer, or being loving).

Finally, the conclusion will summarize my argument, finalize my analysis, and discuss further areas of research.

1

The Rise of the Abbasids and the Golden Age of Islam

After the death of the prophet Mohammad, Muslims expanded beyond the Arabian Peninsula to the Levant, Mesopotamia, and North Africa. The Umayyad dynasty (AD 661–750) followed the period of the *Rashidun* caliphs (the rightly guided caliphs) and moved their capital to Damascus. After the fall of the Umayyads, the Abbasids ruled (AD 750–1258) in Baghdad through a military revolution. "It was the armies of the Muslims of Khurasan," says Hugh Kennedy, "which defeated the forces of the Umayyads and swept the new dynasty to power in 750."[1] The number of the Abbasids' troops in the late eighth century was around 100,000.[2] This military power led to many uprisings within the ruling parties. Most of the Abbasid caliphs died through military coups, treason, and treachery.

Like the Umayyad, the Abbasids practiced hereditary rule to keep the caliphate within the family. They even appointed several sons as crown princes, which in many cases led the elder crown prince to isolate his younger brothers in order to deliver the regime to his own son instead of his brothers. This situation resulted in many military coups within the same family.[3] Moreover, the Abbasid dynasty included religiously mixed caliphs.

[1]Hugh Kennedy, *When Baghdad Ruled the Muslim World: The Rise and Fall of Islam's Greatest Dynasty* (Cambridge, MA: Da Capo Press, 2004), 44.
[2]Kennedy, *When Baghdad Ruled*, 44.
[3]Amina Bittar, *The History of the Abbasid Dynasty* (Damascus: Damascus University Press, 1997), 322.

Many of them were religious, prayed regularly, censured or curtailed musical practice, and did not serve wine at their tables.[4] Others were less religious; they kept concubines and paid more attention to knowledge, music, and translation of literature from different languages to Arabic. This shift in focus led to several improvements in science, language, and art.

The translation movement from Greek to Arabic started under the Umayyad period. The initial Arab conquests in Syria, Palestine, and Egypt, and the move of Arab rulers and tribesmen into Greek-speaking areas, made the transition from Greek to Arabic inevitable, both in government circles and in everyday life. Greek was widely used in Syria and Palestine as the official language of commerce and business and as the language of learning of Christian clerics.[5] However, most—if not all—of the translation activities during the Umayyad period are "instances of random and ad hoc accommodation to the needs of the times, generated by Arab rule over non-Arab peoples."[6] Most of the materials were administrative, political, and commercial documents. They were translated for the purpose of expanding the communication between the new rulers and the allophones.[7]

After the Abbasid revolution and the transfer of the seat of the caliphate to Iraq, the cultural orientation of Islam changed drastically. Hārūn al-Rashīd (AD 766–809) established *Bayt al-Ḥikma* (the House of Wisdom), which reached its pinnacle under the reign of his son al-Ma'mun (AD 813–833) with the involvement of Aramaic speakers, Christians, Jews, and Persian scholars.[8] Several resources mention that *Bayt al-Ḥikma* started as a royal library. As an institution, it was adopted as part of the Sasanian administrative and bureaucratic state system.[9] "With the books brought from both the church schools within the state's borders and neighboring geographies," says Mustafa Barış, "Bayt al-Hikma grew to be the richest library of medieval period and a science center encompassing intense scientific studies. In the foregoing science center were a director, authors and interpreters with

---

[4]Kennedy, *When Baghdad Ruled*, 13.

[5]Dimitri Gutas, *Greek Thought, Arabic Culture: The Graeco-Arabic Translation Movement in Baghdad and Early Abbasaid Society (2nd-4th/5th-10th c.)* (London, UK: Taylor & Francis Group, 1998), 17.

[6]Gutas, *Greek Thought*, 24.

[7]Gutas, *Greek Thought*, 24.

[8]Gutas, *Greek Thought*, 19.

[9]Gutas, *Greek Thought*, 56-58.

clerks working under them, scribes copying the books and bookbinders responsible of binding."[10] According to Muhammad ibn Isḥāq Ibn Al-Nadīm, who closely examined *Bayt al-Ḥikma* and utilized its library, forty-six scholars translated from Syriac to Arabic, fourteen from Persian, and three from Sanskrit.[11]

The translation movement would have not flourished without the support of the caliphs, such as Hārūn al-Rashīd and al-Ma'mūn, and the scholarly zeal of Syriac-speaking Christians, who were fluent in Greek, Syriac, and Arabic. Christian theologians who wrote in Arabic in the early Islamic period were associated with monasteries and ecclesiastical institutions. Under the influence of the caliphs and Christian thinkers, intellectual life flourished in Baghdad and beyond. As Griffith mentions, "Some were physicians, some were philosophers, and some were logicians, mathematicians, copyists, or translators. Some were also Christian apologists and theologians. . . . All of them contributed something to the newly flowering culture of the classical period of Islamic civilization."[12]

The Status of Christian Scholarship During the Early Abbasid Period

Under the Byzantine rule and the invasion of Islam into the Levant, Christians were divided into three major groups. The monasteries of Jerusalem, the Judean desert, and (to a certain extent) the ecclesiastical establishment in Edessa in Syria were filled with Greek and Syriac-speaking confessors of the Chalcedonian faith. They were known later in the ninth century by the name Melkites[13] "because of their acceptance of the doctrinal decisions of the imperially sponsored, sixth ecumenical council in Byzantium, Constantinople III (681 CE), along with its five equally imperially sponsored predecessors."[14] After the invasion of the Muslims to the Levant, the Melkites

[10]Mustafa Necati Barış, "First Translation Activities in Islamic Science History and their Contribution to Knowledge Production," *Cumhuriyet Ilahiyat Dergisi* 22, no. 1 (2018): 716.

[11]Muhammad ibn Isḥāq Ibn al-Nadīm, *The Fihrist of Al-Nadīm: A Tenth-Century Survey of Muslim Culture*, vol. 2 (New York: Columbia University Press, 1970), 586-90.

[12]Sidney H. Griffith, *The Church in the Shadow of the Mosque: Christians and Muslims In the World of Islam* (Princeton, NJ: Princeton University Press, 2008), 106.

[13]The word *Melkite* comes from the Arabic word *malik*, which means "king."

[14]Sidney H. Griffith, "The Melkites and the Muslims: The Qur'ān, Christology, and Arab Orthodoxy," *Al-QanṬara* 33, no. 2 (2012): 414.

adopted the Arabic language in the ninth century. John of Damascus (AD 655–749) was the first theologian/apologist who wrote against Islam in Greek, and Theodore Abū Qurrah (AD 750-820) was the first theologian to write in Arabic. He even translated the Greek secular work of the pseudo-Aristotelian treatise *De virtutibus animae* into Arabic and submitted it to Ṭāhir ibn al-Ḥusayn, the caliph al-Ma'mūn's famous general.[15]

The second Christian group that had knowledge of Greek were Jacobites. They took their name and existence after Jacob Baradeus (AD 500–578), who was credited with organizing the Syrian Orthodox "Jacobite" Church.[16] This group is pejoratively called Monophysites by the Chalcedonians, who thought that Monophysites believe in the single nature of Christ, particularly Jesus' divinity being the principle of the union of his two natures, in which his humanity is absorbed.[17] They were separated from the Chalcedonians in the sixth century because they thought mistakenly that Chalcedon was Nestorian.[18] However, Baradeus continued to travel throughout Egypt, Syria, Mesopotamia, Armenia, Arabia, and many other countries, ordaining numerous bishops and priests.[19] As he traveled, his preaching was all the more effective because of his fluency in Greek, Syriac, and Arabic.

It is worth noting that in the age before the printing press, copyists and booksellers were closely related professions. Yaḥyā Ibn ᶜAdī, for instance, who received most of his education in Baghdad, was a member of the Jacobite church and quite knowledgeable in Syriac and Arabic. He devoted considerable time to copying manuscripts. Even though he was Christian, he did not restrict himself to writing only about Christianity or Christian theology. On the contrary, he boasted of being a scribe, copying Islamic manuscripts. He states,

[15]Griffith, *Church in the Shadow*, 107.

[16]J. W. Childers, "Baradeus, Jacob (c. 500–578)," in *The Encyclopedia of Christian Civilization*, ed. G. T. Kurian Wiley (Malden, MA: Wiley-Blackwell, 2012).

[17]Dietmar W. Winkler, "Monophysites," in *Late Antiquity: A Guide to the Postclassical World*, ed. G. W. Bowersock, Peter Robert Lamont Brown, and Oleg Grabar (Cambridge, MA: Harvard University Press, 1999).

[18]A. A. Luce, *Monophysitism Past and Present: A Study in Christology* (New York: The Macmillan Co. 1920), 1.

[19]Philip Wood, "Christians in the Middle East, 600–1000: Conquest, Competition and Conversion," in *Islam and Christianity in Medieval Anatolia*, ed. A. C. S. Peacock et al. (New York: Taylor & Francis Group, 2015), 24.

> I have transcribed with my hand two copies of the Tafsīr [Quranic Commentary] of al-Tabarī [d. 923], which I have taken to the kings of the frontiers, and I have copied innumerable works of the Muslim theologians. In fact, I have forced myself to write a hundred pages each day and night, though I felt this to be little.[20]

Ibn ᶜAdī did not speak or read Greek; instead, he worked from existing translations into his native Syriac and was a major ambassador for Greek ideas into the Christian and Islamic worlds.[21]

In addition to the Melkites and the Jacobites, the Church of the East made up the community of scholars inspiring the next generation of thinkers to follow their footsteps in learning, writing, and translating philosophy. The Church of the East lived in Iraq, yet they had their own Greek and Syriac learning tradition. Gutas states that the same Greek-Syriac learning atmosphere existed in Monophysite and Church of the East congregations throughout the area,

> If we are to judge by scholars who appeared during the early ʿAbbasid period with a solid background in Greek learning; witness Dayr Qunnā south of Baghdad on the Tigris [*EI* II, 197] the site of a large and flourishing Nestorian monastery, where Abū-Biŝr Matta ibn-Yunus (*EI* VI, 844-51), the founder of the Aristotelian school in Baghdad early in the tenth century, studied and taught.[22]

Many cities in the Levant and Mesopotamia maintained a Greek-Syriac learning tradition, which the Church of the East contributed effectively to in the pre-Islamic era.

The previous analysis shows the important role that the Christians played in launching Arabic language, philosophy, and science. These scholars participated in the translation movement out of altruistic motives for the improvement of society and the promotion of their own religion. The translation movement created new developments in studying philosophy in the Arabic world, which in turn allowed some Christian and Muslim

---

[20]"Yahya ibn ᶜAdi," in *Encyclopedia of World Biography Online*, vol. 37 (Detroit: Gale, 2017). Accessed December 7, 2020. https://link.gale.com/apps/doc/K1631010726/BIC?u=vic_liberty&sid=BIC&xid=c5dd4b6a.

[21]Mohd. Nasir Omar, "The Life of Yahya Ibn ʿAdi: A Famous Christian Philosopher of Baghdad," *Mediterranean Journal of Social Sciences MCSER* 6 no. 2 S5 (2015): 310.

[22]Gutas, *Greek Thought*, 14.

scholars to dialogue and debate. Both Christian and Muslim scholars leveraged their skills to employ philosophical, theological, and logical ideas to support the faith of their communities.

The Status of Christian Societies Under the Abbasids

Some Christians held notable positions in the government under the Umayyads, valuable in service because of their knowledge of Greek and the previous positions they held during the Byzantine's power. When the Arabs came to the Levant and Mesopotamia, they ruled as a minority community over established societies. Their expertise in the existing administrative systems helped them to establish their own methods and maintain order over the newly conquered lands.[23] Thus, non-Muslims were in demand as professional state administrators, and they often rose to influential and important positions, especially at the beginning of the Islamic conquest. However, several conditions changed when the Abbasids took over after the Umayyads. While many of the Christians did work for the Abbasid caliphs in translation, this does not mean they had total freedom or that all Christian communities were treated respectfully during the extended period of the Abbasid reign. On the contrary, even with Christians in key positions of influence, they were unable to prevent Abbasid rulers from imposing new restrictions on Christians and non-Muslim communities.

One of the restrictions that Abbasids applied on local non-Muslims in the Levant and Mesopotamia is called the *dhimma*—a covenant of protection between Muslims and certain tolerated non-Muslim religious communities (Christians, Jews, Zoroastrians, and Sabaeans) living permanently within its boundaries.[24] Muslims were a minority at the beginning of the conquest; however, their number increased rapidly as many locals converted to Islam after being given the choice of conversion, paying taxes, or being killed. The people who refused to convert and opted to pay taxes are called *ahl al-dhimma,* or *dhimmis*. They did not have to pay any *zakat* (alms) on their properties, vines, crops, or livestock like Muslims did, but they had to

---

[23]Mun'im Sirry, "The Public Role of Dhimmīs during ʿAbbāsid Times," *Bulletin of SOAS*, 74, no. 2 (2011): 188.

[24]Norman A. Stillman, "Dhimma," in *Medieval Islamic Civilization*, ed. Joseph Meri, vol 1, (New York: Taylor and Francis, 2016), 205.

pay *jizya*—a poll tax imposed on non-Muslims in lieu of military service. Women and senior citizens did not pay *jizya*, only men who were able to hold the sword and fight.[25]

Jizya is a Qur'anic command that Mohammad himself imposed on non-Muslims during his *ghazawat* (raids). In Surah 9:29, Mohammad commands the Muslims to "fight those who do not believe in Allah, nor in the latter day, nor do they prohibit what Allah and His Messenger have prohibited, nor follow the religion of truth, out of those who have been given the Book, until they pay the tax in acknowledgment of superiority and they are in a state of subjection."[26] The amount of *jizya*, however, is not defined in the Qur'an. The Ḥadīths mention briefly that Jews and Christians should pay a tenth of their profits if they are making trade outside their area of residence.[27] *Muwatta Malik* includes a Ḥadīth stating that *jizya* is imposed on

> the people of the Book to humble them. As long as they are in the country they have agreed to live in, they do not have to pay anything on their property except the jizya. . . . This is because jizya is only imposed on them on conditions, which they have agreed on, namely that they will remain in their own countries, and that war will be waged for them on any enemy of theirs, and that if they then leave that land to go anywhere else to do business they will have to pay a tenth.[28]

Non-Muslims (mostly Christians and Jews) who lived under Islamic rule paid a certain amount of money on their properties in exchange for protection, but if they traveled from their area of residence to do business in other Islamic regions, they had to pay one-tenth of their trade, whereas Muslims did not. In another Ḥadīth, Mohammad explains that tithing is not imposed on Muslims: it is only for the Jews and the Christians.[29]

---

[25]Christian C. Sahner, *Christian Martyrs under Islam: Religious Violence and the Making of the Muslim World* (Princeton, NJ: Princeton University Press, 2018), 6.

[26]Unless otherwise noted, all qur'anic passages referenced are in *The Quran*, ed. M. H. Shakir (Medford, MA: Perseus Digital Library, 2016).

[27]Ḥadīths are the collective records of the traditions of Prophet Mohammad's words and acts. Many of the Ḥadīths are treated as authentic (which goes directly in unbroken chain to the prophet himself) and second in authority to the Qur'an. These Ḥadīths are called *Ḥadīth Ṣaḥīḥ* (correct Ḥadīth). This study will use only *Ḥadīth Ṣaḥīḥ*.

[28]Mālik Ibn Anas, *Al-Muwatta of Imam Malik ibn Anas: the first formulation of Islamic law*, Book 17, Ḥadīth no. 46. Accessed December 14, 2020. https://sunnah.com/urn/506220.

[29]Tirmidhī, Muḥammad Ibn, *'Īsá*, "Jami' at-Tirmidhi," Book 7, Ḥadīth no. 634. Accessed December 14, 2020, https://sunnah.com/tirmidhi/7.

As for the people of the Book who do not travel and remain in their area of residence in the Islamic regions, their *jizya* was not standardized, and its conditions fluctuated. The amount was left to be negotiated with individual Muslim monarchs. Al-Qurṭubi records several cases he heard from different resources about *jizya,* detailing how Mohammad and the caliphs after him treated the non-Muslims among them.[30] He recalls al-Ṭabari saying that *jizya* should be at least one dinar with no maximum amount, while others say it should be more than one dinar or be based on whatever the Muslim potentate defines.[31]

As Islamic dominance in the region increased with time, Islamic law and administrative practice evolved, and the rule of *dhimma* became more closely defined. At the beginning of the Abbasid's reign, the tribute paid by the non-Muslims varied from one province to another, depending on the conditions of the Arab commanders. Eventually, Islamic law required all adult dhimmi males to pay *jizya* "of five dinars for the wealthy, three for the middle class, and one for the working poor (although not for the total [*sic*] indigent), as well as a land tax (kharaj) for those who owned real estate."[32] Hārūn al-Rashid was the first Abbasid caliph to discuss the proper administration of the *jizya*. During his time, *dhimmis* were required "to pay a five percent tariff on their merchandise, as opposed to the Muslims, 2.5 percent."[33] Some historians like to argue that *dhimmis* were not oppressed, mistreated, or taxed beyond their means and that *jizya* was not as restrictive as we might think today, especially since Muslims themselves are required to pay *zakat* (alms). Amira Bennison, in her comment on *Muwatta' Malik's* Ḥadīth, states that "the distinction between the two was therefore not so much a matter of quantity but quality: Muslims paid taxes for the benefit of their own souls and the needy amongst them, while non-Muslims were obliged to pay their masters taxes of no particular benefit to themselves, except to guarantee their protected status."[34] While these are helpful observations,

---

30 Muhammad Iben Ahmad Al-Qortobi, *Tafsir Al-Qortobi* (Ar-Riyadh, Saudi Arabia, 2003). Accessed December 13, 2020. https://quran.ksu.edu.sa/tafseer/qortobi/sura9-aya29.html#qortobi.

31 Al-Qortobi, *Tafsir Al-Qortobi.*

32 Stillman, "Dhimma," 206.

33 Stillman, "Dhimma," 206.

34 Amira K. Bennison, *The Great Caliphs: The Golden Age of the 'Abbasid Empire* (New Haven: Yale University Press, 2009), 123.

Bennison completely overlooks the fact that *jizya* was mandated as a way out of conversion or death. It is true that *dhimmis* were not obligated to go to war, but they also missed the booties of war that their Muslim neighbors gained. Bennison also does not discuss the percentage that the *dhimmis* were asked to pay, which is double the amount that the Muslims paid in regular circumstances—and four times the amount paid if they were traveler merchants.

If there is any doubt left about the intention of *jizya*, note that *dhimmis* were required to pay their *jizya* publicly "in broad daylight, with hands turned palm upward, and to receive a smart smack on the forehead or the nape of the neck from the collection officer."[35] As these actions clearly demonstrate, *jizya* not only served as a means of protection, but it was also intended to humiliate the *dhimmis*.

In addition to their obligation to pay the *jizya*, Christians were subject to persecution and subordination. Ira M. Lapidus explains that in the eighth century, "Muslims increasingly treated Jews and Christians as subordinate minorities, forbidding non-Muslims to ride horses, bear weapons, ring church bells, stage processions, or display religious symbols in public."[36] Bennison admits that *ahl al-dhimma* were sometimes required to wear "distinctive garments or markers of their various faiths—coloured shoulder strips, shawls and belts were all stipulated at different times—and forbidden to build ostentatious places of worship, ring bells or sound clappers, sell wine and pork in Muslim areas, carry weapons or hold positions of power over Muslims."[37] During al-Mutawwakil reign, *dhimmis* were not persecuted or forced to convert to Islam but rather were subject to public shaming. Kennedy mentions that in AD 850, al-Mutawwakil issued a decree that forced all *dhimmis* "to wear yellow on their clothes. Upper-class *dhimmis* had to wear yellow hoods and simple belts. They also were required to ride with wooden stirrups and sport two pommels on the backs of their saddles. Their slaves were to wear yellow patches on their fronts and backs, not less than four finger spans (8 centimeters) across."[38] These markers represent

[35]Stillman, "Dhimma," 206.

[36]Ira M. Lapidus, *A History of Islamic Societies*, 3rd ed. (New York: Cambridge University Press, 2014), 155.

[37]Bennison, *Great Caliphs*, 122.

[38]Kennedy, *When Baghdad Ruled*, 240.

another way Muslims discriminated against the non-Muslim communities, creating a system by which they could restrict freedom of movement.

After the establishment of the Islamic government, the Abbasid caliph al-Mutawakil (AD 847–862) "banned non-Muslims from holding state office. Not only did he forbid the employment of non-Muslims in government offices, he also ordered that all churches built since the commencement of Islam should be demolished and imposed several other discriminatory regulations on them."[39] The hagiographical literature of Christian communities from this time period is rife with stories of Christian martyrs executed by Muslim authorities while confessing their Christian faith, opposing Islam, converting Muslims from Islam, or preaching against Islam.[40] The church's hagiography tells several stories about people who lost their lives during the Abbasid dynasty. Christian C. Sahner records that "these martyrs were a varied group, including monks, soldiers, shopkeepers, village priests, craftsmen, princes, and bishops. They were women and men, young and old, peasants and nobles. Although capital punishment disproportionately affected certain groups, especially the clergy, martyrs hailed from across the social spectrum of the early medieval Middle East."[41] This is not to say that Muslims were killing people by the sword in a massive way; rather, it is to show that the historical picture is more complicated than one might assume at first glance. Capital punishment, while real and furious, was also largely bureaucratic in nature and relied on state institution. Sahner states that "the Umayyads and Abbasids were not much interested in persecuting Christians, at least systematically. In fact, the state took a rather laissez-faire attitude toward the governance of *dhimmis* . . . It allowed them to live as they wished provided they paid the *jizya* . . . and accepted their subordination as laid down by the law."[42] The newly established religion and law led to massive conversion to Islam, especially for people who were not firm in their faith or did not have the means to pay *jizya*.

---

[39]Sirry, "public role," 188.

[40]Mark N. Swanson, "Saints and Sainthood, Christian," in *Medieval Islamic Civilization*, ed. Joseph Meri, vol 2, (New York: Taylor And Francis, 2016), 688.

[41]Sahner, *Christian Martyrs under Islam*, 2.

[42]Sahner, *Christian Martyrs under Islam*, 6.

The Christian Thinkers in the Council of the Caliphs

The Abbasid regime founded its influence on the idea of proselytism. By definition, proselytism is "One religion, and within that religion, one version of it, is true."[43] This idea, when it is imposed on a local community by a foreign ruler, generates opposition—both inward-facing within the religion itself and outward-facing toward the adherents of other religions who resist. The leaders of the subjugated religion do not only resist because they believe that their own religion is true but also because they are losing power and followers. Right after the Abbasid's control was consolidated and its firm political power established, the stage was set for confrontations between the Abbasid religion—defined as Islam—and the other religions in the area. Most of the debates that transpired in the History of Islam took place between the traditionalists and many other parties. Caesar Farah illustrates how the different views in early Islamic theology were formed into a standard belief system:

> Qadarite, for instance, stressed the doctrine of free will, while the Jabrites denied it; the Sifatites argued for the eternal nature of the attributes of God, while the Mu'tazilites denied they were eternal; the Murji'ites stressed that human actions must not be subject to human judgment, while their opponents, the Wa'dites, insisted on the condemnation of man in this life, before the Day of Judgment; the Kharijites played down the importance of the role of secular leadership, i.e., the caliphate which they considered merely a human institution, while the Shi'ites went so far as to consider their imam as divine.[44]

At the time, the three major debates among Muslims were as follows: (1) Faith versus works. The Kharijites equated faith and works, insisting that "there could be no compromise, no middle ground. A Muslim was either rigorously observant, a true believer, or not a Muslim at all."[45] (2) Predestination versus free will. The Qadarites argued for *khalq alaf'al* (that man determines his own fate) against Jabrya, who followed the majority of the Kharijites and believed in *jabr* (predestination). (3) Qur'an—the created

---

[43]Gutas, *Greek Thought*, 64.

[44]Caesar Farah, *Islam: Beliefs and Observance* (Hauppauge, NY: Barrons Educational Services, 2000), 207.

[45]John L. Esposito, *Islam: The Straight Path*, 4th ed. (New York: Oxford University Press, 2011), 69.

Word—versus Qur'an—the uncreated word of God. Mu'tazilites and Jahmites argued against traditionalists that God's speech is as eternal as any of his attributes, and they are inseparable from his essence. Mu'tazilites viewed God speaking or revealing as an anthropomorphic act, which ultimately would destroy the unity of God because there would be two eternal entities (God and his word) rather than one that existed eternally.[46]

On the Christian side, there arose a need to defend Christian belief against Islamic objections. At the center of the debate was the Trinity: both communities believed they did not worship the same God, although they both called him *Allah* in Arabic. Due to the spread of heresies in the early church period, defending ecclesiastical doctrine was not a foreign practice among Christians. However, Sara Leila Hussaini suggests that the Trinity itself was not widely discussed among Arab Christians before the rise of Islam because "the doctrine had been largely settled within the tradition by the end of the fourth century, and the expression of God as Father, Son and Holy Spirit as 'one ousia and three hypostases' would have been accepted in most Christian communities."[47] However, it is important to mention that the doctrine of the Trinity cannot be separated from the doctrine of Christology (the two natures of Jesus Christ as the Son of God and Son of Man). The Melkites, Jacobites, and Church of the East were in constant contact with each other to defend their conflicting Christology, both among themselves and with many Muslim scholars who debated them.

During the Abbasid dynasty, the new challenge that faced Christians was the need to communicate their beliefs in Arabic. Muslims were not willing to learn the local language of the land, but they were spreading Arabic, the language of the Qur'an, in schools and public systems. Christian scholars needed to write their apologies in Arabic because Muslims did not speak, read, or write Greek or Syriac. The church faced a palpable need to move to the Arabic language in their ecclesiastical worship. It needed to reach out to Arabic-speaking/reading Christians and defend the tenets of orthodoxy

[46]Ignác Goldziher, *Introduction to Islamic Theology and Law* (Princeton, NJ: Princeton University Press, 1981), 95.

[47]Sara Leila Hussaini, *Early Christian-Muslim Debate on the Unity of God: Three Christian Scholars and Their Engagement with Islamic Thought (9th Century C.E.)* (Danvers, MA: Brill, 2014), 23.

from the new Islamic religion. Switching to Arabic would also be necessary in order to maintain the church's existence and enlarge as a community.[48] As a result, the first Abbasid century saw an unprecedented rise in Arabic Christian apologetic writings directed against Islam.[49] The Melkites were at the forefront of the shift from Greek into Arabic, and their monasteries in the Judean desert produced the first translations of the Gospels and patristic literature.[50] John of Damascus's writings were the first books to be translated into Arabic, and Theodor Abū Qurrah was the first Christian theologian to write in Arabic.

Al-Ma'mūn received a thorough education in the most important fields of learning of his day. His father, caliph Hārūn al-Rashīd, used the best teachers in the country to teach his sons the Arabic language, literature, music, and poetry.[51] Concerning the religious sciences, al-Ma'mūn was trained in *Ḥadīth* and studied *fiqh* (Islamic law) under the experts in the field. Among other things, he was known for hosting debates between Muslims and representatives of other faiths at his court.[52] Under his supervision, many debates took place between Christian and Muslim scholars. But before we examine the debates that took place under the council of al-Ma'mūn, we need to understand the Qur'anic conception of the Trinity.

It is important to mention that in AD 833, al-Ma'mūn initiated what is called *miḥna* (inquisition) between Sunnis and Mu^ctazilites. During this time, the *miḥna* was carried out to ensure that all Muslim scholars professed the doctrine of the created (as opposed to uncreated and eternal) nature of the Qur'an. The Muᶜtazilites believed that the Qur'an had been created at a certain point in time by God to confess that God is the only divine and eternal being.[53] Al-Ma'mūn imprisoned or exiled those who did not comply, most famously Aḥmad Ibn Ḥanbal (AD 780–855), a respected *Ḥadīth* scholar and founder of the Ḥanbalī legal school, who actively

[48]Sidney H. Griffith, "Eutychius of Alexandria on the Emperor Theophilus and Iconoclasm in Byzantium: A Tenth Century moment in Christian Apologetics in Arabic," *Byzantion* 52 (1982): 161.

[49]Gutas, *Greek Thought*, 64.

[50]Lapidus, *History of Islamic Societies*, 158.

[51]John Abdallah Nawas, *Al-Ma'mun, the Inquisition, and the Quest for Caliphal Authority* (Columbus, GA: Lockwood Press, 2015), 21.

[52]Hussaini, *Early Christian-Muslim Debate*, 31.

[53]Kennedy, *When Baghdad Ruled*, 250.

opposed the Mu^c^tazilite's doctrine.[54] Though his definitive motive is unclear, it is likely that al-Ma'mūn wanted to restrict the religious and the secular affairs and keep them under his direct control. Hussaini believes that even for a short time "the Muᶜtazila enjoyed a 'golden period' of theological and political dominance, which had implications for the nature of Christian-Muslim debate during this period."[55] The *miḥna* period and the ideology of the Muᶜtazilites allowed the use of human reason to investigate the divine mysteries. This period in the Abbasid dynasty produced several theological writings on both the Islamic and the Christian sides.

The Widely Recorded Islamic Perception of the Trinity

Against the backdrop of Arabic-Islamic rule, it is no surprise that the doctrine of the Trinity would become the center of the debate between Muslims and Christians. Muslims believe in a strict form of monotheism called *tawḥīd* (divine unity), which is one of the cornerstones of the Islamic faith. The first pillar of Islam, the *shahada,* witnesses that "there is no God but Allah," indicating the existence of one God. Muslims believe that God is one, without associates, separation, or division of parts. Allah is also indivisible, eternal, merciful, and transcendent, and possesses ninety-nine beautiful names (*Asmā' Allah al-Husnā*), which reflect his essence, nature, and acts. This belief is supported in the Qur'an. Allah says, "Take not two gods, He is only one Allah; so of Me alone should you be afraid" (Surah 16:51). Any belief that is contrary to what Allah requires is considered blasphemy and *shirk* (associating someone with Allah in worship), which is the unforgivable sin. The next sections shall examine the Quranic and the Islamic medieval understanding of the Trinity and objections thereof.

The Qur'anic understanding of the Trinity. Mohammad was in direct contact with Christians, and they probably shared some of their beliefs with him. However, the Qur'an includes several verses that do not reflect orthodox Christian belief about the doctrine of the Trinity (the Nicene belief) but rather directly criticize it. The *locus classicus* of denying the Trinity in the Qur'an is found in Surah 4:171, where Mohammad exhorts the Christians to stop being dishonest and declare the truth that "the Messiah, Isa

---

[54]Hussaini, *Early Christian-Muslim Debate*, 31.
[55]Hussaini, *Early Christian-Muslim Debate*, 32.

son of Marium is only a messenger of Allah and His Word which He communicated to Marium and a spirit from Him; believe therefore in Allah and His messengers, and say not, Three." Here Mohammad speaks directly to the people of the Book (Christians) and calls Isa (Jesus) the Messiah, but he orders them not to say "three." Some new translations render *three* as the Trinity.[56] The word *thalātha* (three) in Arabic shares the same root of the word *Trinity*, but the specific Christian phrase for the Trinity—*Uqnūm* (singular), *Aqanīm* (plural)—does not appear in the Qur'an. It seems obvious that the meaning of the phrase "say not, Three" implies the belief that Christians are not monotheists because "three" indicates the understanding of polytheism.

Mohammad also thinks that the Trinity includes three gods: Allah, Jesus, and Mary. In Surah 5:116, he recounts a conversation in which Allah asks Jesus, "did you say to men, take me and my mother for two gods besides? Allah he will say: Glory be to Thee, it did not befit me that I should say what I had no right to (say); if I had said it, Thou wouldst indeed have known it; Thou knowest what is in my mind, and I do not know what is in Thy mind, surely Thou art the great Knower of the unseen things." Most commentators project this text to the Day of Judgment. Jesus denies that he taught the crowd about his and his mother's divinity. The followers of Jesus are accused of taking Jesus and Mary *as gods* in derogation of Allah. The implied relationship—father, mother, child—is very foreign to the Christian identity. This verse contradicts the Nicene understanding of the Trinity that all Christians agree upon.

The inclusion of Mary in the Trinity occurs at different occasions in the Qur'an. Mohammad teaches the Muslims that "Certainly they disbelieve who say: Surely, Allah—He is the Messiah, son of Marium," and he teaches them to reply: "Who then could control anything as against Allah when He wished to destroy the Messiah son of Marium and his mother and all those on the earth? And Allah's is the kingdom of the heavens and the earth and what is between them; He creates what He pleases; and Allah has power over all things" (Surah 5:17). It is highly unusual for Christians to express their faith by saying "Allah—He is the Messiah." Proclaiming Christ's deity is not

[56]Check out A. Yusuf Ali's translation of the holy Qur'an and Muhamad Asad's translation of the Qur'an.

the same as saying "God is Christ." It is not that simple. James White explains that "we do not believe the Son exhausts all that can be said about God. The proper and balanced assertion is 'The Messiah is divine and human,' and, even more to the point, 'The Son of God is eternally divine and became man in the person of Jesus the Messiah.'"[57] The contention of Surah 5:17 denies Mary and Jesus' divinity and attributes the power of creation and destruction to Allah only.

The writer of the Qur'an provides several other reasons not to believe that Jesus is God. First, Jesus himself states that he is not God. Mohammad quotes Jesus directly as stating, "O Children of Israel! serve Allah, my Lord and your Lord. Surely whoever associates (others) with Allah, then Allah has forbidden to him the garden, and his abode is the fire; and there shall be no helpers for the unjust" (Surah 5:72). Al-Ṭabarī explains that Jesus asked people not to worship him but to direct their worship to Allah because he is his God, his king, his master, his creator, and theirs as well.[58] Al-Qurtubī echoes al-Ṭabarī in his explanation and adds that the Jacobites are the ones who told Mohammad that God is Jesus, son of Mary. Al-Qurtubī repudiates the divinity of Jesus by asking a question: "If Jesus says O Lord! And O God! then how can he call himself God? and how can he ask himself? This is impossible."[59] Ibn Kathīr agrees with al-Ṭabarī and al-Qurtubī, adding the other two sects of Christianity to the conversation (the Melkites and the Church of the East) and calling their belief *shirk* (polytheism) to emphasize that the Christian belief is considered an unforgivable sin—people will lose their eternal life in heaven if they persevere in this belief.[60]

The second reason the writer of the Qur'an gives against the divinity of Jesus is that Isa is a mere messenger, a normal man who eats, drinks, and sleeps. "The Messiah, son of Marium is but a messenger," says Mohammad,

---

[57]James White, *What Every Christian Needs to Know about the Qur'an* (Grand Rapids, MI: Bethany House Publishers, 2013), 90.

[58]Muhammad Ibn Jarīr al-Ṭabarī, *Tafsīr al-Tabarī*. Accessed December 12, 2020. https://quran.ksu.edu.sa/tafseer/tabary/sura5-aya72.html#tabary. Ibn Jarīr al-Ṭabarī was one of the earliest and trusted commentators on the Qur'an with al-Qurtubī and Ibn Kathīr. He is not to be confused with Ibn Raban al-Ṭabarī.

[59]Muhammad Ibn Ahmad Al-Qurtubī, *Tafsir Al-Qortoby*. Accessed December 28, 2020. https://quran.ksu.edu.sa/tafseer/qortobi/sura5-aya72.html.

[60]Abi Al-Fida' Ismaeel Ibn Kathīr, *Tafsir Ibn Katheer*. Accessed December 29, 2020. http://quran.ksu.edu.sa/tafseer/katheer/sura5-aya72.html.

"messengers before him have indeed passed away; and his mother was a truthful woman; they both used to eat food. See how We make the communications clear to them, then behold, how they are turned away" (Surah 5:75). Al-Qurṭubī explains that God shows them shreds of evidence against their beliefs. He tells the Christians,

> You admit that Jesus was a fetus in his mother's womb, cannot cause harm or benefit, and if you decided that Jesus does not hear, or see, and does not know, harm, or benefit, then how did you take that to mean he is God? Allah is the one who hears, which means he is still hearing, knowing, causing harm and benefit, and who has these attributes is the real God.[61]

Al-Qurṭubī believes that the evidence is clear: Jesus was born, acted, and lived his life like a normal man. He had human desires and needed what human's need; therefore, he cannot be God. All above-mentioned Islamic scholars—al-Ṭabarī, al-Qurtubī, and Ibn Kathīr—display great ignorance of, or at the very least completely overlook, the classical Christian orthodox understanding of the Trinity—one *ousia*, three *hypostases*. Instead, they just reflect and expand on their own interpretations of the Trinity.

Finally, the Qur'an conveys a literal, materialistic, and anthropomorphic understanding of the title "Son of God." The writer of the Qur'an states that "the Originator of the heavens and the earth! How can He have a child, when there is for Him no consort, when He created all things and is Aware of all things?" (Surah 6:101). Although Mary's name is not mentioned directly in this passage, the verse's allusion is clear: Allah married Mary and had a child called Isa. Ibn Kathīr, al-Qurtubī, and al-Ṭabarī agree that the meaning of *wife* is meant to be understood literally. Since Allah created the heavens and the earth, he does not need a wife and does not need to have a son who looks like him.[62] He can create whatever he wants and nothing in creation is like him. The writer of the Qur'an thinks of a physical relationship between God and his wife (Mary) and a literal pregnancy and birth. The same idea is

---

[61]Muhammad Ibn Ahmad Al-Qurtubī, *Tafsir Al-Qortoby*. Accessed December 28, 2020. https://quran.ksu.edu.sa/tafseer/qortobi/sura5-aya76.html#qortobi.

[62]Muhammad Ibn Ahmad Al-Qurṭubī, *Tafsir Al-Qortoby*. Accessed December 28, 2020. https://quran.ksu.edu.sa/tafseer/qortobi/sura6-aya101.html; Muhammad Ibn Jarīr al-Ṭabarī, *Tafsīr al-Tabarī*. Accessed December 12, 2020. https://quran.ksu.edu.sa/tafseer/tabary/sura6-aya101.html#tabary; Abi Al-Fida' Ismaeel Ibn Kathīr, *Tafsir Ibn Katheer*. Accessed December 28, 2020. https://quran.ksu.edu.sa/tafseer/katheer/sura6-aya101.html#katheer.

repeated in Surah 112:1-4. Mohammad teaches his followers to say that "Allah, is One. Allah is He on Whom all depend. He begets not, nor is He begotten. And none is like Him." The literal understanding of the Qur'an conveys a distorted picture of the orthodox Trinity that most Christians agree upon.

To conclude, the Quran neither mentions the Trinity nor comes close to accurately defining what Christians mean by it. The writer of the Qur'an considers Christians to be polytheists, understands the Trinity in a physical sense and in mathematical terms (i.e., 1+1+1=3)—three beings are divine, namely Father, Mary, and Jesus. God the Father married Mary and had a baby, named Isa (Jesus). The title *Father* is not mentioned in the Qur'an, but it is implied in the physical relationship—Father (Allah), Mother (Mary), and Child (Jesus). The Nicene profession of the Trinity is not mentioned anywhere in the Qur'an even though it was conducted and widely agreed upon among Christians many years before the Qur'an was written.

Omitting the correct theological concept of the Trinity from the Qur'an is a historical weakness because the Qur'an was written approximately 300 years after the Nicene Creed. Thus it is reasonable to conclude that the Qur'anic way of understanding the Trinity is nonhistorical. No early church father used the concept of the Trinity in the way that Mohammad understood it. Tertullian (AD 155–220), for example, was the first church theologian who introduced the word *Trinity* while explaining the unity of God in the third century.[63] He did not believe that God is three separate persons and Mary is one of the divine persons. Augustine (AD 354–430) also believed that "the Trinity is the one and only and true God,"[64] contradicting the Qur'an and its belief.

Other Islamic resources, such as Ḥadīths, Islamic commentators, and Islamic theologians (*Mutaklimīn*) express the same understanding of the writer of the Qur'an about the doctrine of the Trinity. In *Ṣaḥīḥ Bukhārī*, Mohammad tells his people about the end of times and how Allah shall conduct his judgment. He states, "Then it will be said to the Christians, 'What did you use to worship?' They will reply, 'We used to worship Messiah, the son of Allah.' It will be said, 'You are liars, for Allah has neither a wife

[63]Tertullian, *Against Praxeas* 3. Accessed March 25, 2021. www.tertullian.org/articles/evans_praxeas_eng.htm.

[64]Augustine of Hippo, *On the Trinity* (Buffalo, NY: Christian Literature Company, 1887), 1.2.4.

nor a son.'"[65] This Ḥadīth duplicates the Qur'anic understanding of the doctrine of the Trinity, venerating Mary by making her part of the Trinity and God's wife.

The medieval Islamic understanding of the Trinity. Under the Abbasid dynasty in the ninth century, several scholars left written apologies against the Trinity. This section shall examine three of them. The intended purpose of this section is to inform the reader of the varieties of Islamic objections to the Trinity.

Alī Ibn Rabban al-Ṭabarī (783–858). The first apology was written by Alī Ibn Rabban al-Ṭabarī, a Christian, the son of a Jewish scholar, and a Muslim later on in his life—he converted to Islam at the age of seventy.[66] His father was a religious leader in a Syriac-speaking community.[67] Al-Tabarī was a senior member of the Muslim governor's administration and a trusted supporter. According to Ibn al-Nadīm, al-Ṭabarī converted to Islam at the prompting of the caliph al-Muᶜtaṣim (AD 833–842) and came to court during caliph al-Mutawakkil (AD 847–861), who later on made him a table companion.[68] Al-Ṭabarī's polemic objections to the Trinity are unique because they are written from the perspective of a former Christian. It is hard to know why he converted to Islam, but he states that "the eternal One has called me to write this book of mine as a renunciation of the religion of Christianity (*li-l-tanaṣṣul min dīn al-Naṣrāniyya*)."[69] He also thanks al-Mutawakkil for his help in writing the book. It seems that he probably felt the need to prove his belief to the caliph. Thus he wrote his polemic against the Trinity to return a favor or gain his trust.[70]

Al-Ṭabarī's methodology seems to authenticate many sayings of Jesus, especially the ones that indicate his humanity. He starts his polemics against

[65]Muḥammad ibn Ismāʻīl Bukhārī, *Ṣaḥīḥ Bukhārī*, Ḥadīth no. 7439. Accessed April 28, 2020, https://sunnah.com/bukhari/97.

[66]Mark Beaumont, "Muslim Readings of John's Gospel in the ᶜAbbasid Period," *Islam and Christian-Muslim Relations*, 19:2 (2008): 180.

[67]Rifaat Ebied and David Thomas, eds., *The Polemical Works of ʿAlī al-Ṭabarī* (Boston: Brill, 2016), 2. Sami K. Hamarneh, "Al-Ṭabarī," in *Encyclopedia of the History of Science, Technology, and Medicine in Non-Western Cultures*, ed. H. Selin (Dordrecht: Springer, 2008), https://link.springer.com/referenceworkentry/10.1007/978-1-4020-4425-0_9188.

[68]Muhammad ibn Isḥāq Ibn al-Nadīm, *Fihrist*, ed. M. Riḍā-Tajaddud (Tehran: Dar al-Masirah, 1971), 354.

[69]Ebied and Thomas, *Polemical Works*, 41.

[70]Beaumont, "Muslim Readings," 181.

the Trinity by dissecting the nature of Jesus Christ and who He is. He lays out twelve points to refute the divinity of Jesus. For the purpose of this study, only the major objections in relation to the Trinity will be listed. For instance, al-Ṭabarī accuses the Christians of being polytheists, believing "in three or even four gods, Father, Son and Holy Spirit, and an eternal human who is Jesus Christ."[71] Al-Ṭabarī separates the title "Son" and the person "Jesus Christ," making them two different beings. While he does not elaborate on this point, he accuses Christians of believing in four divine beings. This section could be understood as his personal understanding or addition to the Christian belief.

Unlike the Qur'an and many other Islamic scholars, al-Ṭabarī cites several Christian sources.[72] He focuses in his Christology on what Jesus says according to his humanity to prove that he cannot be God. For instance, al-Ṭabarī quotes John 20:17, in which Jesus says, "I am ascending to my Father and your Father, to my God and your God," and concludes that Jesus is a mere human, for he is calling God his God.[73] He also quotes Jesus declaring that his mission on earth is to do the will of God, not his own (Jn 6:38). Al-Ṭabarī deduces that since Jesus is fulfilling not his will but God's will, then he is a different person from God and cannot be God.[74]

Al-Ṭabarī mentions the three major branches of Christianity that existed during the Abbasid dynasty. Because of his Christian background, it seems that he was aware of the christological differences among these branches. To know whether Jesus is divine or not, al-Ṭabarī teaches his followers to ask all types of Christians about the eternality of the creator:

> Can he [God] be changed from the condition of his eternity and substantiality, and can illnesses and death affect him or not? If they say that he is changed and dies, their belief has died, and the person who says this is like the person whom God almighty in his Book likens to animals. . . . The eternal Creator cannot be changed and does not die, they are at variance with their Creed, and in their eyes the one who is at variance with it does not believe in it, for it says that Jesus Christ is Creator not created, and is true God from true God, of the

[71] Ebied and Thomas, *Polemical Works*, 69.

[72] Al- Ṭabarī does not include biblical references, but he seems to quote the biblical translation that was available to him.

[73] Ebied and Thomas, *Polemical Works*, 73.

[74] Ebied and Thomas, *Polemical Works*, 73.

> substance of his Father, and that he was killed and crucified and made to suffer. Thus, their God was changed and died.[75]

Al-Ṭabarī believes that God cannot be likened to creation (human or animals) and his nature cannot be changed. When he looks at Jesus, he sees a person who gets hungry and thirsty, suffers, and is crucified. For these reasons, Jesus cannot be God.

Most Islamic scholars either ignore the Nicene Creed in their polemics or deem it as a hoax, so they do not quote it to explain the Christian belief. Al-Ṭabarī, on the other hand, is one of few Islamic scholars who use the Nicene Creed in his polemics against the Trinity.[76] While he acknowledges that all Christian denominations agree on the Nicene Creed, he attributes contradictions to the first part of the creed:

> The beginning of the Creed is, "We believe in one God, the Father, Possessor of all things, Maker of what is seen and unseen." And then, with this they stop referring to God and begin with a new reference, saying, "We believe in one Lord, Jesus Christ, true God from true God, of the substance of his Father." But this is a contradiction of the first part of what they say, and no one with any justness or understanding will think this fanciful. For they say, "We believe in one God," and then immediately after this and in the same way they say, "We believe that Jesus Christ is the Creator of all things by his hand." In this they affirm another Creator different from the first Creator.

This is another attempt to prove that Christians believe in two different beings, God the Father and God the Son. Al-Ṭabarī's understanding of the creed implies literal polytheism. Since the Father is a creator and the Son is a creator, then there is no one God, but two.

Last, al-Ṭabarī contests the meaning of the words *Father* and *Son*. He argues that the meanings of *father* and *progenitor* can be understood both literally as referring to procreation and metaphorically "as when a child uses 'father' for his uncle or the person who brings him up or teaches him or educates him or does him good, and he will also call the elders of his family and his grandparents 'fathers': thus, Adam is called 'the father of humanity.' And I have heard Christian scholars say that God is really called 'father' because

[75]Ebied and Thomas, *Polemical Works*, 73-74.

[76]Al-Ṭabarī does not use the known verbatim of the Nicene Creed. His resources are unknown. He could be paraphrasing what he had memorized earlier in his childhood.

he is the Initiator and Progenitor of things."[77] Al-Ṭabarī does not cite the person who stated this information; instead, he generalizes the meaning and assumes that it is accepted by all Christians. He continues with the same reasoning, explaining that the metaphorical meaning of *Son* is "someone adopts someone, that is, he brings him up, teaches him, educates him and does him good. And people of culture are called 'sons of culture' and its 'brothers.'"[78] Al-Ṭabarī believes that the metaphorical meanings of the title *Son* contradict the Nicene Creed and the Christian faith "because the followers of Christianity unanimously agree that there are realities to these names, and the realities are not concealed or derived but are obvious and distinct."[79] In Al-Ṭabarī's opinion, if the Son is eternal, then he is not generated, and if he was generated, then he is not eternal. He understands the meaning of the word *generated* in a temporal sense—with a beginning and an end.

Abū ᶜīsā Muḥammad al-Warrāq (AD 864). Abū ᶜīsā Muḥammad al-Warrāq was an independent scholar who lived in the ninth century. Little is known about his life and background, but it seems that he was active in AD 864.[80] It is hard to know his religious background. While the Muᶜtazilites scholars (e.g., ᶜAbd al-Jabbār and al-Masᶜūdī) accused him of being a Shiᶜite, a *zindiq* (irreligious), and *mulḥid* (atheist), the Ashᶜarī said that he was a Manichee; and Ibn al-Nadīm portrays him as an unconventional Muᶜtazilite with such a deep interest in dualist beliefs.[81] David Thomas believes that al-Warrāq "remained a Muslim, probably with Shīᶜī sympathies, though with his own interpretation of faith."[82]

Al-Warrāq left a written work against Christianity called *Radd ᶜalā al-Thalāth Firaq min al-Naṣārā.* The book itself is not now available, but Yaḥyā Ibn ᶜAdī included it in his reply by making a detailed refutation of its arguments.[83] David Thomas managed to edit and translate two volumes of

---

77 Ebied and Thomas, *Polemical Works*, 155.

78 Ebied and Thomas, *Polemical Works*, 155.

79 Ebied and Thomas, *Polemical Works*, 155.

80 David Thomas, "Abū ʿīsā Al-Warrāq and the History of Religions," *Journal of Semitic Studies* 41, no. 2 (1996): 275

81 Muḥammad ibn Hārūn Abū ᶜĪsā Al-Warrāq, *Anti-Christian Polemic in Early Islam: Abū ᶜĪsā al-Warrāq's 'Against the Trinity,'* ed. and trans. David Thomas, (Cambridge: Cambridge University Press, 1992), 10.

82 Thomas, "Abū ʿīsā Al-Warrāq," 1.

83 Al-Warrāq, *Anti-Christian Polemic*, 3.

al-Warrāq's works, one about the Trinity and the other one about the incarnation. Although al-Warrāq was labeled a heretic by many Muslims, he was recognized by others as a reliable authority on non-Muslim religions. Many scholars in the tenth century, such as al-Māturīdī, al-Bāqillānī, and ᶜAbdh al-Jabbār, used his works to defeat other religions; but they attacked him because of his criticism of the Qur'an and the prophet.[84]

Al-Warrāq stands out because he is one of a few scholars who studied the Trinity as Christians explain it. He does not quote the Bible in his book, but he mentions that the referenced explanation about the Trinity comes from a Christian source. His intention in the *Radd* is to expose the downfalls of Christian belief by presenting several dilemmas against the concept of God among the three types of Christian sects (Melkites, Jacobites, and Church of the East). He forms his argument in a series of questions and presents them with several dilemmas to force his audience to review their beliefs (i.e., ask this . . . if they answer no, then . . . and if they answer yes, then . . .).

The first dilemma al-Warrāq presents is related to the nature of substance. While the Church of the East and the Jacobites apply differentiation and number to the hypostases, they equate the substance with the hypostases. In al-Warrāq's opinion, this belief is contradictory because they are "claiming that what is differentiated is what is not."[85] The Melkites, on the other hand, do not believe that the substance is the hypostases, but if they do believe that the substance is the same in some respects "other than the respect in which it is different from them, then if the respect in which it is identical with them is itself, the respect in which it is different from them must be other than itself, requiring an eternal other than the substance."[86] In other words, if the substance is different from the hypostases in a respect that is different from them and itself, then there is another eternal being other than the substance; and if another eternal is admitted, then Christianity becomes a polytheistic belief.

The second dilemma is presented when the Christians say that the substance is different from the hypostases in every respect. Al-Warrāq believes, "then it necessarily follows, since the substance is divine, that neither the

[84]Al-Warrāq, *Anti-Christian Polemic*, 12.
[85]Al-Warrāq, *Anti-Christian Polemic*, 77.
[86]Al-Warrāq, *Anti-Christian Polemic*, 89.

Father nor the Son nor the Spirit is divine; and if each of the hypostases is divine, that the substance is not divine."[87] In other words, whether the Melkites say it is the same or it is different, their belief is wrong.

The third dilemma arises when the Christians say that the substance is neither different from the hypostases nor identical to them. Al-Warrāq asks these questions: "why characterize the substance differently from the hypostases and the hypostases differently from the substance? . . . will people be able to tell at all between the statement: 'two things, one separate from the other, whose names and descriptions are distinct but they themselves are not'?"[88] Al-Warrāq's understanding requires the term *other*, but "the term 'other' cannot be applied to it neither can the terms 'identical and different,' or 'identity' and 'difference.'"[89] Therefore, their claim that the substance is neither identical nor different from the hypostases does not stand.

Al-Warrāq raises a different objection to the divinity of the three hypostases. He is one of a few scholars who acknowledge that Christians believe that the Father, the Son, and the Spirit are divine; however, they do not believe in three divinities but one. They all believe that each of the hypostases is Lord and Creator, not three Lords and three Creators.[90] However, al-Warrāq still thinks of this belief as a contradiction. He explains:

> If the substance is other than the hypostases then its action must be other than theirs and its creation other than theirs . . . if action must be affirmed of the substance and not of the hypostases, then consequently it must be denied of the Father, the Son and the Spirit, which must all be debarred from it . . . if action and creation belong to the hypostases and not the substance which is other than them, then you have claimed that the eternal divinity, which is the general substance and its hypostases, has no action or work or control.[91]

Al-Warrāq seems to consider the substance as a separate being, which is comparable to the three hypostases.

Al-Warrāq presents an objection to the nature of fatherhood and sonship of the Trinity. He asks, "Is it [substance] of the Father's substance or not? If

[87] Al-Warrāq, *Anti-Christian Polemic*, 93.
[88] Al-Warrāq, *Anti-Christian Polemic*, 95.
[89] Al-Warrāq, *Anti-Christian Polemic*, 97.
[90] Al-Warrāq, *Anti-Christian Polemic*, 109.
[91] Al-Warrāq, *Anti-Christian Polemic*, 111.

it is not of his substance then it must be of a substance other than his. . . . If it is eternal then they affirm two eternal substances. . . . If it is contingent, then before the appearance of this substance the Father was not Father and was not entitled to fatherhood."[92] His confusion between the substance and the hypostases continues with his understanding of the fatherhood of the Father and the sonship of Jesus. "If fatherhood is of the substance of the father," says al-Warrāq, "and the substance of the Son is according to you the substance of the Father, then it follows that the Son must be Father and that you must affirm fatherhood of him as you do of the Father, since their substance is one."[93] It seems that although al-Warrāq worked to understand the Trinity according to Christian belief, his grasp of the one divine being and three hypostases remained oblique.

Al-Qāsim Ibn Ibrāhīm al-Husnī, al-Rassī (AD 785–860). Al-Qāsim Ibn Ibrāhīm al-Husnī, known as al-Rassī, was born in AD 785, grew up in al-Medina, and spent eleven years in Egypt.[94] He was contemporary to Hārūn al-Rashīd, al-Ma'mūn, and al-Mutawakkil caliphs during the Abbasid reign. He was persecuted by the Abbasids for practicing secret *da^cwa* (invitation) to the Shi^cites.[95] He gained several supporters, however, and was called the star of Mohammad.[96] While he was in Egypt, he learned about Christianity and debated Christians and Jews. In AD 826, he left Egypt and settled in al-Rass near al-Medina, where he died in AD 860. While he was influenced to a large extent by the Mu^ctazilites, he was one of the founders of the theological traditions of the Zaydi branch of Shi^cite.[97]

Al-Rassī's intent in writing *Ar-Radd ^calā al-Naṣarā* (a reply to the Christians) is to refute the Christian revelation and their doctrine of God. He objects to the names of the hypostases—Father, Son, and Spirit—categorizing them into three different groups: natural names, which are related to the substance; hypostatical names, which are proper names; and incidental

[92]Al-Warrāq, *Anti-Christian Polemic*, 127.
[93]Al-Warrāq, *Anti-Christian Polemic*, 129.
[94]W. Madelung, *Der Imam al-Qasim ibn Ibrdhim und die Glaubenslehre der Zaiditen* (Berlin: De Gruyter, 1966), 86-96. Binyamin Abrahamov, "Al-Ḳāsim Ibn Ibrāhīm's Theory of the Imamate," *Arabica*, T. 34 (1987): 80.
[95]Al-Qāsim Ibn Ibrāhīm al-Husnī Al-Rassī, *al-Rad 'Ala al-Nassara* [The Reply to the Christians], ed. Hanafi Abduallah (Cairo, Egypt: Dar -al=Afaq al-Arabia, 2000), 15.
[96]Al-Rassī, *al-Rad 'Ala al-Nassara.*
[97]Abrahamov, "Theory of the Imamate," 80.

names, which are related to the situation/verb. To him, *Father* and *Son* are incidental names. "If you name the Father as father," says al-Rassī, "because he gave birth, as you stated, he had a son and a child, so these names are not natural nor hypostatical personal names, but they are incidental, when children are born, between the parents and their children, and not natural, or proper names nor in Roma or other than Roma."[98] Al-Rassī categorizes *Father* and *Son* as incidental names and not natural or proper. These names, in his opinion, are used to describe a verb or an action. He compares them to *earth*, *heaven*, or *fire*, which denote something that is its substance—something that can be explained by its name and not by anything else.[99]

In the second part of the book, al-Rassī calls the Christian to *al-Inṣāf* (fairness). He bases his invitation on five common points on which all Christians and Muslims agree: (1) the testimony of Allah, (2) the testimony of the angels, (3) the sayings of Jesus and his testimony, (4) the testimony of Mary the mother of Jesus, and (5) the testimony of Jesus' disciples and their message.[100] He starts by quoting Matthew 1:1: "This is the genealogy of Jesus the Messiah the son of David, the son of Abraham." Al-Rassī uses this verse to prove to the Christians that Jesus is the son of David, not God. He explains that the meaning of fatherhood and sonship is not consistent in the Gospels because Jesus says to his disciples that God is their father (Mt 5:48). Al-Rassī also adds the testimony of Mary, Jesus' mother, to that of the apostle Philip, stating that both give testimony that Jesus is the son of Joseph. However, he never cites any reference from the Gospels.[101] Finally, al-Rassī includes the testimony of the angels to Mary,[102] telling her that she will bear a child, not that she would bear the Son of God.[103] Moreover, while al-Rassī affirms the authenticity of a few verses, he declines the authenticity of others. For example, he declines that Simon Peter may have said that Jesus is the Son of God.[104] It is important to note that Al-Rassī claims to quote the Bible; however, he does not quote from a known Arabic translation. He either cites

---

[98]Al-Rassī, *al-Rad ʿAla al-Nassara*, 40.
[99]Al-Rassī, *al-Rad ʿAla al-Nassara*, 40.
[100]Al-Rassī, *al-Rad ʿAla al-Nassara*, 43-44.
[101]The editor adds two wrong citations in his footnotes (Mt 16:13-16 and Mk 8:27-29).
[102]Al-Rassī does not mention angel Gabriel, but he uses a plural description of angels.
[103]Al-Rassī, *al-Rad ʿAla al-Nassara*, 45.
[104]Al-Rassī, *al-Rad ʿAla al-Nassara*, 46.

the Bible from memory without paying attention to the accuracy of the verses or paraphrases the verses according to his own understanding.

Conclusion

During the eighth, ninth, and tenth centuries, Christian-Muslim relations were complicated. Some of the Christians were professional state administrators under the Umayyads. They were in high demand, both because they knew how to run the government and because they knew Greek, Syriac, and Arabic. Under the early reign of the Abbasids, circumstances changed for the Christians. Some caliphs, like Hārūn al-Rashīd and his son al-Ma'mūn, were not religiously strict. The former started the translation project of *Bayt al-Ḥikma*, which contributed to the development of several sciences, and the latter encouraged debates between Muslim and non-Muslim scholars under his council, which resulted in several religious writings. The translation movement would not have flourished without the support of the caliphs and the contributions of Syriac-speaking Christians.

Although many Christians worked for the Abbasid caliphs in translation, several also lived under restrictions, and various were persecuted. Various social, religious, and financial restrictions were implemented on Christians and *dhimmis* under caliph al-Mutawakil, resulting in persecution to the extent of martyrdom. However, Christian scholars were able to defend and debate Muslim scholars for a short period, especially during al-Ma'mūn's reign. A need to defend the Christian belief against Islamic objections arose, and the Trinity was at the center of the debate as Christian and Muslim scholars worked to demonstrate that they did not worship the same God.

During this time and under these circumstances, many disputations were written between Muslims and Christians. From the Muslim side, the majority of them are directed against the Trinity and the Christian understanding of the nature of God. Some objections are based on a fundamental misunderstanding of what the Christians actually teach because they are based on nonhistorical arguments, others are rooted in semantic confusion, and others are based on personal observation, accusing Christians of being nonrational.

The nonhistorical objections ignore the Gospels and the Nicene Creed's explanation of the Trinity. They ridicule the Christian belief, label it as contradictory, and add what does not belong to it. In the Qur'an, Mohammad clearly confuses the doctrine of the Trinity with the notion of divine cohabitation, deifying Mary from whom Christ was born, and making her a member of the holy Trinity. He also describes the Christian faith in a polytheistic way, including God, Mary, and Jesus to the Godhead.

The semantic objections are more christological in nature because they are related to the literal and metaphorical meanings of the titles "Father" and "Son." These objections convey a literal, materialistic, and anthropomorphic perception of the title "Son of God." Muslims argue that the Christian belief includes God having a wife or a son in a literal sense. When the title "Father" is used literally, it must mean progenitor, which indicates procreation. When it is used metaphorically, it conveys the idea of God being the Creator of all things. "Son," on the other hand, may be understood in an adoptionist sense if it is used metaphorically. According to the Muslims, this thinking contradicts the Nicene Creed because while Christians claim to believe in one God, they announce two creators. Moreover, some scholars went further to argue that Christians' explanation of the terms "Father" and "Son" indicates more than three persons. Some scholars separate the "Son" and "Jesus," making them two persons, resulting in great confusion as to what Christians actually teach regarding the Trinity.

The "being nonrational objection" is agreed upon by most ancient, medieval, and contemporary Muslim scholars.[105] They accuse Christians of being nonlogical in their explanation of the Trinity because they believe in three persons and call them one God. The animus with which Islamic tradition views core Christian doctrines is still very much alive today.[106] Most Muslims and Christians who have entered into serious conversation have found the doctrine of the Trinity to be a "dead end." I do not intend to solve this dilemma; instead, I seek to add to the conversation.

[105] ᶜabd al-Majīd al-Sharafī, *The Islamic Thought about the Reply to the Christians: To the End of the Tenth Century* (Tunisia: al-Dar al-Tunisya LilNashir, 1986), 6. Al-Sharafī concludes that most of the Islamic replies to the beliefs of the Christians after the tenth century were copying the arguments of the previous centuries, especially the ninth and the tenth centuries.

[106] Hugh Goddard, "Muslim and Christian Beliefs," in *Contemporary Muslim-Christian Encounters: Developments, Diversity, and Dialogues*, ed. Paul Hedges (New York: Bloomsbury Academic, 2015), 294.

2

The Iconoclastic Effect of the Qur'anic Perception of the Trinity

IN THE PREVIOUS CHAPTER, I presented the Qur'anic understanding of the Trinity, which includes Mary as a divine person within the Godhead. Several scholars have been studying the Qur'anic reference of Mary for decades by using different methods and ending with different conclusions. This chapter surveys these studies briefly, examines the historical and theological beliefs about the *Theotokos* icons in the history of Christianity, and finally moves to argue the effect of the *Theotokos* icon on the Qur'anic perception of the Trinity for the purpose of studying the possible reasons why Mary is divinized in the Qur'an.

Survey of Previous Research

Previous studies suggest several reasons for the Qur'anic belief about the Trinity. For example, Abū Mūsa al-Ḥarīrī, a Christian Arab scholar, suggested that Mohammad learned about Christianity from Waraqa bin Nūfal, an Ebionite monk who followed the Gospel according to the Hebrews.[1] Early Fathers dedicated the name Ebionite to a Christian Jewish group who used the Gospel of Matthew and considered Paul an apostate from the law. The Ebionites did not believe in the divinity of Christ but accepted Jesus as a mere man. Al-Ḥarīrī relied heavily on Islamic resources to learn about

[1]Abū Mūsa Al-Ḥarīrī, *Qiss was nabi [A Monk and A Prophet]* (Diar Aqil, Lebanon: Dar Liajil al-Ma'rifa, 2005), 2.

Waraqa. He reports that Waraqa was the only one who translated the Gospel of the Hebrews into Arabic because of his extensive knowledge of Arabic, Aramaic, and Hebrew.[2] Many Islamic resources mention him copying the Gospel and translating it from Hebrew to Arabic.[3]

According to al-Ḥarīrī, Waraqa was well educated and knowledgeable in Gnosticism.[4] This reason pushed al-Ḥarīrī to jump to the conclusion that the Gospel of the Hebrews is the only Gospel that was known to Waraqa and it is the Gospel that he used to teach Mohammad. Al-Ḥarīrī states, "The Arabic Qur'an mentions one Gospel, which proves that 'the Gospel of the Hebrews' was the only one known, especially because we find a complete match in the information concerning doctrines, dogmas, forms of worship, and the religious calendar . . ."[5] It is true that several similarities exist between the Ebionites' belief about Jesus and the Qur'an's teachings about Jesus; however, their beliefs are not identical. For instance, the Ebionites denied the virgin birth and believed that Jesus was the biological son of Joseph and Mary; whereas the Qur'an approves the virgin birth of Jesus. Al-Ḥarīrī's study seems to rely heavily on Islamic resources without taking into consideration other historical factors, such as the beliefs of the specific Arab Christians in South Arabia that Mohammad encountered. Al-Ḥarīrī even jumps abruptly to the conclusion that Waraqa was the president of the church in Makkah during the life of Abdul Mutalib (Mohammad's uncle) and for a long period of time during Mohammad's life.[6]

Other scholars think that the Qur'anic view of the Trinity was influenced by Christian sects/cults that exalted Mary far above her usual Christian status.[7] William Montgomery Watt, Scottish Anglican Islamologist, suggests that Mohammad's attack on the Trinity was not against an orthodox Christian formulation but rather against a heterodox community—people

---

[2]Al-Ḥarīrī, *Qiss was nabi*, 33.

[3]Bukharī, *Ṣaḥīḥ Bukharī*, Hadīth no. 3392. Accessed March 3, 2021. https://sunnah.com/bukhari:3392. Muslim, *Ṣaḥīḥ Muslim*, Hadīth no. 160a. Accessed March 13, 2021. https://sunnah.com/muslim:160a. The extent of the Gospel according to the Hebrews is no longer known. Few quotations are preserved in the writings of Clement of Alexandria (second century), Origen (third century), Eusebius (fourth century) and Cyril (fourth century).

[4]Al-Ḥarīrī, *Qiss wa Nabi*, 32.

[5]Al-Ḥarīrī, *Qiss was nabi*, 35-36.

[6]Al-Ḥarīrī, *Qiss was nabi*, 37.

[7]John Kalner, *Ishmael Instructs Isaac: An Introduction to the Qur'ān for Bible Readers* (Collegeville, MN: Liturgical Press, 1999), 272.

who believed in God and yet introduced false doctrines.[8] He explains that the idea that Mary was part of the Trinity "may have come from an obscure set of Collyridians, heard of in Arabia more than two centuries before Muhammad."[9] Collyridians were a cultic group in Arabia, composed mainly of women who worshiped Mary the mother of Jesus.[10] Epiphanius of Salamis writes in his *Panarion* about a group of women who came from Thrace to Arabia who seemed to adopt a particular form of devotion to Mary, offering her loaves of bread on appointed days (called in Greek *Kollyris*).[11] Furthermore, Jamāl al-Dīn Qāsimī, a Syrian Muslim scholar, supports Watt's idea and argues for the possibility that Surah 5:73 refers to the Collyridians as a Christian sect. He states, "Among the Christians there was a group (firqa) called 'Collyridians' who said that gods are three: the Father, the Son, and Mary."[12] Despite the claim "Arabia is the mother of heresies,"[13] this view has no historical evidence in early Islamic and Christian literature. There is no evidence that Mohammad was in touch with the Collyridians, and Epiphanius's polemic implies they were an obscure sect of no great importance.[14]

As for the origin of the Quranic reference to Mary as one of three gods, Watt mentions another possible explanation by referring to the goddess connotations of Mary found in the relatively early Christian Apocrypha.[15] There is evidence that before the fourth century, scribes in ancient Syria described the Holy Spirit not only as a female but also as a mother.[16] Susan Ashbrook

[8]W. Montgomery Watt, *Muslim-Christian Encounters: Perceptions and Misperceptions* (New York: Routledge, Taylor & Francis Group, 1991), 23.

[9]Watt, *Muslim-Christian Encounter*, 23.

[10]G. Kruger, s.v. "Collyridian," *New Schaff-Herzog Encyclopedia*. Accessed February 11, 2021. https://ccel.org/ccel/schaff/encyc03/encyc03/Page_162.html.

[11]Epiphanius, *Panarion* 73.23.

[12]Jamāl al-Dīn Al-Qāsimī, *Maḥāsin al-ta᾽wīl*, vol. 6, (Cairo: Dārihyā᾽ al-kutub al-ʿarabiyya, 1957), 2008.

[13]Samuel M. Zwemer, *Arabia: The Cradle of Islam*. (New York: The Caxton Press, 1900), np.

[14]Michael P. Carroll, *The Cult of the Virgin Mary: Psychological Origins* (Princeton, NJ: Princeton University Press, 1986), 44-45.

[15]Marvin Meyer, *Gospel of Thomas* (Polebridge Press, 1992, 1994), 101. "For my mother gave me falsehood, but my true mother gave me life," *The Nag Hammadi Library*. Accessed February 12, 2021. www.gnosis.org/naghamm/gosthom-meyer.html. Wesley W. Isenberg, *Gospel of Philip*, "Some said, Mary conceived by the Holy Spirit. They are in error. They do not know what they are saying. When did a woman ever conceive by a woman?" *The Nag Hammadi Library*. Accessed February 12, 2021. http://gnosis.org/naghamm/gop.html.

[16]Sebastian Brock, *Holy Spirit in the Syrian Baptismal Tradition*, vol. 9 (Piscataway, NJ: Gorgias Press, 2013), 3-8.

Harvey explains that the Syriac church emphasized the birth of Jesus, his baptism in the Jordan, and his descent to Sheol as imagery in relation to baptism, whereas the Greco-Latin churches highlighted the "resurrection, of baptism as a dying and rising, and the baptismal water as the grave, following on the Pauline teachings of Rom 6:4-6 especially."[17] Ashbrook Harvey continues, "In early Syriac tradition Baptism was above all a rebirth, following John 3:3-7, and the baptismal water was the 'womb' that bore true sons and daughters for the heavenly kingdom. Baptism became the 'Mother of Christianity,' as Mary has been the Mother of Christ."[18] It seems that cults understood the baptismal imagery in this way: as Mary gave birth to Jesus through her womb, Christ gave birth to Christians through the womb of the baptismal waters. Thus, womb imagery might have been used in Gnostic and apocryphal literature to identify Jesus' mother with the Holy Spirit, possibly due to the feminine form of the word *Spirit* in Syriac.[19] Ashbrook Harvey indicates that the shift to the masculine form of the word *Spirit* that occurred during the fifth century was to bring the Syriac churches into closer conformity with those of the Greco-Latin West.[20]

Recent critical scholarship of the Qur'an as represented by the works of Sidney Griffith and Gabriel Reynolds displays a shift from the heretical Quranic explanation to the emphasis on the rhetorical language of the Qur'an. According to these scholars, the misunderstanding of the Trinity should not be understood as referring to heretical sects but rather "as a rhetorical device developed by the Qur'an to win over an argument in such a polemical environment."[21] For example, when Mohammad claimed that Christians said "God is Jesus, the son of Mary" or "God is the third of three," he was not simply repeating these narratives, but he was using polemical statements to allude to, add to, and even correct them. Sidney Griffith states that "the Qur'an's seeming misstatement, rhetorically speaking, should therefore not be thought to be a mistake, but rather a polemically inspired

[17]Susan Ashbrook Harvey, "Feminine Imagery for the Divine," *St Vladimir's Theological Quarterly* (1993): 119.

[18]Harvey, "Feminine Imagery," 119.

[19]Watt, *Muslim-Christian Encounter*, 23.

[20]Harvey, "Feminine Imagery," 121.

[21]Mun'im Sirry, "Other Religions," in *The Wiley Blackwell Companion to the Qur'an*, eds. Andrew Rippin and Jawid Mojaddedi (Hoboken, NJ: Wiley Blackwell, 2017), 329.

caricature, the purpose of which is to highlight in Islamic terms the absurdity, and therefore the wrongness, of the Christian belief, from an Islamic perspective."[22] Reynolds echoes Griffith, saying that

> Christians refer to Christ as the son of God, and the Qur'an explicitly rejects this appellation (Q 9:30), yet it also insists (against the Jews) that Christ had no father at all (Q 3:59), and so it cannot refer to him as "Son of *his father*." Thus, the Qur'an refers to Jesus as the son of *his mother*, and thereby encapsulates its argument against both Christians and Jews.[23]

Given their knowledge of Arabic culture and the way Arabs argue, Griffith and Reynolds's suggestion seems very reasonable; however, taking into consideration the types of Christianity available to Mohammad in Arabia and the context of his conversations with Christians might reveal a better understanding of his statements about Christianity. In my estimation, there is no problem with any of the above-mentioned approaches. They are all prospects that scholars should pursue, but my study seeks to propose different possibilities. According to my research, a different explanation may account for the Qur'anic misunderstanding that scholars have not presented yet.

THE THEOTOKOS ICON: A HISTORICAL BACKGROUND

The *Theotokos* icon was common among Christians in the Levant, Egypt, and Ethiopia. The few icons that survived were dated between the fourth and seventh centuries, indicating that such icons were widely spread among Christians well before the rise of Islam. One example of these is a fourth-century image of Mary and Child seated on a throne, which was discovered in the city of al-Fayyum in Egypt and is now in the Staatliche Museum in Berlin.[24] Another is a fifth- or sixth-century image of a venerated virgin and child appearing on a fragmentary papyrus leaf from the Alexandrian Chronicle in the Pushkin Museum in Moscow.[25] A sixth-century ampulla

[22]Sidney H. Griffith, "Al-Naṣārā in the Qur'ān: A hermeneutical reflection," in *New Perspectives on the Qur'ān: The Qur'ān in Its Historical Context*, ed. Gabriel Said Reynolds (London: Routledge Taylor & Francis, 2011), 311.

[23]Gabriel Said Reynolds, "On the Presentation of Christianity in the Qur'an and the Many Aspects of Qur'anic Rhetoric," *Al-Bayan—Journal Of Qur'ān And Hadîth Studies* 12, (2014): 48-49.

[24]Pierre du Bourguet, *L'art Copte* (Paris: Ministere D'Etat Affaires Culturelles, 1967), 92.

[25]André Grabar, *Christian Iconography: A Study of its Origins* (London: Princeton University Press, 1980), 321.

from Palestine, now residing at Monza in the Treasury of the Collegiale, depicts the mother Mary and baby Jesus sitting in the same posture.[26] There is also a surviving seventh-century image of Mary holding her child in an apse in Saqqara in Egypt.[27] Besides these, excavators found a sixth-century mural painting of Mary (though her face did not survive) in Kom el-Dikka, Alexandria. She was seated on a throne and accompanied by angels, and the Child is seated in a frontal position on her left knee. According to Thomas Mathews and Norman Muller, the image is an important testimony to the veneration of Marian images in early Byzantine and Egyptian churches.[28] The icons and images mentioned here are few among many that survived.

In a study about the term *Theotokos*, J. A. McGuckin expresses his belief that "the word is an ancient Alexandrian theologoumenon that made its way by the third century to an international arena because of its use by leading Logos theologians in Egypt, Palestine, and Rome."[29] Building on McGuckin's study, Mathews and Muller conclude that Marian icons started in Egypt with the goddess Isis, who had been called both the Mother of the God (because she was the mother of the divine Horus) and the Great Virgin (because she miraculously conceived her son after he had died).[30] The historicity of this theory is beyond the scope of this study. Nonetheless, if Mathews and Muller's conclusion is right, then it is reasonable to say that when the Roman Empire was following pagan religions, people made images and venerated their pagan gods. In the same manner, once the Roman Empire moved to Christianity, people began making and venerating Christian figurative art. Without conscious thought about their pagan origins, they began forming a new theology about the holy images.

In the wider Christian world, a large number of the sixth- and seventh-century churches included mosaics, an art form that displayed the brilliant work of the era. In a church in Thessaloniki, now transformed into a mosque,

---

[26]Grabar, *Christian Iconography*, 320.

[27]Martyrium A. Grabar, *Recherches sur le culte des reliques chretien antique*, vol. 2 (Paris: Collège de France, 1946), 572.

[28]Grabar, *Recherches*, 572.

[29]J. McGuckin, "The Paradox of the Virgin-Theotokos: Evangelism and Imperial Politics in the 5th-Century Byzantine World," *Maria, A Journal of Marian Theology* 2, no. 1 (2001): 12.

[30]Thomas Mathews and Norman Muller, "Isis and Mary in Early Icons," in *Images of the Mother of God: Perceptions of the Theotokos in Byzantium*, ed. Maria Vassilaki (New York: Taylor & Francis Group, 2005), 4.

"the Ascension of Christ is portrayed on the vault of the cupola, while on the apse, the Virgin, seated on a gem-encrusted throne, bears the Baby Jesus in her arms."[31] A similar iconography occurs in a mosaic of Mary and Jesus in the chapel of San Zeno in Santa Prassede in Rome (AD 817–824).[32] In conclusion, the *Theotokos* icons were widely spread among Christians in most churches in different styles, shapes, and sizes before the seventh century. Christians adorned, venerated, and used them in their worship.

The Theotokos Title: A Theological Background

The theological argument before the sixth century. The theological conversation about the *Theotokos* started during the Council of Ephesus in AD 431, when Cyril of Alexandria advocated for venerating Mary by giving her the title *Theotokos* (the one who conceived or gave birth to God). Cyril anathematized Nestorius, the patriarch of Constantinople, who advocated for the *Christotokos* (the one who gave birth to Christ). The council ended up voting in favor of Cyril and for use of the title *Theotokos*.

Cyril taught that the Word of God was conceived in Mary's womb in order to sanctify humanity. The immortal God united himself to mortal human flesh (even in death) to accomplish the incorruptibility and imperishability of the flesh in his own body for the whole human race.[33] By uniting himself to human death in Christ, God who is immortal overcame death and thus enabled flesh to be set beyond death and corruption.[34] Sarah Jane Boss describes it well when she says that Jesus "took what was ours to be his very own so that we might have all that was his."[35] In order to accomplish this purpose, God used Mary to bring forth corporally God made one with flesh. Cyril states,

> For this reason we also call her Mother of God, not as if the nature of the Word had the beginning of its existence from the flesh. For "In the beginning was the Word, and the Word was God, and the Word was with God," and he

[31]Charles Bayet, *Byzantine Art* (New York: Parkstone International, 2008), 26.

[32]G. R. D. King, "The Paintings of the Pre-Islamic Ka 'ba," *Muqarnas* 21 (2004): 222.

[33]St. Cyril of Alexandria, *Festal Letters 8*, ed. John J. O'Keefe, (Washington, DC: Catholic University of America Press, 2009), 148-52.

[34]Cyril, *Festal Letters 8*, 148-52.

[35]Sarah Jane Boss, "The Title Theotokos," in *Mary: The Complete Resource*, (New York: Oxford University Press, 2007), 52.

> is the Maker of the ages, coeternal with the Father, and Creator of all; but, as we have already said, since he united to himself hypostatically human nature from her womb, also he subjected himself to birth as man, not as needing necessarily in his own nature birth in time and in these last times of the world, but in order that he might bless the beginning of our existence, and that that which sent the earthly bodies of our whole race to death, might lose its power for the future by his being born of a woman in the flesh.[36]

Cyril of Alexandria calls Mary the Mother of God not because he thought she was divine but because Jesus is God, and she played a role in the divine plan for saving humanity. To Cyril, refusing to call Mary the Mother of God equals denying Jesus' divinity. Cyril sent letters of condemnation to Nestorius, stating that "if anyone refuses to confess that the Emmanuel is in truth God, and therefore that the holy virgin is Mother of God (θεοτόκος), for she gave birth after a fleshly manner to the Word of God made flesh; let him be anathema."[37]

It was in honor of the definition by the Council of Ephesus of Mary as *Theotokos* that Pope Sixtus III built the most important shrine to Mary in the West, the Basilica of Santa Maria Maggiore in Rome.[38] The theological argument and the council of Ephesus helped to spread the icon of the *Theotokos* among churches in the West and the East after the sixth century, especially after Mary officially became known as the Mother of God.

The theological argument after the sixth century. After the council of Ephesus, the veneration of Mary started developing into different cults. According to Hans Belting, in the seventh century "a new and decisive phase of the Virgin's cult began when the capital and the hard-pressed empire needed a support in the age of wars against the Avars and the Persians, and ultimately against Islam."[39] By AD 626, after the great siege of the city of Constantinople by the Avars and the Persians, Mary had emerged as the

[36]St. Cyril of Alexandria, "The Epistle of Cyril to Nestorius with the XII Anathematisms," in *The Seven Ecumenical Councils*, ed. Philip Schaff and Henry Wace, trans. Henry R. Percival, vol. 14 (New York: Charles Scribner's Sons, 1900), 205.

[37]The Council of Ephesus, "Counter-statements to Cyril's 12 Anathemas," *New Advent*. Accessed February 23, 2021. www.newadvent.org/fathers/2701.htm.

[38]Jaroslav Pelikan, "The Theotokos, the Mother of God," in *Mary Through the Centuries* (New Haven, CT: Yale University Press, 1996), 56.

[39]Hans Belting, *Likeness and Presence: A History of the Image before the Era of Art*, trans. Edmund Jephcott (Chicago: The University of Chicago Press, 1996), 35.

special protectress. People believed that her icon saved them from their enemies,[40] which made her veneration even stronger.

According to Leslie Brubaker and John Haldon, the earliest images to acquire cult status were the *acheiropoeta* of images (made without hands). They are of two kinds: either they are images believed not to be made by human hands or they are the mechanical impressions of the divine face or the body—miraculous impressions of the celestials.[41] Three *acheiropoeta* manifested during the second half of the sixth century:

> The so-called mandylion of Edessa, an imprint of Christ's face on a piece of linen, was a contact relic, the sanctity of which was multiplied by the miraculous portrait that immediately appeared on it. It is first attested c. 590 by Evagrios, and at about the same time we hear of two more *acheiropoieta* of Christ: one, in Memphis (Egypt), is mentioned by the so-called Piacenza pilgrim c. 570, the other in kamoulianai (Syria), is described in a Syriac epitome of a chronicle by Zachariah of Mitylene written by an anonymous monk in 569. Like relics, *acheiropoieta* had intercessory and salvatory power: they superseded the role of Roman urban palladia—statues that housed the soul of the city—and channeled divine force to Christian community. Evagrios credited the Edessa portrait with the salvation of that city, and, in 626 an *acheiropoieton* image of Christ (perhaps the Kamoulianai portrait) famously saved Constantinople from the Avars.[42]

The fact that churches and individual people perceived this as a miracle played a great role in increasing veneration of images and leading to the formation of several cults. This concept persisted until the last quarter of the seventh century because it was believed that the holy images and relics had miraculous or intercessory powers.[43]

In most pre-iconoclastic representations, Mary is depicted as holding Jesus, the Child, and presenting him to the world. She is not only venerated because of her role in the incarnation but also as an intercessor. Among the

[40]Averil Cameron, "The Theotokos in Sixth-Century Constantinople: A City Finds its Symbol," *The Journal of Theological Studies* 29, no. 1 (1978): 79.

[41]Ernst Kitzinger, "The Cult of Images in the Age Before Iconoclasm," *Dumbarton Oaks Papers* 8 (1954): 128-29.

[42]Leslie Brubaker and John Haldon, *Byzantium in the Iconoclast Era C. 680–850: A History* (Cambridge: Cambridge University Press, 2011), 35-36.

[43]Brubaker and Haldon, *Byzantium*, 35-36.

many examples of pre-iconoclastic imagery that have been given, Mary is also "identified by an inscription as ΗΑΓΙΑ ΜΑΡΙΑ and is flanked by the archangels. A suggestion of her role as intercessor is made by the enthroned figure of Christ placed directly over her."[44] There is an icon by the south door of the church of Hagia Sofia in Constantinople (modern Istanbul) depicting the Virgin with Constantine and Justinian on either side of her. In her lap sits the Christ child. This mosaic has stood in its place for over one thousand years. While it is not known when it was created and concealed under the whitewash and plaster, the current image dates back to the tenth or eleventh century, witnessing the important role that medieval Christians gave to Mary.[45]

By the seventh century, churches had begun incorporating Christian symbols in their designs (such as the shape of the cross and Christ's image) because they resemble the physical likeness and the work of God in human form. Ernst Kitzinger reports that the cult of Christian images increased and intensified from the middle of the sixth century until the imposition of iconoclasm in AD 730.[46] It is beyond the scope of this research to study the history of iconoclasm; however, it is important to mention that many Christians saw iconoclasm as a response to a strong and steady rise in the importance of sacred images from the sixth century onwards.

By contrast, Palestinian iconoclasm, according to Brubaker and Haldon, "was not consistently applied; and, in Palestine, it seems to have been a localized response rather than the realization of some anti-image edict by the ruling caliph."[47] Under the Umayyads in Damascus and during the period of Leo III's rule in the Byzantine empire, five churches attest to active construction and a skilled artisanal workforce employed by Christians. People facing day-to-day consequences of Umayyad rule were in a different situation from people living under Byzantine rule. Iconoclasm in Palestine was neither inspired by Byzantine iconoclasm nor spurred by any official Islamic policy. The Byzantine iconoclasm was not accepted by Christian churches

[44]Ioli Kalavrezou, "Images of the Mother: When the Virgin Mary Became 'Meter Theou,'" *Dumbarton Oaks Papers* 44 (1990): 168.

[45]Nicholas N. Patricios, *The Sacred Architecture of Byzantium: Art, Liturgy, and Symbolism in Early Christian Churches* (New York: I.B. Tauris, 2014), 346-47.

[46]Kitzinger, "Cult of Images," 128-29.

[47]Brubaker and Haldon, *Byzantium*, 107.

in the East after AD 754. It was condemned in AD 760, 764, and 767 by Eastern synods and patriarchs.[48] The Byzantine iconoclasm did not affect the prevalence of the *Theotokos* as drastically as one might think. While the Western iconoclasts rejected the images of Christ, Mary, and the saints, the Eastern iconophiles acknowledged, defended, and even actively advanced the decoration of their churches with pictorial renderings of secular themes.[49]

Mohammad's Experience with the Christians During His Life

The Arabic appellation for Christians (*masīḥīyūn*) never appears in the Qur'an. The writer of the Qur'an used instead several other terms that we understand to refer to Christians. For instance, the most common appellation that Mohammad and Muslims deploy is *Naṣārā*. According to Griffith, "In the early Islamic period, Arabic-speaking Christians and Muslims alike regularly used the Qur'an's term *Naṣārā* as the functional equivalent of the name 'Christians' (Χριστιανοι *masīḥīyyūn*) for the several ecclesial communities of the followers of Jesus of Nazareth (Acts 11:26), who lived in the world of Islam."[50] Today, Arab Christians do not use this word to refer to their religion; however, many Muslims still use it to refer to Christians. It is also important to note that the English translation of *Naṣārā* always appeared as *Christians* in the Islamic scripture. *Naṣārā,* however, is not the only appellation that is used to refer to Christians. Labels such as "Scripture People" (*ahl al-kitāb*) and "Gospel People" (*ahl al-injīl*) have been used as well (Surah 5:47, 59, 65, 68, 77, 57:29).

The appellations above and the evidence of an exchange of information between Muslims and Christians suggest that Mohammad was in contact with Christians in different places and at different times throughout his life. According to Muhammad Hamidullah, Makkah was a developed city that contained people from different religions.[51] While Medina was a less-developed

---

[48]Brubaker and Haldon, *Byzantium*, 114.

[49]Moshe Barasch, *Icon: Studies in the History of an Idea* (New York: New York University Press, 1995), 265.

[50]Griffith, "Al-Naṣārā in the Qur'ān," 303.

[51]Muhammad Hamidullah, "Aqdam Dustur Musajjal fi-l-ʿAlam," *Islamic Scholars Conference* 1 (1937): 98. Accessed February 14, 2021, retrieved from https://abulhasanalinadwi.org/book/aqdam-dastoor-musajjal-fil-aa/.

city, compared to Makkah it was "a single house that encompasses people of diverse beliefs within its walls."[52] Islamic literature mentions several Jewish tribes such as Banī Quraẓa and Banī Nuḍair who lived in Medina, and it also affirms that Mohammad was in contact with Christians. Actually, Mohammad met with Christians in several places: in the Levant, Makkah, and Medina. Both Surah al-Nisā' and Surah al-Mā'da are Madni Surahs (written in Medina) that include speeches related to Christians (Surah 4: 171; 5:78). This evidence indicates that Mohammad was in contact with Jews and Christians, and this contact was formative to Islamic identity.

In the Levant. Mohammad's initial interaction with Christians possibly occurred early in his life when he traveled to the Levant with his uncle for trade. Most Syrian monasteries appear to have been situated near the major trade routes because these monks sought interaction with travelers. According to Islamic biographer Ibn Isḥāq, Mohammad traveled to Syria with his uncle on a merchant caravan. While they were near Buṣra in Syria, they met with monk Baḥīrā "who was well versed in the knowledge of Christians. A monk had always occupied that cell. There he gained his knowledge from a book that was in the cell so they allege, handed on from generation to generation."[53] Christian literature written between the sixth and the tenth centuries does not mention Baḥīrā nor the encounter between him and Mohammad. Richard Gottheil has translated Syriac and Arabic documents about the legend of Sergius Baḥīrā, who is believed to be the same monk that Mohammad met in Syria; however, he dates these documents to the late eleventh and probably early twelfth centuries.[54] These documents seem to be written for polemic purposes, emphasizing that Baḥīrā was the original channel for Muhammad's revelations. As Guillaume mentions in his introduction to the *Life of Muhammad*, it is hard to authenticate this story.[55] The part that describes Baḥīrā owning an ancient book that was handed down from one generation to another does not give enough information regarding whether this book is an apocryphal book, such as the Gospel according to the Hebrews, one of the four Gospels, the Diatessaron, or another book.

[52]Hamidullah, "Aqdam Dustur Musajjal fi-l-ʿAlam," 99.

[53]A. Guillaume, *The Life of Muhammad: A Translation of Isḥāq's Sirat Rasūl Allah* (New York: Oxford University Press, 1998), 79.

[54]Richard Gottheil, "A Christian Bahira Legend," *Zeitschrift für Assyriologie* 13 (1898): 192.

[55]Guillaume, *Life of Muhammad*, xix.

Despite the lack of detail, this story does offer a glimpse of Mohammad coming into contact with Christians of some sort—however, it is hard to know whether they were orthodox or heretical.

In Arabia. It is possible that the first thorough interaction between Mohammad and Christians took place in Arabia. Most Islamic scholars agree that Khadija, the first wife of Mohammad, was a Christian, and her cousin was a monk. Khadija was a rich merchant woman in Makkah who hired Mohammad to transport and sell her goods in Syria after she heard about his admirable character. After their marriage, Khadija arranged for Mohammad to meet with her cousin, monk Waraqa bin Nūfal, who was introduced in Islamic literature as a "blind, elderly Christian sage with profound knowledge of the Bible."[56] Like the story of monk Baḥīrā, the narrative of the life of Waraqa is equivocal. Some Islamic sources suggest that Waraqa died shortly after recognizing Mohammad as a prophet.[57] Others suggest that Waraqa learned from those who followed the Torah and the Gospel, wrote the Gospel to the Hebrews, and helped Mohammad launch his new religion.[58] A study written by Brian C. Bradford suggests that the Hebrew books Waraqa read "could have included groups who possessed a *Hebrew Matthew*, the *Diatessaron*, *According to the Hebrews*, or any of the other texts that have been shown to have Qur'anic parallels."[59] Finally, the abovementioned study by al-Ḥarīrī affirms that Waraqa was not a Christian but an Ebionite monk who helped Mohammad to launch his new religion and that all the references to the word *Naṣāra* in the Qur'an were added later by 'Uthmān.[60] Regardless of the background of Waraqa (orthodox or nonorthodox), the salient point for our discussion is that Mohammad's biography shows that he was in contact with Christians, that he probably met with them in their churches, and that Waraqa was one of them.

The second contact between Mohammad and Christians is well-documented in Islamic literature. While Christians were not numerous in

---

[56]Recep Senturk, *Medieval Islamic Civilization: An Encyclopedia*, vol. 1, ed. Joseph Meri (New York: Taylor & Francis, 2006), 167.

[57]Bukharī, *Ṣaḥīḥ Bukharī*, Hadīth no. 3. Accessed February 16, 2021. https://sunnah.com/bukhari:3.

[58]Bukharī, *Ṣaḥīḥ Bukharī*, Hadīth no. 3.

[59]Brian C. Bradford, "The Qur'anic Jesus: A Study of Parallels with Non-Biblical Texts" (PhD diss., Western Michigan University, 2013), 141.

[60]Abu Musa Al-Ḥarīrī, *Priest and Prophet* (Diar 'Akil, Lebanon: Dar Li'ajl al-Ma'rifa, 2005), 272-82.

Makkah, South Arabia was home to several well-organized Christian communities. Excavations in the city of Sana'a in Yemen revealed a big cathedral called Qalis church, which represents a strong Christian presence in South Arabia. Islamic sources tell the story of King Abraha al-Ashram, who built a great cathedral in Sana'a and called it Qalis.[61] Ibn-al-Kalbī cites Abraha explaining to the king of Ethiopia after having completed the building of the church, "I have built to you a church / the like of which no one has ever built. I shall not let the Arabs alone until I divert their pilgrimage away from the house to which they go and turn its course to this church."[62] It seems that the purpose of Abraha was to create a turning point in the pilgrimage in Makkah to Sana'a by making a great cathedral that competes with *Ka*^{c}*ba,* instituting a great center for Christianity in South Arabia. This story informs the reader that Christianity was well-established in the Arabian Peninsula before the birth of Mohammad.

In addition to Sana'a, a famous area in South Arabia called Najrān has surfaced in both Christian and Islamic hagiographies. Christianity was well-rooted for more than a century in this area before the birth of Mohammad. According to Ifran Shahid, "Najrān converted to Christianity in the first half of the fifth century by Ḥayyān, one of its merchants, who brought the Christian Gospel from Ḥīra before the birth of the Monophysite movement."[63] Philostorgius writes in his *Church History* about Theophilus, who was sent to the Ḥimyarite ruler Ta'ran Yuhan'im, who then converted to Christianity.[64] As a result of his conversion, three churches were constructed, one in the capital city of Ẓafār, one in Aden, and one near the mouth of the Persian Gulf.[65] Moreover, The Najrānite Christian community was linked with Abyssinia (Ethiopia), which had strong political relations in Yemen in AD 525, a connection that subsequently strengthened the Christian life in Najrān.

[61]Hishām Ibn-al-Kalbī, *The Book of Idols*, trans. Nabih Amin Faris (Princeton, NJ: Princeton University Press, 1952), 40.

[62]Ibn-al-Kalbī, *Book of Idols*, 40.

[63]Irfan Shahid, *Byzantine and the Arabs in the Sixth Century*, vol. 1 (Washington, DC: Dumbarton Oaks Research Library and Collection, 1995), 711.

[64]C. Jonn Block, "Philoponian Monophysitism in South Arabia at the Advent of Islam With Implications for the English Translation of Thalātha' In Qur'ān 4. 171 And 5. 73," *Journal of Islamic Studies* 23, no. 1 (2012): 71.

[65]Irfan Shahid, *Byzantine and the Arabs in the Fourth Century* (Washington, DC: Dumbarton Oaks Research Library and Collection, 1984), 89.

According to Islamic resources, Najrān used to have its own *Kaᶜba* to compete with the one in Makkah.[66]

The struggle between Christianity and Judaism before the rise of Islam reached its climax in the sixth century in Najrān. A major Ethiopian military intervention "brought about the downfall of the Ḥimyaritic kingdom of South Arabia and spread the Christian faith as well as the dominion of the Negus across the Red Sea."[67] Recently discovered Syriac manuscripts reveal several events of severe persecution that happened in the city of Najrān in AD 523 against the Christians, led by a pagan king who converted to Judaism.[68] Thus, Najrān became the Arabian martyropolis, a place of pilgrimage for the Arabic Christian tribes in the Arabian Peninsula.

Several historians believe that Christians in Najrān were Monophysites.[69] Monophysites believe that Jesus Christ only has one nature, the divine nature, and that his humanity was either dissolved in a sea of divinity or absorbed into the divine at the moment of incarnation.[70] According to Shahid, "It was in the reign of Anastasius and through the vision of Philoxenus that Najran acquired its strong Monophysite character, which determined the confessional stance of South Arabia for a century till the rise of Islam."[71] If this claim is true, then it is reasonable to conclude that the Christians of Najrān—or the ones who were in contact with Mohammad, at least—were Monophysites. This piece of information should clue us in on why primary Christian terms such as Trinity, Father, and Holy Spirit were not mentioned in the Qur'an, and why Mary was understood to be included in the Trinity.

It seems that Monophysites had an opposite christological belief from the Muslims, who denied the divine nature of Jesus and emphasized his

---

[66]Ibn-al-Kalbī, *Book of Idols*, 40.

[67]Irfan Shahid, *The Martyrs of Najran: New Documents* (Bruxelle, Belgique: Société des Bollandistes, 1971), 7.

[68]There are several Syriac letters that document several stories about martyrdom and persecution against the Ḥimyarite Christians in Najrān. Ignatious Yaᶜqūb, *al-Shuhada' al-ḥamiriyoon al-'Arab fi al-Watha'iq al-Syrianiya* [the Arab Himyarites Martyrs in Syriac Manuscript] (Damascus: Syrian Patriarchate of Antioch, 1966), 24-82.

[69]Tereza Heintaler, al-Massiḥiyiin al-'arab Qabil al-Islam [The Arab Christians before Islam], trans. Lamis Fayed (Cairo: Dar al-Nashir al-Usqufiya, 2017), 203. Yaᶜqūb, *al-Shuhada'*, 13-14. Shahid, *Martyrs of Najran*, 36-37.

[70]A. A. Luce, *Monophysitism Past and Present: A Study in Christology* (New York: The Macmillan Co. 1920).

[71]Shahid, *Arabs in the Sixth Century*, 711.

humanity, claiming that he was just a prophet. Monophysites, on the other hand, denied the human nature of Jesus after the incarnation and emphasized the divine nature. Their major concern when they shared their belief with others was the divine nature of Christ. The emphasis on Jesus' divinity is obvious in the Syriac documents of the mass martyrdom of the Najranites. These documents include several stories recounting that many men and women were martyred because they refused to deny the divinity of Christ. The Jewish king killed the women's husbands and gave the women another chance, saying:

> You have seen with your very own eyes your husbands put to death because they refused to renounce Christ and the cross, and because they blasphemously claimed that Christ is God and son of Adonay. But do you have pity on yourselves now, and on your sons and your daughters: deny Christ and the cross, and become Jewish like us; then you shall live. Otherwise you will certainly be put to death.[72]

The women were scared neither of death nor being burned alive. They replied, "Christ is God and Son of the Merciful One; we believe in him and we worship him; for his sake we will die. Far be it from us to deny him or to go on living after the deaths of our husbands. No, like them and alongside them we shall die for Christ's sake."[73] As mentioned above, Christian terms such as Trinity, Father, and Holy Spirit are not mentioned in this story. These women acknowledged their belief in the Father by referring to him as the Merciful One and emphasized the divinity of Jesus by being willing to die for his sake. It is interesting to see the Najrānites willing to die for the sake of Jesus, not the Father or God. The prominence they gave to Jesus' divinity in contrast to the Trinity might explain the Islamic denial of Jesus' divinity and the omission of the Trinity in the Qur'an. Mohammad's emphasis on God's unity, solidarity, and singularity speaks directly against the Monophysite belief in Jesus being divine. Mohammad probably refused Monophysitism because it conveys double divinities.

The scholarship of C. Jonn Block renders this circumstance increasingly likely. He reports that a certain kind of Monophysitism was short-lived in

[72]Sebastian Brock and Susan Ashbrook Harvey, *Holy Women of the Syrian Orient* (Oakland, CA: University of California Press, 1998), 108.

[73]Brock and Harvey, *Holy Women*, 108.

the late sixth century, a variant of orthodox Monophysitism. He calls it "Philoponian Tritheism."[74] It was "dominant in South Arabia, in which Christians worshipped three distinct gods. No longer one nature and three persons, the Philoponians recognized doctrinally three distinct natures. The doctrine came from John Philoponus and was spread by the bishops Conon and Eugenius."[75] The theology of John Philoponus propagated three individual natures for the three persons of the Trinity and further denied any common substance between them. Philoponus states in a surviving fragment of his book *On the Trinity*:

> They [divine persons] do not have equality of substance with respect to their properties, that is, in those things by which this one is Father, this one Son, and this one Holy Spirit. In accordance with these [distinctions], they are different in species and separate from one another. . . . It is the same with "animal," which is generally said of all animals, though they vary by species. When "rational" or "irrational" is added to "animal," then they are differentiated in species from one another: one animal is rational, another animal irrational. Therefore, when "Father" and "Son" and "Holy Spirit" are added to "divinity," it makes God the Father not the same as God the Son and the divine Spirit. And so, each one of them is subsequently different from the other two.[76]

It seems that Philoponian Tritheism acknowledges the existence of the Father, Son, and Holy Spirit as three individuals, and it does not accept the creedal position on the Trinity. If the people of Najrān were following this particular type of Monophysitism, then it makes sense that Mohammad understood trinitarianism as believing in three gods, as he expresses in the Qur'an (Surah 2:135; 3:67; 4:171).

Islamic resources record that the Christians of Najrān visited and communicated their belief to Mohammad on several occasions. This study will focus on two of them. The first group of Christians from Najrān visited the prophet when he was living in Makkah.[77] They asked him questions about Islam, and at the end of the meeting, they listened to him reciting the Qur'an:

---

[74]Block, "South Arabia at the Advent of Islam," 51.

[75]Block, "South Arabia at the Advent of Islam," 51.

[76]Ellen Muehlberger, trans., "John Philoponus, Fragments on the Trinity," in *The Cambridge Edition of Early Christian Writings*, ed. Andrew Radde-Gallwitz (Cambridge: Cambridge University Press, 2017), 359.

[77]Guillaume, *Life of Muhammad*, 179.

"their eyes flowed with tears and they accepted God's call, believed in him, and declared his truth."[78] It seems that this group returned to Najrān and reported what happened to their leaders, who in turn sent another larger and more religiously knowledgeable group to converse with Mohammad.

The second group of Najrānites visited Mohammad after he moved to Medina. This cohort of sixty included fourteen of their best men, their prince, their bishop, and their pontiff.[79] Mohammad allowed them to pray in the mosque when their time of prayer came. After a long theological discussion, the Najrānites recognized Mohammad as a prophet, but they decided to hold to their religion.[80] Al-Waḥidī details the conversation they had with Mohammad when he asked them to surrender to Allah. They said, "We have surrendered to Allah before you." Mohammad replied, "You lie! Three things prevent you from surrendering to Allah: your worship of the cross, eating pork and your claim that Allah has a son." They asked him back, "Then who is the father of Jesus?" Mohammad refused to give them an answer and asked to come back the next day.[81] Al-Waḥidī mentions that Allah, on this occasion, revealed Surah 3:59 as an answer to the Najrānites.[82] Allah said, "Surely the likeness of Isa is with Allah as the likeness of Adam, He created him from dust, then said to him, Be, and he was" (Surah 3:59). The reason behind revealing this Surah might seem contradictory to the Islamic explanation of the origin and the virgin birth of Jesus; however, it is not the purpose of this study to make such analysis. What the reader needs to note is that the Najrānites had a long theological conversation with Mohammad about the nature and the origin of Jesus. Mary and her divinity were not mentioned in this conversation, according to Islamic writings, which suggests another source for Mohammad's belief that Christians held to her divinity.

---

[78]Guillaume, *Life of Muhammad*, 179.

[79]Abī Ḥasan ʿalī al-Waḥidī, *Asbāb al-Nuzūl* [The Reasons of Revelation], ed., ʿiṣām al-Ḥmīdān (Dammam, Saudi Arabia: Dar al-Iṣlāḥ, 1992), 97. The Arabic version of al-Waḥidī even mentions some names: the prince's name is Abdul Massīḥ, the bishop's name is Al-Ayham, and the pontiff's name is Abū Ḥāritha ibn ʿalqama. The English version is published by "*The Tafsirs*," but it does not include the names of the Najranites' deputation. www.altafsir.com/Tafasir.asp?tMadhNo=1&tTafsirNo=86&tSoraNo=3&tAyahNo=59&tDisplay=yes&UserProfile=0&LanguageId=2. Accessed February 17, 2021.

[80]Guillaume, *Life of Muhammad*, 179.

[81]Al-Waḥidī, *Asbāb al-Nuzūl*, 97.

[82]Al-Waḥidī, *Asbāb al-Nuzūl*, 97.

Ibn Kathīr records a detailed explanation of this verse and the conversation between Mohammad and the Najrānites.[83] While the Christians insisted on their belief in the divinity of Jesus, Mohammad could not provide evidence for his opposing belief. In order to save the situation, he invited them for *al-Mubāhaleh* (Surah 3:60-61). This term means "to curse one another and then appeal to Allah"[84] for an answer. In other words, when performing *al-Mubāhaleh,* one party curses the belief and the people of the other party and asks Allah to intervene by revealing who is the winning party. The Najrānites were safe and peaceful people who had experienced mass martyrdom in their history. They feared losing and asked Mohammad to give them another option. He offered three alternatives: to convert to Islam, to pay *jizya*, or to go to war.[85] The Najrānites decided to pay *jizya*. It is commonly believed that they were the first to pay *jizya* among non-Muslims, for *jizya* became a decree after opening Makkah in Surah 9:29.[86]

The interactions with Christians described above are not the only ones that scholars know of. Historians record more collaborations between Mohammad and Christians. Since they are of less significance, this study will only mention them briefly. The biography of Mohammad refers to him discussing the Christian religion while sitting at the Marwa (a spot in Makkah), at the booth of a young Christian slave called Jabr, learning what he has to say about Christianity.[87] It is also said that Mohammad learned about Christianity from his Coptic concubine, Mariyah.[88] He listened to Christian sermons by the bishop of Najrān while attending a merchant festival near Makkah.[89] All these interactions are documented in both Islamic and Christian sources, and they agree that Mohammad visited Christian monasteries, possibly churches, and conducted theological discussions about

[83]Abū al-fidā Isma'īl Ibn Kathīr, *Tafseer al-Qru'an al-Atheem* [The Explanation of the Great Qur'an] (Beirut: Dar Ibn Ḥazm, 2000), 369-71.

[84]*Al-Mawsoo'a al-Lahootiya* [Theological Encyclopedia], s.v. "Mubāhaleh," vol. 36, (Kuwait, al-Awqāf Ministry, 1996).

[85]*Al-Mawsoo'a al-Lahootiya*, [Theological Encyclopedia], s.v. "Mubāhaleh," vol. 36, (Kuwait, al-Awqāf Ministry, 1996).

[86]Ibn Kathīr, *Great Qur'an*, 371.

[87]Guillaume, *Life of Muhammad*, 180.

[88]'A'isha 'abd al-Rahman, *Nisa' al-Nabi* [The Prophet's Wives] (self-published), 218-21. Guillaume, *Life of Muhammad*, 653.

[89]Geoffrey Parrinder, *Jesus in the Qur'an* (London: Oneworld Publications, 2013), 163.

their christological beliefs. None of these recorded interactions directly mention Christians teaching Mohammad about the divinity of Mary.

Mohammad's Awareness of Christian Iconography, Especially the Theotokos

It is highly likely that Mohammad saw the *Theotokos* image during his visits to Buṣra or the Levant as a boy. According to Mathews and Muller, "In Byzantine art the most important Mary and Christ icons were also door images, namely the *proskynetarion* icons of the icon screen, which are located left and right respectively of the door to the sanctuary."[90] If this is true, then Mohammad might have seen the image of the venerated Mary and Child for the first time in a Christian monastery in Syria.

Al-Balādhurī, a Muslim historian who collected documents and possessed the text of the peace treaty between Mohammad and the Christians of Najrān about *jizya,* offers an insightful note regarding Mohammad's awareness of Christian iconography usage. The peace treaty made in exchange for the Najrānites' safety includes a note about Christian images. After Mohammad defined the amount of *jizya*, the treaty mentions that "Najrān and their followers are entitled to the protection of Allah and the security of Muhammad the prophet, the Messenger of Allah, which security shall involve their persons, religion, lands and possessions, including those of them who are absent as well as those who are present, their camels, messengers and images."[91] Al-Balādhurī indirectly suggests that the Christians of Najrān had images and relics most likely in their churches, and Mohammad was aware of them because he mentioned that they were to be protected with the other properties belonging to Christians.

Another Ḥadīth suggests that Mohammad saw the *Theotokos* image in al-Kaᶜaba in Makkah. Most Islamic studies reveal that Makkah was a metropolitan center for pagan religions.[92] It is said that the interior of al-Kaᶜaba was filled with pictures and relics of many gods. One of the pictures that Islamic resources mention is a sculpture of Mary and her Son Jesus.

---

[90] Mathews and Muller, "Isis and Mary," 9.

[91] Abū al-ᶜabās al-Balādhurī, *Kitāb Futḥāt al-Buldān The Origins of the Islamic State*, trans. P. K. Hitti (New York and London, 1916), 100. In the footnote of the same source, the writer explains that *tamathīl* means sculptures.

[92] Ibn-al-Kalbī, *Book of Idols*, 28.

Al-Azraqī makes a detailed description of the exterior and the interior decorations of al-Kaᶜaba, saying, "They paint on its pillars pictures of the prophets, trees, and angels; there was the picture of Abraham the friend of God (as an old man) dividing the arrows, a picture of Issā the son of Mary and his mother, and a picture of the angels."[93] Al-Azraqī includes several other authenticated and non-authenticated Ḥadīths related to the same topic. The authenticated Ḥadīths are the ones that have an uninterrupted chain of speakers going back to the prophet or one of his close *ṣaḥāba* (followers). Al-Azraqī includes several authenticated Ḥadīths stating that the relic of Jesus and his mother was inside al-Kaᶜaba, engraved on one of the pillars.[94] For instance, Ḥadīth no. 180, which is classified as authenticated, states that "Abū al-Walīd told us, my grandfather said, whose own source was Da'ūd b., whose source was ᶜamrū bin Dinār, 'Before the demolition of al-Kaᶜaba, I have seen (the sculpture) of Issā bin Maryam and his mother.'"[95] Al-Azraqī includes also several Ḥadīths about Mohammad ordering ᶜOmar his companion (who became the second caliph) to obliterate all the relics and images of al-Kaᶜba. Few of these Ḥadīths suggest that Mohammad asked to eliminate all relics and images except the one of Jesus and his mother.[96] It does not concern this study whether Mohammad actually destroyed the images or not: the main concern is to know whether he saw these images. It seems that most of these Ḥadīths affirm that Mohammad saw the *Theotokos* sculpture. Ḥadīth no. 179 references Jesus seated on Mary's lap, and they both were ornamented and embellished.[97] The iconography of the seated Virgin with Jesus in her lap adorned is a universal piece of Christian art. This Ḥadīth echoes the aforementioned resources and affirms that it was already widespread among Christians in the seventh century, even in Makkah.

Other Islamic sources suggest that Mohammad gained an awareness of the Christian images, relics, and statues from his wives who went to Ethiopia at the beginning of Mohammad's *daᶜwa* (calling). When Mohammad started

---

[93] Abī al-Tawlīd Al-Azraqī, *Akhbar Makkah wa ma ja'a fiha min Akhbar* [*The News of Makkah and Its Ruins*], (edited and published by Abdula Dahīsh, 2003), 248.

[94] Al-Azraqī, *Akhbar Makkah*, Ḥadīth no. 179, page 250.

[95] Al-Azraqī, *Akhbar Makkah*, 251.

[96] It should be mentioned that the unauthenticated Ḥadīths suggest that Mohammad ordered to keep Jesus and his mother's relics. Al-Azraqī, *Akhbar Makkah*, Ḥadīth no. 181, page 251, Ḥadīths no. 185, 187, page 253.

[97] Al-Azraqī, *Akhbar Makkah*, 250.

calling his tribe Quraysh to Islam, he and many of his companions faced persecution. These circumstances led a large number of his followers to migrate to Ethiopia in approximately AD 615. Early Muslims *muhājirūn* (immigrants) encountered Christian paintings in the churches of Ethiopia as they sought refuge and help from Negus the king of Ethiopia. They even expressed their admiration of these images at the deathbed of Mohammad. This information is reported by authentic Islamic sources. In *Ṣaḥīḥ Bukharī*, "Um Habiba and Um Salama mentioned a church they had seen in Ethiopia in which there were pictures. They told the Prophet (ﷺ) about it."[98] Imam Khatib at-Tabriz includes a similar Ḥadīth, stating that ᶜAisha (the wife of the prophet) said that "when the Prophet was ill some of his wives mentioned a church called Mariya. Umm Salama and Umm Habiba who had gone to Abyssinia mentioned its beauty and the statues it contained."[99] While these Ḥadīths do not prove that Mohammad saw the paintings in the Ethiopian churches, it shows that he was aware of their glory and beauty from his wives and friends.

The Islamic Belief About Images, Icons, and Figurative Arts

Islam is a monotheistic religion that believes in one God, Allah, the creator. It claims a kind of restorative bridge to Abraham, and it follows the footsteps of Moses in prohibiting the use of holy religious images because of their association with idolatry and apostasy. Apart from the warning against idolatry, the Qur'an does not include an explicit prohibition of images. The Ḥadīths, however, contain clear and consistent statements against them. *Ṣaḥīḥ Bukhārī* mentions that "the people who will receive the severest punishment from Allah will be the picture makers."[100] Any kind of picture (pictures of plants, animals, or humans) that might distract the faithful person is forbidden in Sunni Hadīths. *Ṣaḥīḥ Muslim* also includes many similar

[98]Bukharī, *Ṣaḥīḥ Bukharī*, Hadīth no. 427. Accessed February 2, 2021. https://sunnah.com/bukhari:427. Muslim, *Ṣaḥīḥ Muslim*, Ḥadīth no. 528a. Accessed February 2, 2021. https://sunnah.com/muslim:528a.

[99]Imam Khatib at-Tabriz, *Mishkat al-Masabih*, vol. 22, Hadīth no. 195, accessed February 20, 2021, https://sunnah.com/mishkat:4508.

[100]Bukhārī, *Ṣaḥīḥ Bukhārī*, Ḥadīth no. 5950, accessed March 9, 2021, https://sunnah.com/bukhari/77.

Ḥadīths, stating that "all the painters who make pictures would be in the fire of Hell. The soul [of the figure represented in the image] will be breathed in every picture prepared by him and it shall punish him in the Hell, and he (Ibn ᶜAbbas) said: If you have to do it at all, then paint the pictures of trees and lifeless things."[101] Even the painters of figurative art representations will face severe punishment and torment in hell because they have tried to imitate the creation of Allah.

The Islamic prohibition of images is a result of the unique view of Allah, the creator. All creation is under the influence of his creative power. Allah is the only creator responsible for imparting life in the world by breathing into his creation. The supreme meaning of the Arabic key term *rūḥ* (spirit) in Islam was thus "never first the soul or the lifebreath of man, but the spirit of God, which at most, as in the conception of Mary, can be breathed into a man."[102] Any attempt to imitate Allah—the only soul maker—is considered blasphemous. Any anthropomorphic representation of the transcendental Allah is considered an attack of his innermost being/person. For this reason, Islam can be classified as "a phenomenon of iconophobia rather than a phenomenon of iconoclasm."[103]

Vasile-Octavian Mihoc compares the decorations of the mosques to the decorations of the churches, stating,

> While the walls of the churches are adorned with pictures, the mosques present the Muslim faithful with phrases from the Qur'an, as once Mohammed did, thus instrumentalizing the iconic dimension as the bearer of the divine message. As a result of the anchoring of the earthly counterpart of the Qur'an in the heavenly archetype, "the mother of the script" (*umm al-kitab*, Q 43:4), this imagery was clear: the written word becomes an opening toward the transcendent, a non-figural icon of the divine.[104]

The Arab geographer Muḥammad Ibn Aḥmad al-Muqaddasī (AD 991) mentions that the Dome of the Rock in Palestine and the Umayyad mosque

[101]Muslim, *Ṣaḥīḥ Muslim*, Hadīth no. 2109c, 2110a, 2110b, accessed March 9, 2021, https://sunnah.com/muslim/37.

[102]Ignác Goldziher, "Zum Islamischen Bilderverbot," *Zeitschrift der Deutschen Morgenländischen Gesellschaft* 74 (1920): 288.

[103]Vasile-Octavian Mihoc, "Aesthetics as Shared Interfaith Space between Christianity and Islam," *Ecumenical Review* 71, no. 5 (2019): 683.

[104]Mihoc, "Aesthetics," 683.

in Damascus served as a counterbalance to the abundantly decorated churches.[105] This is to say that Muslims substituted the figurative art of the divine with Arabic calligraphy to imitate Christianity without offending the inner being of Allah.

With the Muslim conquest of the Levant, Muslims found the cross and Christian images a stumbling block and folly. Politically speaking, the cross retained imperial/military connotations, and within the new Islamic order, it was a symbol of a hostile and despised power. Muslims saw the Christian icons as visual references to the doctrine of the Trinity and the incarnated God. They accused Christians of worshiping the materials rather than the reference that these images implement. The fact that Christians venerated the holy icons by kissing and prostrating themselves before them no doubt convinced many Muslims that their worship was little different from the idols which the pagan Arabs had worshiped before the coming of Islam.[106] In reality, Christians believe that the relics and images are pure materials that do not possess any divine quality. Images were created as expressions of divine essences intended to help the worshiper remember the person behind the material.

ᶜAbd al-Malik and al-Walīd, the Umayyad rulers who conquered Palestine and Syria, were aware of the differences between Muslims, Christians, and Jews, especially in their manner of worship and decorating sacred spaces. They, however, wished to compete with and surpass monuments like the Church of the Holy Sepulchre and the Cathedral of Saint John in Damascus, which they turned later on into the Umayyad Mosque.[107] The Umayyad caliphs built their shrines and decorated them in a way that aligns with their theological convictions. Just as the Christian iconography and church decoration communicated doctrinal beliefs, so Islamic decoration of certain shrines and mosques asserted emerging theological views—the interior inscriptions of the Dome of the Rock, which is a calligraphic

[105]Muḥammad Ibn Aḥmad al-Muqaddasī, *Kitab Ahsan al-taqasim fi maʿrifat al-aqalinm*, ed. M. J. de Goeje (Leiden: Brill, 1967), 159.

[106]Mark N. Swanson, "the Cross of Christ in the Earliest Arabic Melkite Apologies," in *Christian Arabic Apologetics during the Abbasid Period (750–1258)*, ed. Samir Khalil Samir and Joren S. Nielsen, vol. 63, (New York: Brill, 1993), 116.

[107]Nancy Khalek, "Icons John the Baptist and Sanctified Spaces in Early Islamic Syria," In *Damascus after the Muslim Conquest: Text and Image in Early Islam* (Oxford: Oxford University Press, 2011), 96.

statement used to express doctrinal statement. In the heart of the Christian East, those inscriptions declared Islamic opposition to the Trinity by making multiple references to the absolute unity of Allah and the status of Jesus as a prophet.[108]

Conclusion

Several studies have attempted to discover the reason behind the misunderstanding of the Trinity in the Qur'an. While this study acknowledges the previous efforts of several scholars and studies, it follows a different route to examine the iconographic effect on Mohammad's understanding of the Trinity. This study explores the effect of the *Theotokos* icon and the possible reason behind Mohammad's assumption of Mary's inclusion in the Trinity.

In the seventh century, Mohammad started the Islamic religion, which emphasized the absolute unity of Allah and rejected the divinity of Jesus. Mohammad had several interactions with Christians during his life. His first wife was a Christian, and one of his concubines was a Coptic Christian. The most important and thorough interaction he had with Christianity involved the Christians of Najrān. A number of Islamic resources place the Surahs that talk about the Trinity (Surah 4:171 and 5:73) within the context of the prophet's meeting with the Christians of Najrān. Many historians think that Najrānites were Monophysites, who believed in the Trinity but emphasized the divine nature of Christ and underestimated his human nature. Mohammad rejected their belief in the divinity of Jesus and called for absolute oneness because he could not reconcile Jesus' deity with the divinity of Allah.

The Najrānites challenged Mohammad by asking him who is the father of Jesus. At first, Mohammad did not know how to answer them. The next day, Allah revealed to him that the resemblance of Jesus is like the resemblance of Adam. This is to say that Jesus had no father: he is fatherless, and God is not his father. This message is also conveyed every time Jesus is called

---

[108]John of Damascus and Theodore Abū Qurrah were both iconophiles, defending the veneration of icons because they saw it as a public form of worship and exercising religion. The prostration to Jesus' icon and the cross was seen as an act of respect and worship of the person of Jesus, not to the icon itself. Muslims, however, perceived this act as being similar to the polytheistic worship of idols. Despite the fact that the iconoclasm argument is related to the icon's investigation, which this study has presented, John and Theodore's defenses were chronologically after Mohammad, and, consequently, they did not affect his understanding of the Trinity.

"the son of Mary" in the Qur'an, which Mohammad purposely used several times (2:87, 253; 3:45; 4:157, 171; 5:17, 46, 72, 75, 78, 110, 112; 9:31). In comparison to other prophets, only Jesus is called by the name of his mother. The Qur'an does not call Abraham or Moses by the names of their fathers or mothers. It seems that Mohammad was trying to make a point when he called Jesus "the son of Mary" as if he were stressing Jesus' origin by calling him "the fatherless Jesus."

Islamic writings include some of Mohammad's sources about Jesus; however, there is no historical evidence that Mohammad learned about the divinity of Mary from Christians. There is no record, neither in Islamic resources nor in the early history of Christianity, of Christians believing or teaching the divinity of Mary. On the contrary, there is historical evidence that early Fathers condemned such teaching and considered it heretical. The lack of resources makes it reasonable to think that Mohammad's understanding of Mary and her role was acquired by inference rather than conversations with Christians.

In comparison to biblical data, Mohammad seems to be confused about Mary's family. He conflates Mary the mother of Jesus with Mary the sister of Moses (Surah 19:28; 66:11). Certain aspects of the story of Mary the mother of Jesus were mentioned several times in the Qur'an, such as information about her family, her experience with Zakaria, and her pregnancy; but her divinity was alluded to only once (Surah 5:116). By contrast, the number of times the divinity of Jesus was mentioned surpasses the few times Mary is mentioned. This is probably because Christians (likely Monophysites) did not mention Mary much, instead focusing on Jesus, his virgin birth, and his divinity. What Mohammad learned about Mary was mostly inferences from the *Theotokos* icons we know he saw in Kaᶜba, Buṣra, and other places.

Extant icons in Egypt inform us of the early evolution of the son-and-mother pairing, beginning in pagan art and possibly evolving to Christian art (as Jesus and Mary's pairing) in the Levant, Ethiopia, and South Arabia by the sixth century. However, theological conversations among Christians took place at the council of Ephesus. In AD 431, Mary was given the title *Theotokos* (bearer of God) against the title *Christotokos* (bearer of Christ). After the council of Ephesus, the veneration of Mary started developing into different cults, especially in Byzantium, which led to the iconoclastic age. While the iconoclasm took effect in the Byzantine churches, it was rejected by the Eastern churches, and as the construction of new churches continued even in South Arabia, Holy images and relics were included in the new churches' decorations.

Islamic writings show that the relic of Jesus and his mother in al-Ka^{c}ba was not isolated but was part of a movement that has started, spread, and continued among the Christians in many locations. While the Islamic description of the relic of Mary and her son in al-ka^{c}ba is terse, it is similar in some ways to the description of the *Theotokos* icon. The Ḥadīth provided by al-Azraqī states that Mary is seated, Jesus is on her lap, and both of them are ornamented. This description is very similar to the *Theotokos* icon, in which Jesus and Mary are seated on a throne, Jesus is in Mary's lap, and they both look adorned and venerated because of the halos around their heads. Christians throughout history have developed the habit of standing in front of these icons, touching, crying, praying, and asking for personal blessings and physical healing. While Muslims (including Mohammad) know Christians divinize Jesus, they see Christians performing the same worship/adoration acts in front of the image of Mary. Thus, it is reasonable to conclude that a misconception can be acquired easily by someone who is not deeply rooted in Christian theology. In other words, it is easy to believe that Christians divinize Mary as well as Jesus because of the adorned guise that the paintings conveyed and the divinized worship acts that the Christians performed in front of the holy images.

The Islamic understanding of iconography is similar to the Jewish understanding. Icons and images are linked to spiritual idolatry. The Islamic prohibition of images is a result of the unique view of Allah. He is the only creator, and any attempt to imitate his creation is a direct blasphemous act against his inner being. The fact that Christians venerated the holy icons by kissing and prostrating themselves before them no doubt convinced the Muslims that Christians worship the idols. Perhaps this is why Mohammad presumed that Christians venerated Mary. Unfortunately, extant literature about the Christians of Najrān does not provide information about their iconography belief, what it meant to them, or how important it was in their worship. The aforementioned Islamic testimonies about the Christian churches in Arabia and the surviving ancient ruins of some of these churches suggest that Christians in Arabia venerated and used images, relics, and statues. Maybe Mohammad not only saw the holy icons but also witnessed Christians venerating, kissing, and bowing in front of the holy images, leading him to conclude that Christians divinized Mary as they divinize Christ.

In a nutshell, clues from Islamic and Christian literature as well as history point to the idea that Mohammad learned about the divinity of Jesus from Christians—most likely Monophysites—but none of the Christians he met actually believed in the divinity of Mary. There is no historical evidence that Christians taught Mohammad that Mary was divine. Therefore, it is reasonable to conclude that Mohammad reached this conclusion by inference—by observing Christian holy images and their adoration, especially to Mary and Jesus' relics. The *Theotokos* icon is painted in a way that gives equal adoration to Jesus and Mary: both are enthroned and venerated with halos around their heads. When Christians bow and kneel in front of the *Theotokos*, they convey the idea that they are worshiping and praying to two divine beings, Jesus and Mary, and since Christians believe in *three*, then Mohammad, by inference, thought Mary is part of the Trinity.

3

The Christian Explanation of the Trinity in the Eighth, Ninth, and Tenth Centuries

HAVING PRESENTED A POSSIBLE ANSWER to the Qur'anic perception of the Trinity and the divinity of Mary, the current chapter focuses on the scholarly Islamic objections to the Trinity—the ones presented in chapter one of this volume. By relying on English and Arabic resources, this chapter introduces the life, background, and trinitarian arguments of three Arab Christian scholars (John of Damascus, Theodore Abū Qurrah, and Yaḥya Ibn ᶜAdī) who defended the Trinity in the eighth, ninth, and tenth centuries and answered many Islamic objections to the Trinity.

John of Damascus (AD 675–754)

John's life and educational background. John was born in a great Damascene family that participated in the negotiation of the peaceful surrender of Damascus to the Muslim army. Sarjun, John's grandfather, negotiated the terms of surrender with Khalid Ibn al-Walīd and helped the Christians keep fifteen of their churches.[1] John grew up under Islamic rule and spent the early part of his life working as a member of the financial administration in Damascus, probably under ᶜabd al-Malik (AD 685–705).[2] Daniel Sahas

[1]Joseph Nasrallah, *Mansoor ben Sarjon al-Ma'roof bil Qidiis Youhana al-Dimashqi: 'Asroh, Hayatoh, Mo'alfatoh* [*Mansoor the Son of Sarjon the Damascene: His Time, Life, and Writings*], trans. Antoin Wehbi (Beirut, Lebanon: Al-Maktaba al-Boulisya, 1991), 42-46. Daniel J. Janosik, *John of Damascus: The First Apologist to the Muslims* (Eugene, OR: Pickwick, 2016), 25.

[2]Janosik, *John of Damascus*, 27.

suggests that John may have attained a higher position than his father, a personal secretary to the caliph, while continuing with the financial responsibilities his father left to him.[3]

While John lived under Islamic rule, his father made sure he received a good education. Several sources report that John learned philosophy and Greek from a Sicilian monk who was captured by Muslims, brought to Syria, and later on freed by John's father.[4] Although most of John's writings were in Greek, it is hard to know whether this story is authentic or not. Frederic Chase, who wrote the introduction and translated three of John's writings into English, states that John's understanding of classical Greek philosophy was clearly demonstrated in his books.[5] He also concludes that John's writings are "sufficient to show that his traditional reputation as an eloquent, learned, and devout preacher is fully justified."[6] Later in his life, John retreated to the monastery of Mar Sabas in southern Palestine.[7]

According to Janosik, it is likely that John remained working under the Umayyad government through the reign of Walid I (AD 706–715), entering Mar Sabas monastery to start his monastic life in AD 716.[8] During this time, John wrote several poems and many liturgical, philosophical, and theological books, including *The Fount of Knowledge*, which is mostly Greek philosophy. He also wrote *The Orthodox Faith*, which is also called "Dialectic."[9] It is considered the first *Summa* because it includes a summary of dogmatic faith of the early Fathers and is designed to help Christians know their faith. *On Heresies* is a summarized work similar to Irenaeus's and Hippolyte's works against heresies. Finally, John wrote a short article

---

[3]Daniel J. Sahas, *John of Damascus on Islam: The Heresy of the Ishmaelites* (Leiden, Netherlands: E. J. Brill, 1972), 42.

[4]Kamal al-Yazaji, *Youhana al-Dimishqi: Ara'oh al-Lahootiya wa Masael 'ilm al-Kalam* [John of Damascus: His Theological Opinions and the Issues of Theology] (Beirut: Manshūrat al-Nūr, 1984), 34-36. Nasrallah, *Mansoor ben Sarjon*, 84.

[5]Frederic H. Chase, trans., *John of Damascus: The Fathers of the Church Writings*, vol. 37 (Washington, DC: Ex Fontibus, 2012), xxviii.

[6]Janosik, *John of Damascus*, xv.

[7]There is no historical evidence indicating whether John of Damascus was a monk in Mar Sabas. Sidney H. Griffith, *The Church in the Shadow of the Mosque: Christians and Muslims in the World of Islam*, (Princeton, NJ: Princeton University Press, 2008), 40; Janosik, *John of Damascus*, 31.

[8]Janosik, *John of Damascus*, 31.

[9]J. B. O'Connor, "St. John Damascene," *The Catholic Encyclopedia: New Advent*. Accessed April 27, 2021. www.newadvent.org/cathen/08459b.htm.

called "The Discussion of a Christian and a Saracen,"[10] recounting a conversation between a Muslim and a Christian. His writings still prove influential today, and his teachings continue to be used throughout the Eastern Orthodox world.

History indicates that John was neither a miracle worker nor a martyr. Nevertheless, the reason behind his desire to shift to monastic life is uncertain. Some resources mention that he decided to leave his position under the Umayyad's rule after he was persecuted by the caliph. The story asserts that after John sent his iconography defense to the Byzantine emperor, the latter created a forged letter that counterfeited John's handwriting and was sent to the Muslim ruler of Damascus leaking strategic information about the status of the city and its army. When the Muslim ruler confronted John, he denied writing these letters but acknowledged that the handwriting seemed similar to his. The caliph ordered John's hand amputated as a punishment. After the amputation, John prayed to Mary the mother of Jesus to intercede for him. The next morning, his hand was miraculously healed. When the Muslim prince saw his hand healed, he asked John about the doctor who helped him. John replied, "My Christ is a medical Seer. He is omnipotent. It was not difficult for him to heal me, so he was fast in his accomplishment."[11] It is important to mention that while Joseph Nasrallah quotes the details of this story, including John's prayer to Mary, he states that the event is closer to legend than history, especially considering that it was not mentioned in any earlier historical literature, and it is written by unknown authors.[12]

During John's time in the monastery, he preached in several churches. According to Frederic Chase, John "was a preacher of the first order and, although his style is at times more effusive and exalted, he may be said to

---

[10]It is also called "The Dispute." This study will be using J. P. Migne's translation: John of Damascus, "The Discussion of a Christian and a Saracen," trans. J. P. Migne, *Patrologia Graeca* 94 (1864): 266-73. The authorship of this document is not definitively known. It was first ascribed to John of Damascus by Robert Grosseteste, who translated it in the thirteenth century. Louth and Sahas suggest that the content of "The Dispute" was used by the Arab Christian theologian Theodore Abū Qurrah in the ninth century. Therefore, it is plausible that Abū Qurrah based his writing on John's oral teaching. Sahas, *John of Damascus*," 102. Louth, *St John Damascene*, 77-78. Janosik, *John of Damascus*, 136. J. P. Migne divides John's argument and Abū Qurrah's in his translation.

[11]Al-Yazaji, *Youhana al-Dimishqi*, 45.

[12]Nasrallah, *Mansoor ben Sarjon*, 100-103.

rank with the great Chrysostom."[13] In the title of one of John's homilies, he is described as "a presbyter (priest) of the Holy resurrection of Christ," which may refer to the Church of the Holy Sepulchre in Jerusalem.[14] This sort of evidence indicates that he was ministering in Jerusalem and other areas outside Mar Sabas monastery. Because he defended the Christian faith in the eighth century against Islamic objections, John is now considered the first apologist to the Muslims.[15]

The formation of Islamic theology. As stated in chapter one, during the eighth, ninth, and tenth centuries, Islamic theology developed through conversations and debates between *ahl al-ra'y* (the people of opinion), who were mostly Muᶜtazilites, and *ahl al-Ḥadīth* (the people of *Ḥadīth*), who were called Traditionalists. The former group based their opinions on reason, whereas the latter relied on literal reading and application of the Qur'an and Ḥadīth.[16] While these debates were conducted, a new party emerged "with its tendency to take the middle ground between the Muᶜtazilites and the Traditionists, Ashᶜarism came to dominate the theological scene in much of the Sunni world."[17] Ashᶜarites and Muᶜtazilites debated different topics, but the most important subject concerning this study is the nature of the Qur'an—the created word versus the uncreated word of God. Ashᶜarites argued against Muᶜtazilites that the Qur'an is uncreated—and therefore, it is eternal.[18] There is no time in history when God existed without his word. Similar to God's speech are God's attributes. Ashᶜarites argued that since God's speech is eternal, his attributes (omnipotence, power, knowledge, etc.) are eternal as well.[19] Allah was, is, and always will be omnipotent, all-powerful, and perfect in knowledge. All his attributes and speech are eternal and inseparable from his essence.

Muᶜtazilites, on the other hand, refused to believe in the eternality of the Qur'an. They viewed God speaking or revealing as an anthropomorphic act, which—if taken literally—ultimately would destroy the unity of God. If

[13]Frederic H. Chase, trans., *Saint John of Damascus Writings* (New York: Fathers of the Church, 1958), xxiii.
[14]Louth, *St John Damascene*, 7.
[15]Janosik, *John of Damascus*, 1.
[16]Abdullah Saeed, *Islamic Thought: An Introduction* (Florence: Taylor & Francis Group, 2006), 47.
[17]Saeed, *Islamic Thought*, 71.
[18]Saeed, *Islamic Thought*, 68.
[19]Saeed, *Islamic Thought*, 68.

God's discourse is as eternal as God's being, then there would be two eternal entities (God and his word) rather than one that existed eternally. Since the Qur'an is Allah's speech, then it must be eternal like his nature.[20] The eternality of the Qur'an also implies that it is uncreated because it is part of Allah's nature (like his attributes). Muᶜtazilites rejected this view because, in their opinion, it leads to *shirk* (polytheism) and ultimately destroys the unity of God. If the Qur'an existed apart from God (which it did on *Al-Lawh Al-Mahfūẓ*),[21] then there would be two eternal entities rather than one, and the unity of Allah would be compromised.[22] The seeds of this argument were planted during John's days, but the argument was only officially formulated in the eleventh century.[23]

John's trinitarian argument. As stated in the previous chapters, the Islamic invasion of the Levant carried with it several political, economical, and religious consequences. While many Christians considered the Islamic conquest as a judgment from God, others lost their faith because of persecution and the *jizya* mandate. Many thought it was economically wiser and physically safer to ally with the stronger, winning party than with the losers. Their faith was not well-rooted in the church's teachings, and their economical situation was given a priority over their spiritual beliefs. John was quick to notice the spiritual weakness of his own people and the need to define the Christian faith. While he writes about the fundamentals of the orthodox Christian faith in his book *The Orthodox Faith*, he teaches about heresies and Islam in his book *On Heresies*. John probably lists Islam as a heresy because during the first half of the eighth century, Islam was still in

---

[20]Janosik, *John of Damascus*, 86.

[21]Most Sunnis believe that the Qur'an is eternal, but it was descended from heaven in three stages: the first one is when the Qur'an descended to *Al-Lawh Al-Mahfūẓ* (the Book of Decrees/the Preserved Tablet) (Surah 57:22; 85:22). *Al-Lawh Al-Mahfūẓ* is a tablet that Allah had saved in the highest heaven, where all the ecumenical events that have happened and all that will happen are kept in the tablet forever. The second descension was when the Qur'an descended as a whole to *Beit Al-Iza* (the House of Glory), which is another place in heaven, where angel Jibril has access to the words of the Qur'an. Finally, the third descension took place when the verses of the Qur'an came down to the heart/mind of Mohammad. While the Qur'an descended as a whole to *Al-Lawh Al-Mahfūẓ* and to the dwelling place of Jibril in *Beith Al-Iza*, it partially and gradually came down to Mohammad.

[22]Duncan Black Macdonald, *Development of Muslim Theology, Jurisprudence, and Constitutional Theory* (New York: Charles Scribner's Sons, 1903), 135.

[23]George Makdisi, "Ashʿarī and the Ash'arites in Islamic Religious History I," *Studia Islamica* 17 (1962): 37.

its formative stage. Its rules, traditions (*Ḥadīth*), and even the written Qur'an were still developing at that time as the Arabs were expanding into new lands, powers, and territories. According to Janosik, "Islam was not very distinct from Christianity in the time of John of Damascus and it is only in the latter half of the eighth century, when the earliest biographies on Muhammad were being written and the first Ḥadīths were being penned, that the finalization of the Qur'an was also taking place."[24] Many theological schools were yet to form in the later centuries, and the theological and cultural distinctions between Islam and Christians were yet to become more defined.

Writing in an Islamic context, John needed to be careful about the way he unfolded his arguments. At the same time, he needed to be explicit to help Christians distinguish between what they believed and what their Muslim neighbors believed. In his book *On the Orthodox Faith*, John's prologue of his *Summa Theologica* started by mentioning the incomprehensibility of God due to the limited knowledge of human beings, which is common ground between Christians and Muslims.[25] John explains that no one has seen God; therefore, no one can fully know him. Only Jesus "who is in the bosom of the Father, he has declared him . . . the Holy Spirit knows the things of God, just as the spirit of man knows what is in man."[26] John gives the divine revelation a high position, advising his students against declaring things about God beyond what is being revealed to humanity.

On the nature of the deity and the Trinity, John lists several attributes of the Godhead to emphasize the oneness of God. While some of these attributes are common between Muslims and Christians, others are exclusive to Christianity; therefore, they are misunderstood by the Muslims. For example, John stresses the idea of God being one, "one substance, one godhead, one virtue, one will, one operation, one principality, one power, one domination, one kingdom; known in three prefect Persons and adored with one adoration, believed in and worshiped by every rational creature, united without confusion and distinct without separation."[27] His intention is to teach his

---

[24]Janosik, *John of Damascus*, 98.

[25]Frederic H. Chase, trans., "The Orthodox Faith," in *Saint John of Damascus Writings* (New York: Fathers of the church, 1958), 165.

[26]Chase, "Orthodox Faith," 165.

[27]Chase, "Orthodox Faith," 177.

students the theistic nature of their belief against the Islamic accusation of being *Mushrikūn* (polytheists).[28] John uses the word *one* in a numerical sense, which is the same way that Muslims use it to convey the theistic nature of Christianity.

After establishing the oneness of God, John moves to write about the three persons of the Trinity. He affirms the Nicene Creed, the Chalcedonian confession of Christology, and the Eastern Orthodox understanding about the Holy Spirit (*anti-filioque*).[29] John describes the Father as being "the cause of all things, begotten of no one, who alone is uncaused and unbegotten, the maker of all things."[30] Muslims would accept this description and apply it to Allah; however, they reject the term "Son of God" (Surah 112:3). As stated earlier, Muslims understand the theological terms literally, which John took notice of, and he developed a special way of teaching the Christians how to understand and explain their orthodox faith. Regarding the term "the Son of God," John elucidates that Jesus has the same essence of the Father and is eternal with the Father because he "was begotten of the Father before all the ages, light from light, true God from true God, begotten not made; consubstantial with the Father, by whom all things are made."[31] John continues, "We say that he is before all ages, we mean that His begetting is outside of time and without beginning, for the Son of God was not brought from nothing into being."[32] John affirms that the term "Son of God" has a special meaning in the Christian worldview. It is not literal, physical, or sexual, but eternal. The Son is as eternal as the Father and from the same nature of the Father. While the Father is unbegotten, the Son is begotten. Begotten does not mean that Jesus had a beginning nor had a different nature from the Father. The Son was not God who has converted to a human and lived among us on earth while leaving the universe

---

[28]Chase, "Orthodox Faith," 176. It is important to note that John mentions Sabellius in this book; however, his explanation of the Trinity helps Christians to convey their orthodox belief to their Muslim neighbors as well because it clears out many misconceptions that Muslims have about the Trinity.

[29]It is important to mention that John's method in explaining the Trinity is biblical and creedal at the same time. He combines the biblical verses with the creedal statements and adds his own words in between to clarify meaning, without referring to the Nicene Creed or the Chalcedonian Creed.

[30]Chase, "Orthodox Faith," 178.

[31]Chase, "Orthodox Faith," 177-78.

[32]Chase, "Orthodox Faith," 177-78.

unattended. On the contrary, Jesus is eternal with the Father and was even involved in creation.

The eternal state of the Father and the Son connotes immutability. The Father cannot be called a Father without a Son. The same thing goes for the Son; he cannot be called Son without having a Father. Since their relationship is mutual, simultaneous, and has no beginning or ending, it is by necessity unchanging. "The Father and the Son begotten of Him," John states, "exist together simultaneously, because the Father could not be so-called without a Son. Now, if he was not Father when he did not have the Son, and then later became Father without having been Father before, then he was changed from not being Father to being Father, which is the worst of all blasphemies."[33] The concept of God's mutability is rejected in Christianity because it connotes an inferior nature of the divine. If God's nature is subject to change, then God can improve and develop. At one point he cannot do something, and at another point he is able to do it. The changing nature of God connotes progressive development within the divine essence; therefore, it is rejected totally in Christianity.

To explain what Christians believe about God *begetting*, John contrasts *begetting* and *creation*. While "begetting means producing of the substance of the begetter an offspring similar in substance to the begetter," creation "is the bringing into being, from the outside and not from the substance of the creator, of something created and made entirely dissimilar."[34] This is another way to say that Jesus is not created; he is eternal with the Father because he and the Father have the same essence. Jesus is not created because there was no time in history when Jesus was not.

John's belief about the Holy Spirit follows the Eastern Church's tradition, which is anti-*filioque*. While the Holy Spirit proceeds from the Father, he abides in the Son.[35] Ascribing divine attributes that are similar to the Father and the Son affirms the divinity of the third person of the Trinity; therefore, John calls the Holy Spirit "uncreated, complete, creative, almighty, all-working, all-powerful, infinite in power; who dominates all creation but is not dominated; who deifies but is not deified; who fills but is not filled; who

[33]Chase, "Orthodox Faith," 178.
[34]Chase, "Orthodox Faith," 178-79.
[35]Chase, "Orthodox Faith," 183.

is shared in but does not share; who sanctifies but is not sanctified . . ."[36] Although the Holy Spirit is divine in nature, he "is distinctly subsistent and exists in His own Person indivisible and inseparable from the Father and the Son."[37] The Holy Spirit participated in creation by giving subsistence to all things. In a nutshell, the three *Aqanīm* differentiate in their manner of existing—the Father is uncaused and unbegotten, the Son is begotten of the Father, and the Holy Spirit proceeds from the Father.[38]

The attributes of God is another related topic to the Trinity that John focuses on. He presents the omnibenevolence of God, attributing goodness to God and making him the source of all goodness. John states that God is "light itself and goodness and being in so far as having neither being nor anything else that is from any other; the very source of being for all things that are, of life to the living, of speech to the articulate, and the cause of all good things for all; knowing all things before they begin to be."[39] If God is the source of goodness, then he is not the source of evil; he does not have evil in his nature; therefore, he does not tempt people with evil. This is a point of difference between Islam and Christianity, and it is related to the morality of God.

Another divine attribute that is important to the conversation between Muslims and Christian is the transcendence of God. This doctrine is a fundamental issue and a point of difference between Islam and Christianity. John explains that God is transcendent; he is "removed far beyond all things and every substance as being supersubstantial and surpassing all, supereminently divine and good and replete; appointing all the principalities and orders, set above every principality and order, above essence and life and speech and concept."[40] Christians do not believe that God is only transcendent; they also believe that he is immanent in his creation. God is above, yet he pervades "all substances without being defiled."[41] Traditional Muslims during John's time, however, held a different concept of the divine. They believed that God is utterly transcendent, and nothing is like him in creation.

---

[36]Chase, "Orthodox Faith," 183.
[37]Chase, "Orthodox Faith," 184.
[38]Chase, "Orthodox Faith," 186.
[39]Chase, "Orthodox Faith," 186.
[40]Chase, "Orthodox Faith," 186.
[41]Chase, "Orthodox Faith," 186.

He is not immanent in his creation, and only Qur'anic attributes can be used to describe him.[42]

John's defense of the Trinity against Islamic objections. In his book *On Heresies*,[43] John teaches students or Christians how to converse with Muslims against the accusation of being *Mushrikūn* (associators) in a more direct way than he did in his book *On the Orthodox Faith*.[44] Being *Mushrikūn* implies that Christians do not believe in one God but three because they are associating Jesus and the Holy Spirit as divine persons with God. After explaining that Christians believe in one God, John advises his students to start the conversation with their fellow Muslims by asking them what the Qur'an says about Jesus. Based on his knowledge of the Qur'an, John anticipates the answer to be that Jesus is "the word of God and his spirit" (Surah 4:171). Based on this answer, John teaches his students to explain:

> The word, and the spirit, is inseparable from that in which it naturally has existence. Therefore, if the Word of God is in God, then it is obvious that he is God. If, however, he is outside of God, then, according to you, God is without a word and spirit. Consequently, by avoiding the introduction of an associate with God you have mutilated Him. It would be far better for you to say that he has an associate than to mutilate Him, as if you were dealing with a stone or a piece of wood or some other inanimate object.[45]

Several presuppositions can be extracted from this text: (1) God should be eternal because eternality is a concept related only to the divine nature, and it is part of God's substance. Any being that is not eternal is not God. (2) God should have a word, and his word should be internal to him (part of his being), which makes his word as eternal as he is. If God does not have a word, then he would be mute and cannot communicate with his creation, and if his word is external to him, then at one point, he did not have a word. (3) God should have a spirit, otherwise he is dead. His spirit

---

[42]Saeed, *Islamic Thought*, 68.

[43]The authorship of chap. 101 of "On Heresies" is debatable; however, Sahas believes that it is "undoubtedly, a work of John of Damascus." See Sahas, *John of Damascus*," 55-58.

[44]The root of *Mushrikūn* is *shirk* in Arabic. It is the ultimate sin in Islam to associate another entity or being with Allah, and thus derogate from the unique sovereignty of God.

[45]Frederic H. Chase, trans., "On Heresies," in *John of Damascus: The Fathers of the Church Writings*, vol. 37 (Washington, DC: Ex Fontibus, 2012), 156.

is as eternal as his word. John assumes that these presuppositions are acceptable by Muslims, and if they deny it, then their concept of the divine is mutilated.

Although both Christians and Muslims use the same words to describe Jesus, their references are different. When a Muslim thinks of "the word of God," she means the book/Qur'an. When John thinks about "the word of God," he means Jesus Christ. Noting this problem, John seeks to establish a common ground between the two worldviews in order to bring out the inconsistencies of the Islamic faith. After pointing out that both religions believe that Jesus Christ is "the word of God," John notes the first inconsistency about the eternality of the Qur'an. The Qur'an and Jesus have eternal natures, which makes something/someone co-existing with God since eternity. Muslims do not see the eternality of the Qur'an as *shirk* (the greatest sin in Islam); however, they see the eternality of Jesus as *shirk*. John rationalizes that the Islamic belief in the eternality of the Qur'an is inconsistent with the Islamic worldview because it makes Muslims associators and *shirk* is the ultimate sin in Islam. When Muslims say that the Qur'an is eternal with God, they are combining two eternal existences together, and this is not acceptable in Islam because only Allah is eternal. John introduces this as a logical dilemma of the Islamic faith, stating that if Muslims accept the view that the "word of God" is internal to him (inseparable from him) and eternal with him, then they fall into the same trap they accused the Christians of: they are associating another eternal being with God. If they say, however, "the word of God" is outside of God and separate from him, then God had no word from eternity—this is a mutilation to the divine essence. John, therefore, concludes that it is logical to believe that the "word of God" is God.

The problem seems to be related to the way Christians and Muslims interpret the meaning of the phrase: "the word of God." Muslims tend to be literal when they talk about "the word of God" because they understand it to be the Qur'an. However, when the Qur'an refers to Isa (Jesus) being "the word of God," they shift to the nonliteral meaning, stating that "the word of God" means the messenger of God—Jesus is the one who delivered "the word of God." In a different conversation, John realizes this problem and addresses it. The resulting article is titled "The Discussion of a Christian and a Saracen."[46] In this article, John teaches Christians how to converse with Muslims and ask different questions that are related to the topic of the word and the Spirit. If a Muslim, probably a Muᶜtazili,[47] says that the Qur'an is created,[48] then John asks, "Who created the Word of God and the Spirit? For if compelled by necessity, he [a Muslim] will reply, 'God Himself created (the Word and the Spirit),' then do you again say, 'Therefore before God created the Spirit and the Word, he had neither Spirit nor Word.'"[49] Muᶜtazilites believed in the createdness of the Qur'an in order to protect *tawḥīd* (the unity of God); however, if God created his word and Spirit, then chronologically speaking, at one point in history, he was without his word and Spirit. This is why John states in *On Heresies* that those who believe in the createdness of the Qur'an have mutilated God.

John foresees that some Muslims might deny the uncreatedness of the Qur'an, stating, "Behold, all the words of God are created. But they are not gods."[50] In the same sense, if Jesus is the created word of God, then he is not God.[51] John explains in his book *The Orthodox Faith* that "things which are changeable must definitely be created,"[52] because they increase or decrease in quality and morality. However, the creator must be unchangeable because he is perfect in his nature. This distinction might serve as a trap to the Muslims who believe in the createdness of the Qur'an, for if God created the word and the Spirit, then how could he have had his Spirit and word before

[46]It is also called "The Dispute." John of Damascus, "Discussion," 266-73. J. P. Migne divides John's argument and Abū Qurrah's in his translation. Sahas, *John of Damascus*, 102. Louth, *St John Damascene*, 77-78. Janosik, *John of Damascus*, 136.

[47]During the Umayyad government, the Muᶜtazilite's belief about the uncreatedness of the Qur'an was considered a heresy because it was linked to man's free will. The Umayyad enforced the belief in the ultimate sovereignty of Allah (Allah controls all men's actions) in order to establish their rules and control their subjects as they wished. A number of Muᶜtazilites were executed because of their beliefs under the Umayyad, such as the leader of the Jahmite groups, Jahm B. Safwan. Janosik, *John of Damascus*, 156 and Sahas, *John of Damascus*, 114-15.

[48]Sahas argues that the Greek word for "created" must have been copied incorrectly because the word "uncreated" fits the context better. Janosik, however, disagrees with Sahas. Janosik, *John of Damascus*, 159.

[49]John of Damascus, "Discussion," 266.

[50]John of Damascus, "Discussion," 267.

[51]This issue reflects the early controversy of the Orthodox Muslims with the Jahmites and the early Muᶜtazilites over the passages where God appears to be speaking in the Qur'an. The Jahmites believed that the words of the Qur'an are the words of God, but they are created in order to convey God's will and his command. Check Harry Austryn Wolfson, *The Philosophy of the Kalam* (London: Harvard University Press, 1976), 266-67.

[52]Chase, *John of Damascus*, 169.

they were created? If he did not have them before he created them, then his nature changed after he had them.

In response to the problem of the createdness of the Qur'an, John clarifies the fundamental rule in biblical interpretation by explaining the difference between the literal and the figurative meanings of the text. He states, "the literalness refers to the established and fixed meaning of a thing. Figurative interpretation, however, involves a secondary meaning."[53] John does not refer directly to the Nicene Creed, but he quotes it, explaining that the Son is begotten, not born; therefore, he is not created. He continues, "I acknowledge only one Word of God Who is uncreated. But I do not call Scripture λόγια, that is 'words' of God; but ρήματα, that is 'formal words' of God."[54] John introduces here two distinctions that lie behind the concept "the word of God," which is "the uttered words of God" versus "the written words of God," and the singular form of "the word of God" (referring to Jesus) versus its plural form "the words of God" (referring to Scripture). The Scripture (the written words of God) is created because it is the words of human beings, but the "word of God," Jesus Christ, is not created (he is begotten), therefore, he is God.

John wanted to teach his students that the Qur'anic expression "the word of God" refers to a person, not words/Scripture.[55] The createdness of the Qur'an was not the common view among Muslims during John's days because it was the persecuted view. However, John still marks it as a potential answer. Muslims might point out that Christians also believe in the creation of "the word of God," not realizing that there is a great distinction between "the words of God" (plural form: his utterances, meaning the Scripture) and "the word of God" (singular form: referring to Jesus Christ). Muslims might claim that either the words are all God's or that "the word of God" (the Christian profession of Jesus) is not God. In John's view, the word (the written word of God) is neither created nor uncreated; however, Jesus (the living Word of God) is the one hypostatic "word of God," a point even the Qur'an admits.

Traditionalist Muslims, according to Sahas, borrowed John's distinction of the singular and plural form of the word/words *of God* and applied it "as a means to reaffirm the eternity and uncreatedness of the Qur'an without

---

[53]Chase, *John of Damascus*, 169.
[54]Chase, *John of Damascus*, 267.
[55]Janosik, *John of Damascus*, 159-60.

any differentiation from its utterance."[56] The later-developed Islamic distinction of the concept of "the words of God" follows the Christian concept of the Scripture: the Qur'an was proclaimed to be uncreated, but its pronouncement by men is created. This distinction was not developed until the end of the ninth century. The later Orthodox Muslims (Ashᶜarites) embraced the belief that God's speech is eternal, but the written Qur'an is just a representation of the eternal Qur'an in heaven.[57]

Harry Austryn Wolfson traces the createdness of the Qur'an to Labīd, who "had taught the createdness of the Torah, and Ṭalūb—insincere convert from Judaism to Islam—who was the first to write about this doctrine. So, the original belief about the pre-existent Qur'an was that it was created and that its uncreatedness was introduced later in consequence of the rise of the belief in uncreated attributes."[58] Saeed, on the other hand, proposes a different theory. He indicates that the Muᶜtazilites' position on the created nature of the Qur'an "was partly a reaction to the Christian notion of the incarnation of Jesus"[59] because it threatens the unity of Allah, who is wholly transcendent and wholly other. If Saeed's theory is true, then John's argument may have played a major role in developing the later theological formation of the Islamic belief. John's argument might have led the Muᶜtazilites, a century after him, to believe that the Qur'an is created so as to avoid the dilemma of acknowledging two eternal beings.[60]

Theodore Abū Qurrah (AD 755–830)

Theodore Abū Qurrah was a Melkite monk who defended the Christian orthodox faith to Muslims, Monophysites, and others. Although historians do not know much about his life before becoming a monk or about how he received his education, they know that he was competent in Syriac, Arabic, and Greek.[61] Abū Qurrah demonstrated good knowledge in philosophy by

---

[56] Sahas, *John of Damascus*, 117.

[57] Jerry R. Halverson, *Theology and Creed in Sunni Islam: The Muslim Brotherhood, Ash'arism, and Political Sunnism* (New York: Palgrave Macmillan, 2010), 16-17.

[58] Wolfson, *Philosophy of the Kalam*, 265.

[59] Saeed, *Islamic Thought*, 66.

[60] Louth, *St John Damascene*, 84.

[61] Ignatius Deek, "Maymar fi Wujud al-Khaliq wa al-Din al-Qawim [An Article about the Creator's Existence and the Right Religion]," in *al-Turath al-Arabī al-Masīḥī* (Jouniey, Lebanon: al-Maktaba al-Boulisiya, 1982), 43.

translating some of Aristotle's books.[62] He also left a wealth of written works and presented the rational and philosophical tenability of the Christian faith before Christian and Muslim officials within the context of his ecclesial and theological tradition.

As stated earlier, Abū Qurrah was the first theologian/apologist of the Eastern Orthodox Church to write in the Arabic language. His writings model John of Damascus's works, which makes scholars think that he had a close association with Mar Saba's monastery theologians.[63] However, Griffith points out that "none of this requires that Abu Qurrah has been in Mar Sabas in John of Damascus' lifetime, as many scholars who have written on the subject have assumed."[64] John of Damascus died before Abū Qurrah was born, but he might have read his writings, since both were Melkites and knew Greek and Syriac.

In AD 780, Abū Qurrah became the bishop of Ḥarrān in Mesopotamia, a position from which he was removed and reappointed in AD 799.[65] The

---

[62]Deek, "Maymar fi Wujud al-Khaliq," 43.

[63]John Lamoreaux disagrees with earlier scholars who suggested that Abū Qurrah was a monk in Mar Sabas Monastery. He has exerted great labor in a historical investigation to highlight the complex relationship between Abū Qurrah and the available resources that talk about his environment. However, the work only seeks to disassociate the bishop of Harrān from Mar Sabas, while the abundant evidence of Abū Qurra's relationship with the Jerusalem patriarchate alleviates some of Lamoreaux's conclusions. John C. Lamoreaux, "The Biography of Theodore Abū Qurrah Revisited," *Dumbarton Oaks Papers* 56 (2002): 25-40. David Bertaina questions Lamoreaux's argument, wondering why Abū Qurrah would "travel throughout Palestine and have a personal familiarity with the patriarchate of Jerusalem if he is only bishop of an insignificant see, particularly since his immediate jurisdiction was under the patriarch of Antioch? Wouldn't Theodore have had a close relationship with the monasteries of Jerusalem? In fact, Mar Sabas monastery did not only include the monastery just southeast of Jerusalem in the Judean desert, but it included a house in Jerusalem (and in Constantinople and Rome as well)." He brings to the attention of the reader the similarity of thoughts between John of Damascus and Abū Qurrah and the fact that his works have been copied and found in Mar Sabas Monastery. David Bertaina, "An Arabic Account of Theodore Abu Qurra in Debate at the Court of Caliph al-Ma'mun: A Study in Early Christian and Muslim Literary Dialogues," (PhD diss., The Catholic University of America, 2007), 214-17.

[64]Sidney H. Griffith, "Images, Islam and Christian Icons: A Moment in the Christian-Muslim Encounter in Early Islamic Times," in *La Syrie de Byzance a l'Islam: VIIe-Ville siècles,* Colloque 1990, ed. Pierre Canivet and Jean-Paul Rey-Coquais (Damascus: Institut Frangais de Damas, 1992), 121-38.

[65]Sidney H. Griffith, "Reflections on the Biography of Theodore Abu Qurrah," *Parole de l'Orient: revue semestrielle des études syriaques et arabes chrétiennes* 18 (1993): 165. A. Van Roey, Nonnus de Nisibe, Traiti Apologltique, Etude, Texte et Traduction (Bibliotheque du Museon, vol. 21; Louvain, 1948), 18. See also Sidney H. Griffith, "The Apologetic Treatise of Nonnus of Nisibis," *ARAM* 3 (1992), 115-38. Deek, "Maymar fi Wujud al-Khaliq," 44-45.

reason for his demotion is not clear; however, Griffith speculates that "it could have been his position in favor of public veneration of the icons that put Abū Qurrah on a collision course with Patriarch Theodoret of Antioch."[66] This hypothesis makes sense, especially given that Abū Qurrah regained his seat with the ascension of Patriarch Job, who liked him, perhaps because both were iconophiles. One of Theodore's main concerns was clearly engaging in intra-Christian polemic in order to promote the belief of Melkite doctrine. In AD 780, Abū Qurrah set off on a journey south to Alexandria and north to Armenia to defend the Chalcedonian orthodoxy.[67] In AD 817 in Armenia, he engaged in a debate in the presence of a prince, debating the Syrian Orthodox deacon Nonnus of Nisibis.[68] He also engaged in a debate with Muslim scholars in the presence of caliph al-Ma'mūn in Ḥarrān.[69]

Abū Qurrah was a well-known writer. He recognized a great need for effective religious teaching in Arabic to support the Christian faith and to proclaim the Gospel in the new social and political contest. He left about twenty compositions in Arabic, and forty-three other Greek texts that are attributed to him, though they are arguably translations from Arabic.[70] At the end of the eighth century and the beginning of the ninth century, Arabic became the *lingua sacra* of the Qur'an and the common language of the Levant. This period was also known for mass conversions to Islam, largely on the part of Greek- and Syriac-speaking Christians in the Levant, Mesopotamia, and Egypt. Many Chalcedonians soon found themselves subject to the rule of an aggressive and expansionist foreign religion—not adherents to an imperial faith, but merely one sect living alongside other Christian sects.[71] In this context, Abū Qurrah saw a great need to teach and write about how to defend and articulate the Christian doctrines against other sects and the Islamic religion.

Unfortunately, based on the available resources, Abū Qurrah's biography is incomplete. However, several scholars—including Muslim scholars—mention

[66]Griffith, "Biography of Theodore Abu Qurrah," 165.

[67]Sidney H. Griffith, *Theodore Abū Qurrah: A Treatise on the Veneration of the Holy Icons* (Louvain, Belgique: Peeters, 1997), 13.

[68]John Lamoreaux, trans., *Theodore Abū Qurrah* (Provo, UT: Brigham Young University Press, 2005), xv.

[69]Griffith, "Biography of Theodore Abū Qurrah," 13.

[70]Griffith, "Biography of Theodore Abū Qurrah," 3.

[71]Lamoreaux, *Theodore Abū Qurrah*, xviii.

Abū Qurrah's writings[72] and his defense of icon veneration.[73] He is also known for his famous debate about the Christian religion at the council of the caliph al-Ma'mūn in Harrān in the year AD 829.[74] This debate helped influence and shape *ᶜlim al-kalām* (Islamic theology) during the early Abbasid dynasty.[75] Historians estimate that Abū Qurrah was about seventy-five years old when the debate took place, and they presume he died not long afterward.[76]

Theodore Abū Qurrah's Trinitarian Theology/Argument

Like John of Damascus, Abū Qurrah had a great zeal for the Christian Chalcedonian faith, which led him to travel to several regions, debate Muslims, and endure persecution and demotion in his priesthood status. While he was busy in mission work, he did not neglect writing and teaching about the Trinity and many other doctrines. As an apologist, Abū Qurrah's main purpose of his written work was to answer those who do not believe in Christianity, especially those who do not believe in the Trinity.[77]

Christians can learn about God via Adam. Abū Qurrah writes little about the Trinity in his treatise *Theologus Auttodidactus* but thoroughly in *On the Trinity. Theologus Auttodidactus* seems to be a preparatory work to other treatises that he wrote. He uses the natural theology approach with those who are skeptical about the existence of God by recognizing that the cognitive faculties of human beings—reason, sense-perception, introspection—can be used to investigate theological matters. "While God is unseen through the likeness of our own nature's virtues," says Abū Qurrah, "Notwithstanding that God transcends and is contrary to our nature, our

[72]Muḥammad ibn Isḥāq Ibn al-Nadīm, *The Fihrist of Al-Nadīm: A Tenth-Century Survey of Muslim Culture*, vol. 1, (New York: Columbia University Press, 1970), 42.

[73]Miriam L. Hjälm, ed., *Senses of Scripture, Treasures of Tradition*, vol. 5, (Leiden, Netherlands: Brill, 2017), 12-13.

[74]Lamoreaux, *Theodore Abū Qurrah*, xvii.

[75]It should be noted that the historicity of this debate is not entirely authenticated. The manuscripts of the debate are found throughout Melkite and Jacobite monasteries; however, the scribe who copied the debate seems to be somehow affiliated to Theodore Abū Qurrah, but not a direct pupil. Abū Qurrah's debate was likely used in a monastic context for educational purposes. It also has served as a rhetorical tool to train monks who were interested in engaging Muslims in apologetics.

[76]Griffith, *Theodore Abū Qurrah,* 13. Deek, "Maymar fi Wujud al-Khaliq," 52.

[77]Qusṭanṭine Bashā, Mayamir Theodore Abū Qurrah Usquf Ḥārān: Aqdam Ta'lif arabi Nasrani [Mayamir Theodore Abū Qurrah Usquf Ḥārān: The Oldest Arabic Christian Writings] (Beirut: Al-Fou'ad Printing Press, 1904), 27.

minds can see both Him and the attributes according to which He is to be worshipped."[78] He gives the analogy of a person looking into the mirror. While he cannot see his real face in the mirror but only its likeness, in a similar way, when he looks at his human nature, he also cannot see the nature of God and his attributes but only God's likeness.[79]

Given the difference between the divine and the human natures, human beings can still learn about the divine nature by observation and reflection. Abū Qurrah uses Adam as a representative of human nature. Adam's nature and virtues allow theologians to see God and have true knowledge of him, despite the fact that God transcends human nature. Abū Qurrah believes that "when with our minds we examine Adam's nature and observe its virtues, we can see God from it and have true knowledge of Him, for that nature is His likeness, notwithstanding that God transcends and is contrary to it."[80]

The gap between the human nature—represented by Adam—and the divine nature is wide. Adam has defects, whereas God does not. Adam exists today but tomorrow is gone. He is learned, wise, powerful, and living today, but tomorrow he is ignorant, unwise, weak, and dead. While Adam's nature is changing and defected, God is not. He is perfect and much more transcendent, unlike human beings. "God is not comprehended through the defects of Adam's nature, nor does God resemble Adam in those defects," says Abū Qurrah, "It is only with regard to his virtues that Adam resembles God."[81] While Adam's virtues can be attributed to God, his defects cannot, because God is holy and perfect. Adam's virtues, however, are minor to the virtues of God, who is maximally greater than any human being. Because Adam acquires such virtues, we know that God does as well. It is just that God enjoys attributes and virtues in a greater and more transcendent way.[82]

---

[78]Lamoreaux, *Theodore Abū Qurrah*, 9.

[79]According to the Routledge *Dictionary of World Philosophy*, the term *Bilā kayfa* literally means "without how," which denotes the Islamic theological principle according to which one should not question revelation when one cannot understand it. This principle was invoked by Abū Ḥasan al-Ashʿarī (AD 935) and others—e.g., Aḥmad Ibn Ḥanbal (AD 855)—regarding the Quran's anthropomorphizing expressions such as "Hand of God," and "Face of God," which attribute human features to God. According to these thinkers, though having a hand and having a face cannot be attributes of God, these expressions have to be taken literally without asking how.

[80]Lamoreaux, *Theodore Abū Qurrah*, 10.

[81]Lamoreaux, *Theodore Abū Qurrah*, 10.

[82]Lamoreaux, *Theodore Abū Qurrah*, 10.

Answers to those who deny that the Father begets, and Jesus is begotten. In a similar fashion, Abū Qurrah uses Adam's resemblance to answer those who deny that God begets a son. He explains that since "Adam begets and is head over one who is from him, He who caused him to beget and to be head must surely Himself beget and be head over One who resembles Him. Nonetheless, this is so in a transcendent and contrary manner."[83] Abū Qurrah believes that the ability to beget surpasses the inability to beget, and since he caused Adam to beget, then He himself should be able to beget and rule over others; otherwise, he is not the highest conceived God. Those who say that God is unable to beget are demeaning his divine nature.

Abū Qurrah does not neglect to mention that Adam's begetting is different from God's begetting. While Adam's begetting of a son took place through a sexual relationship, God's begetting of his Son and the procession of the Holy Spirit do not happen through sex and physical development but in a more transcendent way.

> There are in Adam no virtues more noble or exalted than begetting and headship. After all, if Adam did not beget, he would have neither felicity of life, nor headship, nor speech, nor generosity, nor any of the other virtues attributed to him. His felicity of life would be with the pigs, asses, and other beasts—which is not felicity . . . it would not be headship but degradation and dishonor to be called the head of ticks, pigs, scarabs, and worms.[84]

It is glory, honor, and exaltation when the headship is attributed to Adam over other human beings like him, not a humiliation or a deprivation of human nature. Thus, those who say that God cannot beget attribute deprivation of the divine nature because they make God rule over what is less than he is and unable to rule over what resembles him. Thus, among the many things the mind can infer from the likeness of Adam's nature is that God is three persons: One who begets, another who is begotten, and another who proceeds.[85] This belief does not necessarily undermine the divine nature or disrespect God.

Can God be one and three? In his treatise *On the Trinity*, Abū Qurrah discusses the topic of faith and reason, keeping in mind the variety of

[83]Lamoreaux, *Theodore Abū Qurrah*, 12.
[84]Lamoreaux, *Theodore Abū Qurrah*, 13.
[85]Lamoreaux, *Theodore Abū Qurrah*, 13-14.

audiences he met along the way of his ministry.[86] He knew that some of them were simple in receiving faith while others were more philosophically inclined. As Najib Awad points out, Abū Qurrah "believes that reason is faith's caretaker, which reviews faith and preserves it. Reason is what enables one to investigate what she believes in and to discover its truth or falsehood. It is what guides one to the true faith, even if the content of that belief is not according to what our feelings like and our desires seek."[87] By acknowledging the fact that people are on different levels with their philosophical inquiry, Abū Qurrah continues with the Scripture explaining that Christians believe in Moses' books and all the prophets of the Old Testament; therefore, the Trinity is not a new invention or a new belief that has been recently acquired. The Trinity is implied in the Old Testament. Several texts refer to two persons but do not call them two Lords. For instance, in Psalm 110:1, 3 the writer "called both the one who speaks 'Lord' and the one addressed 'Lord,' but did not count two lords."[88] Similarly, regarding Psalm 45:6-7, "do you not see that he mentions a God whose throne is forever and ever and says that this God has another God who anointed him? As for this anointed one, there can be no doubt for the wise that this is Christ."[89] Abū Qurrah believes that the Trinity is implied in the Old Testament, and many passages describe the Father as God, the Son as God, and the Holy Spirit as God; however, no writer calls them three gods.

After discussing the implication of the Trinity in the Old Testament, Abū Qurrah uses reason to explain this doctrine to those who like reasonable arguments. He realizes that one of the major philosophical errors that people commit is category errors; therefore, he explains the differences between logical and nonlogical names. Logical names indicate persons, such as Peter, Paul, and John; and nonlogical names indicate natures, such as man. The former may be many, while the latter is one.[90] While Peter, Paul, and John are the names of three persons, the number three does not apply to the names; instead, it indicates their human persons. According to Abū Qurrah, it is

---

[86]Bashā, *Mayamir Theodore Abū Qurrah*, 27.

[87]Najib George Awad, *Orthodoxy in Arabic Terms: A Study of Theodore Abu Qurrah's Theology in Its Islamic Context* (Boston: De Gruyter, 2015), 101.

[88]Lamoreaux, *Theodore Abū Qurrah*, 179.

[89]Lamoreaux, *Theodore Abū Qurrah*, 180.

[90]Lamoreaux, *Theodore Abū Qurrah*, 183.

correct to say that Peter is a man, Paul is a man, and John is a man, but it is not correct to say that Peter is mankind, Paul is mankind, or John is mankind.[91] This concept is applied in a similar fashion when a person says, "God is one in three persons: Father, Son, and Holy Spirit." The Father is God, the Son is God, and the Holy Spirit is God, but God is not the Father, God is not the Son, and God is not the Holy Spirit. God is a name that indicates divine nature. Father, Son, and Holy Spirit are names that indicate three divine *Aqanīm* (persons).[92]

> "Person" is a logical name and does not belong essentially to just one of them [persons of the Trinity]. Rather, the name "person" is predicated of the Father and of the Son and of the Holy Spirit . . . as well as of every other indivisible entity. The logical name was introduced solely that number might be applied to it, for it is not right for number to be applied to their common name, that by which their nature is named . . . otherwise, it would follow that there are different natures, as we have already said.[93]

Logical names are meant to describe the name of the person, not his nature; therefore, they can be used in a plural form. However, it is not right to apply numbers/plurality to a particular nonlogical name; otherwise, "number will make each of the numbered entities to be all of them."[94] Abū Qurrah explains that "If you say, 'Here, Peter, James, and John are three,' you make each one to be the three of them [Peter is also James and John]. So also, if you say, 'in heaven, the Father, Son, and Holy Spirit are three,' you make each one to be the three of them."[95] The Christian trinitarian belief, however, does not believe that the Father is the Son and the Holy Spirit, but it indicates that there is unity in diversity and distinction in unification. While each of the Father, Son, and Holy Spirit is God, the Father is not the Son and the Holy Spirit. For this reason, it is necessary to apply logical names to persons, "and that we say that Peter, James, and John are three persons, but that the name 'man' remain singular, neither diffused nor multiplied."[96]

---

[91]Lamoreaux, *Theodore Abū Qurrah*, 183.

[92]It should be noted that Abū Qurrah never explains the term 'Uqūum or Aqānīm by using the Arabic term shakhṣ (pl. 'ashkhās), which was the practice of other Christian writers and of many Muslim scholars who wrote about Christianity.

[93]Lamoreaux, *Theodore Abū Qurrah*, 184.

[94]Lamoreaux, *Theodore Abū Qurrah*, 184.

[95]Lamoreaux, *Theodore Abū Qurrah*, 184.

[96]Lamoreaux, *Theodore Abū Qurrah*, 184.

Abū Qurrah discuss another reason why Christians do not apply plurality to the divine essence by explaining to his audience a philosophical/mathematical principle of plurality. Human beings are counted as many because they are divided in place, will, and state. However, those who are many, but agree in the will or place, are to be counted as one.[97] The three men—Peter, James, and John—are divided in terms of place, will, and state; therefore, it is correct to count them as many. "As for the Father, Son, and Holy Spirit," says Abū Qurrah, "not one is in a place that the others are not in, not one has a form that the others do not have; and the same holds for will and state."[98] Therefore, they are one, and it is wrong to account them as many. What applies to human beings does not necessarily apply to God.

To illustrate this principle more thoroughly, Abū Qurrah offers several trinitarian examples. He depicts the Trinity as three lamps shining in a dark house. "The light of each is dispersed in the whole house, and the eye cannot distinguish the light of one from the light of the others or the light of all from the light of one. So also, the Father, Son, and Holy Spirit are one God, even though each is fully God."[99] In the second example, Abū Qurrah asks his reader to imagine three men standing and reciting a poem while the reader is outside listening. "You hear only a single poem," says Abū Qurrah, "but you do not doubt that each of them recited the complete poem, nor could you say, 'I heard three poems.' This is the case even if in the voices of the men there is some difference."[100] Finally, the last example is related to three pieces of gold. Abū Qurrah states, "If three pieces of pure gold were placed before you, you would say that each of the three is fully gold and would not say that the three are three golds, but rather that they are one gold."[101] Abū Qurrah uses this example to emphasize that it is inappropriate for a number to predicate the name of the nature of God and to say that the three persons of the Trinity (Father, Son, and Holy Spirit) are three gods, even though that each one of them is fully God.

Answering objections. Abū Qurrah anticipates several objections to his explanation. Some may ask, "Was it three or one that created the world? If

[97]Lamoreaux, *Theodore Abū Qurrah*, 184.
[98]Lamoreaux, *Theodore Abū Qurrah*, 184.
[99]Lamoreaux, *Theodore Abū Qurrah*, 184-85.
[100]Lamoreaux, *Theodore Abū Qurrah*, 185.
[101]Lamoreaux, *Theodore Abū Qurrah*, 185.

you say three, they consider this loathsome. If you say one, they consider the other two hypostases nullified."[102] Abū Qurrah believes that the answer should be "one that created the world." In his opinion, this answer does not prevent the other hypostases/*Aqanīm* from being creators nor nullifies them. To prove his point, Abū Qurrah offers a few more examples. When a person says, "Moses speaking the truth," it is right to think that Moses spoke the truth or the tongue of Moses spoke the truth, but it is not right to think that Moses and his tongue spoke the truth because Moses spoke through his tongue.[103] The same concept is applied to the sun and its rays lighting a room, a person seeing another person with her eyes, a carpenter making a door with his hands, and a king and his son striking a person. It is not right in each case to think both have done it (the sun and its rays lighting the room, the person and her eyes seeing another person, a carpenter and his hand making a door, and the king and his son striking a person), but it is right to say that each one separately has acted.[104] Abū Qurrah offers these examples to imply that the Father created the world and the Son created the world. However, it is not right to think that the Father and the Son created the world separately, for the Father created the world through his Son.[105]

Abū Qurrah addresses another objection to the Trinity that non-Christians believe leave Christians with a dilemma. Non-Christians might ask, "Do you deny every God other than the Father? Do you deny every God other than the Son? Do you deny every God other than the Holy Spirit?"[106] If the Christian says, "I deny every God other than the Son," they respond, "The Father and the Holy Spirit, then, must not be God." If, however, the Christian says, "I do not deny every God other than Christ," they respond, "you have, then, multiple gods."[107] Abū Qurrah points to another error non-Christians commit when they ask, "Do you deny every God other than Christ?" The

[102]Lamoreaux, *Theodore Abū Qurrah*, 185.
[103]Lamoreaux, *Theodore Abū Qurrah*, 186.
[104]Lamoreaux, *Theodore Abū Qurrah*, 186.
[105]It is important to emphasize the idea that Abū Qurrah never thought that his examples were perfect. He states, "We do not think that the tongue and the mind or the rays and the sun or the craftsman's hand and the craftsman or the eye and the brain are more closely united than the Father and the Son—and this, because of the refinement of the divine essence, which is unimaginably more refined than the most refined creatures" (Lamoreaux, *Theodore Abū Qurrah*, 186).
[106]Lamoreaux, *Theodore Abū Qurrah*, 188.
[107]Lamoreaux, *Theodore Abū Qurrah*, 188.

questioners have a different assumption about the meaning of the word *Christ*. They are not asking about Jesus' hypostasis but about his nature. "The name 'God' is not distinct to Christ to the exclusion of the Father and the Spirit. The name 'God' is the name of a nature, not a hypostasis."[108] If a Christian affirms she believes in the gospel presented to her, that does not mean other gospels are not full gospels, "for the gospel through which the Holy Spirit speaks is one. Similarly, you say, 'I deny every God other than Christ,' but your words do not entail that the father and the Holy Spirit cease being each a full God."[109] Moreover, the same error is applied when a person is asked which image is his when he looks into a plate that has three mirrors. Abū Qurrah explains that the face is one thing, and the countenance of the person is another. Each person has one face only, and denying the procurance of another image is not denying the image in each of the mirrors.

Abū Qurrah uses a third example to clarify the false presupposition that assumes that to deny every God other than Christ is to deny that the Father and the Holy Spirit are God. A person admires another person's countenance and decides to draw it fully on three pieces of paper. Should the person whose image was drawn deny every other countenance? Abū Qurrah thinks the answer should be "yes, except for the one drawn on this piece of paper [the paper that the artist used]."[110] This is not to deny that the painted countenance on each of the other pieces of paper is the same countenance. However, when the person points out or asks about the countenance drawn on this particular piece of paper, he does not mean the particular drawing (the lines, curves, and dots), but the essence of the person's countenance (dark complexion, black eyes, and aquiline nose)—despite the fact the questioner was pointing with his hand to the lines of the image.[111] The same holds to the affirmative answer to the question: "Do you deny every God other than Christ?" To answer yes does not mean to deny that the Father and the Holy Spirit are God, "for even though the questioner is hinting at Christ with his words, it is not Christ himself that he means when he names 'God,' but the nature of Christ, to which the name 'God' refers."[112]

---

[108]Lamoreaux, *Theodore Abū Qurrah*, 189.
[109]Lamoreaux, *Theodore Abū Qurrah*, 189.
[110]Lamoreaux, *Theodore Abū Qurrah*, 190.
[111]Lamoreaux, *Theodore Abū Qurrah*, 190.
[112]Lamoreaux, *Theodore Abū Qurrah*, 190.

A trinitarian answer to the Muslims. Abū Qurrah affirms the divine simplicity doctrine, which allows no composition in the divine nature to illustrate the Trinity to Muslims. Combining the Qur'anic illustration of Jesus being the word and the Spirit of God with John of Damascus's conundrum, he asks the Muslim this question: has God ever been without his word and his Spirit? The Muslim is compelled to answer negatively; otherwise, she will make God mute or dead. Abū Qurrah introduces a follow-up question: Is the divine word and his Spirit part of God? If the Muslim answers affirmatively, she then ascribes parts to the divine essence, which is proscribed in Islam because it introduces composition to the divine nature. However, if the Muslim answers negatively, then the Christian belief is right. Abū Qurrah states,

> God and his word and his Spirit are one God even as a person and that person's word and spirit are one person. . . . The Son is to God as a person's word is to that person, and the Spirit is to God as a person's spirit is to that person, even though the Word of God is God and the Spirit of God is God—and this, because of how exalted the divine nature is above composition and the like.[113]

The divine simplicity doctrine was emphasized in early Christianity, and it is consistent with the doctrine of *tawḥīd,* which emphasizes the oneness of God in a numerical sense. Abū Qurrah saw similarities between the two doctrines and used them as an analogy to illustrate the Trinity.

Yaḥya Ibn ᶜAdī (AD 893–974)

Though most now know him as Yaḥya Ibn Adī, his full name is Abū Zakariyya (his son's name) Yaḥya Ibn ᶜAdī Ibn Hamid (his father's name) Ibn Zakariyya' (his grandfather's name).[114] He was born in AD 893 to a Jacobite/Monophysite Christian family. He was born in Tikrit, which was the seat of the Jacobite bishopric from the fourth century until the middle of the twentieth century, when the diocese was combined with the one in al-Mosul.[115] He received his education in Baghdad under famous logicians, such as Abu

---

[113]Lamoreaux, *Theodore Abū Qurrah*, 190.

[114]Mentioning the full name alongside the names of his father, grandfather, and son is an Arabic habit indicating historic accuracy.

[115]Mohd. Nasir Omar, "The Life of Yahya Ibn 'Adi: A Famous Christian Philosopher of Baghdad," *Mediterranean Journal of Social Sciences MCSER* 6 no. 2 S5 (2015): 308.

Bishr Matta Ibn Yūnus (AD 940), who was a Nestorian, and Abū Nasr al-Farabī (AD 950), who was a Muslim.[116] Muslim scholars such as Al-Bayhaqī and al-Masᶜūdī state that Yaḥya was the most prominent disciple of al-Farabī.[117] He earned the title of al-Mantiqī (the logician) by his Muslim peers.[118]

Most scholars during the tenth and eleventh centuries were not only philosophers, but they made a living as physicians, teachers, scribes, translators, or booksellers.[119] Yaḥya himself was not a monk; therefore, he needed to find other sources for self-support. He earned a living as a professional copyist and a bookseller, a career that he may have inherited from his father, ᶜAdi Ibn Hamid.[120] Ibn al-Nadīm tells a story about Yaḥya spending too much time copying manuscripts. Yaḥya replies, "Wherefore now do you wonder at my patience? In my own handwriting I have transcribed two copies of the commentary of al-Ṭabarī, which I have taken to the kings of distant regions. I have transcribed so many books of the theologians that they cannot be counted. It is my agreement with myself that I should copy a hundred leaves every day and night, which I feel to be too little."[121] His passion as a copyist might not only be because of a financial need but also because of his hunger and curiosity to gain more knowledge.

In addition to philosophy, Yaḥya learned medicine from the famous doctor al-Razī (AD 925); however, it is not known whether he practiced it or was counted as a physician.[122] After the death of his master Matta Ibn Yūnus in AD 940, and with the absence of his master al-Fārabī (AD 950), who left Baghdad and traveled to study in Syria and Egypt, Yaḥya became the new leader of philosophical studies in Baghdad. He had accumulated several pupils and spent much time teaching and writing about religions

---

116 Max Meyerhof, "'Alī al-Bayhaqī's Tatimmat Siwān al-Hikma: A Biographical Work on Learned Men of the Islam," *The University of Chicago Press on behalf of The History of Science Society* 8 (1948): 160.

117 Omar, "The Life of Yahya Ibn 'Adi," 309.

118 Abū Sulaymān Al-Sijistānī, *Muntakhab Siwan al-Hikma*, ᶜAbd Arahman Badawī (Teheran: Foundation Cultilrelle de l'Iran. 1974), 327. Ibn al-Nadīm, *Fihrist of Al-Nadīm*, 24.

119 Nicholas Rescher, Tatawer al-Mantiq al-'Arabi [*The Development of Arabic Logic*], trans. Mohammad Mahran, (Pittsburgh: University of Pittsburgh Press, 1964), 94.

120 Richard Walzer, "New Light on the Arabic Translation of Aristotle," in *Greek into Arabic: Essays on Islamic Philosophy* (Cambridge: Cambridge University Press, 1962), 77.

121 Ibn al-Nadīm, *Fihrist of Al-Nadīm*, 631.

122 Gerhard Endress, *The Works of Yahya Ibn ᶜAdi: An Analytical Inventory* (Wiesbaden, West Germany: Dr. Ludwig Reichert Verlag, 1977), 124.

and philosophy. In his school, Yaḥya instructed both Muslim and Christian students. Among his famous Muslim disciples were al-Sijistānī (AD 1001), ʿIsa Ibn ᶜAlī Muhammad al-Badihī (AD 990), and Abū Hayyān al-Tawḥīdī (AD 1023); and among his Christian students were Ibn Zurᶜa (AD 1008), al-Ḥasan Ibn Siwār (AD 1017), Ibn al-Khammar (d. AD 1017), Abu ʿAli al-Samh (AD 1027), and Naẓīf Ibn Yomin—all who hailed from different backgrounds and denominations (Melkites, Jacobites, and Nestorians).[123] He also had a Jewish pupil, Wahab bin Thaqīf al-Rumī, and a Sabian student, Abu Isḥāq al-Sabīʾī.[124]

Yaḥya left many writings related to logic, naturalism, math, metaphysics, kalām arguments, ethics, and Christian theology. The first group of his writings was a philosophical translation of Aristotle, Plato, and their followers. He translated many books from Syriac to Arabic and focused especially on Aristotle's Organon and Physics. He and his pupils even compared, corrected, refined, and added their own writings and translations.[125] His philosophical discourses include *Tahdhīb al-Akhlāq* (The Refinement of Character) and *Maqāla fī Siyasa al-Nafs* (A Discourse on the Management of the Soul). The second group of his writings includes several discourses concerning Christian philosophy. Samīr Khalīl lists nineteen treatises in his introduction to *Al-Turāth al-ᶜArabī al-Massīḥī* (Arabic Christian Heritage), a book that belongs to Yaḥya; however, this chapter will focus on *Maqāla fī al-Tawḥīd* (Treatise in Tawḥīd).

Yaḥya Ibn ᶜAdī's Trinitarian Argument

Yaḥya was aware of the Islamic objections to the Trinity as well as his peers' writings and teachings about this doctrine. As a philosopher, he saw a great need to explain, defend, and answer the Islamic objections to the Christian concept of the unity and oneness of God without mentioning or attacking the Islamic concept of *tawḥīd.* His philosophical defense is of a unique nature. According to Samīr Khalīl, Yaḥya might not be the first philosopher

[123] Omar, "The Life of Yahya Ibn ʿAdi," 310. Nadine Abbas, *Nathariyat al-Tawhid wa al-Tathleeth of Yaḥya Ibn Adi fi Kitabihi ʿal-Rad ʿAla al- Warrāqʾ* [Yaḥya Ibn ᶜAdī's Philosophical Theory of Monotheism and Tri-theism in his book *The Reply to al-Warrāq*] (Beirut, Lebanon: Centre de recherche et de publications de L'orient Chretien, 2014), 61-62.

[124] Omar, "The Life of Yahya Ibn ʿAdi," 310.

[125] Omar, "The Life of Yahya Ibn ʿAdi," 311-12.

who has written about the oneness of God, but he is the first to target and expand on this topic.[126]

Yaḥya makes his defense in several treatises and books. Because of the limited space and the nature of the study, this book will concentrate on *Maqala fi al-Tawhid* [Treatise in Divine Unity] and his answer to al-Warrāq, which was compiled and presented in Nadine Abbas's book *Nathariyat al-Tawhid wa al-Tathleeth of Yaḥya Ibn Adi fi Kitabihi 'al-Rad 'Ala al- Warrāq'* [Yaḥya Ibn ᶜAdī's Philosophical Theory of Monotheism and Tri-theism in his book The reply to al-Warrāq']. In his treatise, Yaḥya focuses on the term *wāḥid* (one), which both Muslims and Christians use to express their beliefs in the oneness of God. He presents a philosophical explanation of the term, when it can and cannot be used to describe the divine oneness of God. In his answer to al-Warrāq, Yaḥya focuses on the logical objection to the Trinity. He explains that it is not a logical mistake to believe that God is one substance and three *Aqanīm* because the "one" can be one in one sense and three in a different sense.[127] This section of the study will start with Yaḥya's treatise *Maqala fi al-Tawhid* [Treatise in Divine Unity] to establish the philosophical meaning of the term *wāḥid.* Then it will move to Yaḥya's answer to al-Warrāq to explain the Trinity.

Relying on Aristotelian philosophy and moving away from theology and biblical studies, Yaḥya analyzes the different meanings of the word *wāḥid.* He does not only discuss the oneness of God in terms of its logical sense—how should *wāḥid* be understood in terms of logical or linguistic analysis—but also in terms of the correct understanding of the divine unity. Yaḥya strives to show that in one aspect, the Creator is one; but in another aspect, he is multiple. Influenced by his teacher al-Farābī,[128] Yaḥya presents different meanings of the word *wāḥid*, which vary based on context. Something/someone can be described as *wāḥid* based on its *jins* (genus), *naw*ᶜ (species), *nisba* (relation), *muttaṣil* (continuum), *ḥadd* (definition or limitation), or *ghayr munqasim* (indivisibility). Yaḥya demonstrates that *al-Bari'*

---

[126]Samīr Khalīl, *Maqala fi al-Tawhid Lil Sheikh Yaḥya Ibn Adi (898-974)* [Treatise in Divine Unity to Sheikh Yaḥya Ibn Adi (898-974)] (Jounieh, Lebanon: Al-Maktaba al- Boulissiah, 1980), 115.

[127]It is important to mention that Yaḥya does not use the word "person" to refer to Aqanīm because of the human reference that this term may convey, which could lead one to understand the Trinity in terms of three gods.

[128]Abū Nasr al-Farābī, *The One and the Unity* (Casablanca: Dar Tobqal Publishing, 1990).

(another name that Arab Muslims and Christians use to describe Allah/God, meaning Creator) cannot be *wāḥid* in genus, species, relation, or continuum because they require either the existence of others or a causal connection to exist. However, God is the uncaused cause of everything. He has nothing that caused him, but he is the cause of every other existence.[129] Thus, anything that is caused by another or has any causal connection for its existence cannot be God.[130]

Al-Bari' cannot also be understood as a negation of divisibility (in either an existing or a nonexisting object) or the principle of all divisible things.[131] Regarding the negation of divisibility, *wāḥid* is like the quality of the thing under description—such as its color or its taste—not its quantity. These qualities cannot be divisible. As for the meaning of the principle of all divisible things, *wāḥid* can be understood in two ways: by its substance or by its accident. An example of by its substance would be the point/dot and the unit. It is one and indivisible by nature, but there can be many of them. An example of by accident would be *wāḥid* cannot be the principle of all divisible things because accidents are caused by other causes.

Since none of the previous meanings of *wāḥid* can be applied to *al-Bari'*, Yaḥya strives to show which aspect of the *wāḥid* is applicable—the meaning that can be used to describe God. According to Yaḥya, *al-Bari'* is *wāḥid* in action, substance, and subject.

First, *al-Bari'* is *wāḥid* in action, but not in power. Whatever exists, exists either by action or by power. "If it exists by power," Yaḥya says, "Then every power is directed toward an action, and every power needs—in egress what is in it toward an action—another cause to egress. This necessarily makes the cause caused and this is impossible."[132] The power needs an action to be consummated; therefore, it cannot be uncaused cause, and if the oneness of God is not in power, then it should necessarily be in action. Second, *al-Bari'* is *wāḥid* in substance. "If it is thought of *wāḥid* in multiple senses," says Yaḥya, "Then the unity applies by necessity because *wāḥid* from each multiplicity does exist; this is to say that the existence of multiplicity and its

---

[129]Khalīl, *Maqala fi al-Tawhid*, 223.

[130]Khalīl, *Maqala fi al-Tawhid*, 224.

[131]Khalīl, *Maqala fi al-Tawhid*, 226-28.

[132]Khalīl, *Maqala fi al-Tawhid*, 230. All translations from the Arabic works of Yaḥya are my own, unless otherwise indicated.

substance is a compound union."[133] Everything exists by its substance, whether it is one or multiple. Last, *al-Bari'* is *wāḥid* in subject as long as the subject reflects the definition of *wāḥid* and represents its substance.[134]

According to Yaḥya, *wāḥid* could be understood in different senses; however, a person can discuss the oneness of God only if he has the correct definition of *wāḥid.* When describing Allah, scholars assume different meanings of the term *wāḥid.* Some use it to negate multiplicity, others mean it as "the One who has no one like him," and others use it to convey a strictly numerical sense—one person/one divine being. In Yaḥya's opinion, the previous different meanings of the term *wāḥid* break several laws of logic; and therefore, they do not necessarily apply to God.

Yaḥya accuses those who define God as *al-Wāḥīd* to convey the idea that "there is no one like him" with committing the equivocation fallacy—that is, using similar words to convey opposite meanings.[135] People use the word *Wāḥīd* to refer both to God and to *mawjūd* (the existing thing/creation). For instance, people say we have *Wāḥīd* moon (one moon) in the universe as they say we have *Wāḥīd* (one) God in the universe. Yaḥya's logical argument goes as follows: If *wāḥid* means no one is like God, then *mawjūd* (the existing thing/creation) is not like him. This makes God not equivalent to *mawjūd* and *mawjūd* not equivalent to God in the same respect and aspect. If *wāḥid* (God) is not equivalent to *wāḥid* (not God, but other existing things), then *wāḥid* is not equivalent to *wāḥid.* This makes the existence of *wāḥid* mean that he is not equivalent to the thing that is not equivalent. This makes the two *wāḥids* (that are equivalent and similar things at least in word formation) not equivalent and not similar, and this cannot be because two things that are parallel and similar to each other (*wāḥid* and *wāḥid*) cannot not be (but should be) similar or equivalent in some aspects, but not different in all aspects.[136] Put in a simpler way, Yaḥya tries to show that people can use the same words with different meanings and respects depending on context.

Whereas some people say *wāḥid* means "there is no one like God," others might say, *wāḥid* (God) is "the opposite to all that describes human beings."

---

[133]Khalīl, *Maqala fi al-Tawhid*, 231.

[134]Khalīl, *Maqala fi al-Tawhid*, 231.

[135]*Al* in Arabic is equivalent to the definite article *the* in English. However, when it is added to an attribute describing the divine, it means God is the one being described.

[136]Khalīl, *Maqala fi al-Tawhid*, 170-71.

No attribute of God is similar to human attributes. Yaḥya shows that this understanding of *wāḥid* is wrong because it makes God identical to his creation, with the exception of human beings. "Some of the attributes of being a human being," says Yaḥya, "are that he is not a dominant, not a mare, not a plant, not eternal, is different from every accident, totally different from all that exist except another human being. So, it is necessary that none of these attributes should be applied to *wāḥid*."[137] Yaḥya continues,

> If none of these negative attributes apply to *wāḥid*, then it is necessary to apply the positive attributes that are opposite to it. . . . So, *wāḥid* is not not a plant, but a plant; is not not a quantity, but a quantity; is not not a modality, but a modality . . . in total, since God is not different from all that exists, except another human being, he is necessarily everything that exists, with the exception of not being a human being.[138]

Yaḥya's explanation can be demonstrated in the following equations:

God is not a human being
Human being is not a plant
God is not (not a plant)

Therefore, God is a plant.

The concept of *wāḥid* (the opposite of all that describes human beings) denies that the attributes of human beings are similar to the attributes of *wāḥid* (God), and this denial makes *wāḥid* identical to his creations, but not a human being. This aspect of *wāḥid* must not apply to God because God is not a created being, and he is not part of creation.

By describing God as *wāḥid* in the sense that "there is no one like him," Yaḥya wanted to stress the idea that *wāḥid* should be understood as "there is nothing except him that is similar and equivalent to all his attributes and epithets."[139] It is wrong to say that nothing is similar to God because similarity does not necessarily require parallelism/identification. There are no two similar things/persons that are identical in all their attributes. If two things/persons are similar, it is necessary that they do not match. They are

[137]Khalīl, *Maqala fi al-Tawhid*, 172.
[138]Khalīl, *Maqala fi al-Tawhid*, 173-74.
[139]Khalīl, *Maqala fi al-Tawhid*, 176.

similar in one aspect, but they are not identical, nor do all their attributes match up. Therefore, using the term *wāḥid* to describe God in the sense that "there is nothing like him" in an ultimate sense is wrong.

In the next section of his treatise, Yaḥya moves to explain the meanings of *wāḥid* that are applicable to God. He argues that *wāḥid* could be one in one sense and multiple in a different sense. The numerical nature of *wāḥid* is not the only sense of the oneness. While it is impossible for *wāḥid* to be multiple in genus, species, relation, continuum, and indivisibility, *wāḥid* can be multiple in action (not in power), in substance (not by accident), and in definition (not subject). In order to explain this multiplicity, Yaḥya discusses the attributes of *al-Bari'*—the attributes that may be predicated of the divine essence.[140] *Al-Bari's* attributes can be deduced from his creation because his essence is hidden, but his effect on the creation is evident from his activity. Since God is the creator, every existing being/thing exists because of a cause. As stated earlier, no created thing (individual or material) exists in this world without a cause. God is the cause of every created thing and the only uncaused cause.[141] Being the uncaused cause and the cause of every existent being shows his omnipotence. Furthermore, God caused other things to exist voluntarily because there is no other cause that forced God to create his creation. All that exists came into being out of nothing. All that was once non-existent came into existence because of God's power, and he had no other cause beside himself to create this creation. Thus, it is reasonable to say, "since He was existent before these came into being, the spontaneous and voluntary act of creation reveals His bounty."[142] His omnipotence and his bounty are manifested in his power to create what exists and to choose not to create what does not exist. In a similar way, his wisdom is manifested in the order and the perfection of His work. He created everything to work together and to sustain itself in a very amazing way. These three essential

[140]*Al-Bari'* is another name of God that Arab Christians and Muslims use to describe the Creator.

[141]Yaḥya was a tenth-century scholar and mentioned the cosmological argument a century before al-Ghazālī, to whom the Kalam cosmological argument is attributed.

[142]Gerhard Endress, "Theology as a Rational Science: Aristotelian Philosophy, the Christian Trinity and Islamic Monotheism in the Thought of Yaḥya Ibn ʿAdī," in *Ideas in Motion in Baghdad and Beyond: Philosophical and Theological Exchanges between Christians and Muslims in the Third/Ninth and Fourth/Tenth Centuries*, vol. 124, ed., Damien Janos (Leiden, Netherlands: Brill, 2015), 233.

attributes (*al-jūd* [bounty], *al-Qudra* [power], and *al-ḥikma* [wisdom]) can be derived from his activities in creation—especially that his essence is hidden from human beings, but his effect in creation is manifested through his activities.[143] Yaḥya used the three attributes of God to depict the idea that *wāḥid* can be one in one sense and multiple in a different sense. God is *wāḥid* in being and multiple in attributes.

Like Abū Qurrah, Yaḥya faced several objections from Muslim scholars. In his reply to Abū ᶜīsā al-Warrāq and the dilemmas he presented against the Trinity,[144] Yaḥya uses different arguments to show that God can be one in one sense and multiple in different sense. He interprets the persons of the Trinity as symbolic representations of Aristotelian ideas: the Father symbolizes *al-ᶜaql* (the intellect), the Son symbolizes *al- ᶜāqil* (the intellectually cognizing subject), and the Spirit symbolizes *al-maᶜaqūl* (the intellectually cognized object). According to Abbas, when Yaḥya says "the essence cognizes with its substance all that exist,"[145] he means:

> He cognizes its substance because he is one of things that exist. When He cognizes his substance, He becomes *al- ᶜāqil* [the intellectually cognizing subject] to his substance, and *al-maᶜaqūl* [the intellectually cognized object] to his substance. Then, *al-ᶜaql* becomes the substance of mere intellect (which is the intellect's essence) which is available in three statuses: the status of substance by itself without any other meanings—*ᶜāqil* or *maᶜaqūl*; and a status where it is *ᶜāqil* (the cognizing subject), and a status where it is *maᶜaqūl* (the cognized object).[146]

Yaḥya considers the essence of the intellect by itself the reason for the existence of the other two statuses: the object and the subject of the intellect. The reason behind his understanding lies in the fact that each one of them cannot be depicted without the intellect's essence (*al-ᶜaql*). The intellect cognizing itself (*al-ᶜaqil be ᶜāqilan*) cannot happen without existing of himself or the existing of the cognized object (*maᶜaqūlan*). The act of God cognizing himself makes him the essence and the intellect, which is the subject (because he cognized), and the object (which is himself) at the same time.

---

[143]Endress, "Theology as a Rational Science," 263-64.
[144]These dilemmas are presented in chap. 1 of this volume.
[145]Abbas, *Nathariyat al-Tawhid*, 159.
[146]Abbas, *Nathariyat al-Tawhid*, 159.

Yaḥya's language equates essence (*jawhar*) and substance (*dhāt*). He does not use the word *essence* in a plural form because he believes in divine simplicity—God does not have three parts/essences.[147] Yaḥya instead uses the term *Aqānīm* in reference to the substances or the meanings of the three persons of the Trinity. Each of the substances/*Aqānīm* has its own essence (secondary essence/substance).

In order to understand Yaḥya's language, Abbas makes a distinction between essence and substance to differentiate between primary essence and secondary essence. The latter is the special substance of the Father, not the one related to the Son or the Spirit; whereas the former is the one that belong to all the *Aqānīm*.[148] Yaḥya wanted to show from the formulation of *al-ᶜaql, al-ᶜāqil, al-maᶜaqūl* that the existence of the Father necessitates the existence of the Son and the Spirit. As the existence of the intellect cognizing itself necessitates the existence of *al-ᶜāqil* (the intellectually cognizing subject) and *al-maᶜaqūl* (the intellectually cognized object), so does the existence of the Father necessitate the existence of the Son and the Spirit.[149]

To summarize Yaḥya's standpoint, the Father, the Son, and the Spirit are eternally omnipotent and wise, but the Father is not the Son and not the Spirit. The Father is the *mūlid* of (the one who begets—in the sense of cause) the Son and the source of the Spirit (by procession), especially that the Son is begotten, and the Spirit proceeds from the Father. Moreover, the fatherhood of the Father is from the substance of the Father, not necessarily from the substance of the Son or the Spirit.[150] According to Abbas, the Father is Father because of the Son. The similarity among them is the cause. As the intellect cognizes itself and becomes the cause of the meaning of the intellectually cognizing subject and the intellectually cognized object, the Father is the cause of the birth of the Son and the procession of the Spirit.[151] Applying this concept to the Trinity makes God one in one sense (one in essence) and multiple in different sense (multiple in substances—or *Aqanīm*). The concept of unity and multiplicity in different senses is not a contradiction. It just shows God as one divine being who can have multiple

[147]Abbas, *Nathariyat al-Tawhid*, 164.
[148]Abbas, *Nathariyat al-Tawhid*, 166.
[149]Abbas, *Nathariyat al-Tawhid*, 251.
[150]Abbas, *Nathariyat al-Tawhid*, 301.
[151]Abbas, *Nathariyat al-Tawhid*, 251.

substances, roles, and attributes. *Aqānīm* can be distinct from each other without having different essences.

Conclusion

The previous discussion presents great arguments that call for deeper research. The three scholars used different methods. John and Abū Qurrah's methodologies were theological, whereas Yaḥya's method was philosophical. Despite the different backgrounds of the three scholars (Chalcedonian and Jacobite), all of them agreed on the definition of the Trinity: one divine being manifested in three hypostases/*Aqanīm*. Their agreement shows that all orthodox Christians agree upon the description, the functions, and the role of the *Aqanīm*, which do not match their corresponding human description—they are not like people.

John, Abū Qurrah, and Yaḥya share several common points between Christianity and Islam in order to start their arguments or to solve a problem at hand. For instance, John and Abū Qurrah's starting point regarding the incomprehensibility of God is a shared point among Christianity and Islam. They both admit that God cannot be fully known because of the limitations of human beings. Moreover, while the topic of oneness in Christianity and Islam is mutually believed, it is also a point of tension. Muslims do not understand the trinitarian concept of God nor classify it under theism, which leads them to accuse Christians of worshiping three gods or being *Mushrikūn*. The three scholars were aware of this misunderstanding, so they prioritized the defense of God's oneness over the divine unity of the three hypostases/*Aqanīm*.

Despite the different backgrounds of John, Abū Qurrah, and Yaḥya (Chalcedonian and Monophysite), the three scholars use the word *Aqanīm* to describe the three persons of the Trinity, which is still a common practice among Arab theologians today. The three scholars defend the Eastern model of the Trinity—the anti-*filioque* model; however, they also explain the relational aspect of the nature of God differently. While they affirm the fatherhood of the Father, the sonship of Jesus, and the procession of the Holy Spirit, they show that the intrarelationship of the *Aqanīm* is unique to the divine nature because it cannot happen without their roles. The Father is called Father because he has a son; the son is a son because he is born of the

Father; and the Holy Spirit proceeds from the Father showing how the three *Aqanīm* are living in an eternal relational existence with each other.

John, Abū Qurrah, and Yaḥya shared two main themes while defending the Trinity: the divine oneness and God's attributes. The divine oneness is a crucial topic that is often misunderstood by Muslims. Many Eastern fathers prioritized defending the divine oneness over the eternal relationship of the *Aqanīm* because of the Islamic accusation of being *Mushrikūn.* John relies mostly on the Scripture to show that Christians believe in one God—one divine being, one Godhead, one virtue, one will, one operation, one principality, one power, one domination, and one kingdom. John uses the concept of the oneness of God in a numerical sense, which is similar to the Muslims' understanding and their description of Allah as *wāḥid*—one being.

Abū Qurrah also depends on Scripture to show Muslims that the Trinity is not a newly invented doctrine. It was implied in the Old Testament. He does not stop here, but he proceeds to explain the linguistic aspect of the doctrine by using the distinction between logical and nonlogical names. The former indicates persons such as Peter, Paul, and John, and the latter implies nature. While it is correct to say that Peter is a man, Paul is a man, and John is a man, it is not correct to say that Peter is mankind, Paul is mankind, or John is mankind. In a similar manner, the Father is God, the Son is God, and the Holy Spirit is God, but God is not the Father, God is not the Son, and God is not the Holy Spirit. God is a name that indicates divine nature; and Father, Son, and Holy Spirit are names that indicate three divine *Aqanīm.* Yaḥya does not rely directly on the Scripture; however, he uses the linguistic argument. He discusses the different meanings of the term *wāḥid* to teach that the divine being is one in one sense and multiple in a different sense, and this is not a contradiction. The logical argument for the Trinity indicates that plurality within the unity is possible in the creation and in the Godhead. The numerical sense of *wāḥid* is not the only way to understand this term. There are many other different senses of the term *wāḥid* that can be applied in creation but not to the divine nature. While *wāḥid* in the sense of genus, species, relation, continuum, and indivisibility cannot be applied to God, *wāḥid* in the sense of action, substance, and definition is applicable. Thus, thinking of God in one sense (the numerical sense) is not rationally correct.

The attributes of God represent an important topic shared by Christianity and Islam. Scholars cannot study the nature of God without discussing God's attributes. While Muslims affirm that Allah has ninety-nine beautiful names/attributes, they disagree on the list of these names and many of their meanings. Muslims who follow the doctrine of *Bilā kayfa* are unable to answer many questions related to the morality of Allah because they confirm that Allah's attributes are not like humans' attributes, and Allah cannot be described in a non-Qur'anic way. However, by discussing God's attributes, John, Abū Qurrah, and Yaḥya were able to show that he is maximally good through the doctrine of the Trinity.

John, Abū Qurrah, and Yaḥya discuss the topic in three different ways. While John infers the attributes of God from Scripture and tradition, Abū Qurrah and Yaḥya believe that God's attributes can be deduced from creation. The first attribute discussed is the omnibenevolence of God. The maximally good God in Christianity is shown in different ways. John mentions several attributes. He believes that God is uncreated, eternal, uncircumscribed, unchanging, the source of goodness and justice, and so on. These divine attributes are shared with Muslims; however, some of them are related to the triune nature of God more than others. John, for instance, comments on God's omnibenevolence by attributing goodness to God's essence (not his will, as Muslims do). This distinction makes God maximally good and the source of all goodness. He is the very source of being for all things that exist and the cause of all good things. Being maximally good (omnibenevolence) is reflected in the way God treats his creation and the way he relates to evil in this world. When the goodness of God is ascribed to his essence, his will and power shown in creation will follow.

Abū Qurrah believes that people can learn about God's attributes by observing Adam's virtues. While Adam's defects cannot teach about God, his virtues can do so by affirming the gap between human nature and divine nature. Whatever virtues Adam possesses (bounty, goodness, wisdom, etc.), God possesses in a greater, multiple, and more transcendental manner. Through the virtues of Adam, people can imagine God being maximally good and greater than all human beings. Yaḥya believes that God's essence is hidden, but his effect on creation is evident from his activity. The three essential attributes of God are his bounty, his power, and his wisdom. The three attributes are extrapolated from his creation and show his goodness. His omnipotence and his bounty are manifested in his power to create what exists and of his choice not to create what does not exist. Similarly, his wisdom is manifested in the order and the perfection of his work. Whether the omnibenevolence of God is extracted from the Scripture or from creation, it is related to the essence of God. If God is maximally good, then his nature (whether triune or oneness) should reflect his goodness.

The omnipotence of God is another attribute that is shared between Christianity and Islam. Abū Qurrah emphasizes the omnipotence of God by focusing on the Trinity. He states that begetting surpasses the inability to beget. Any denial of the Father being able to beget undermines the omnipotence of God. Yaḥya, on the other hand, does not link his formula of *al-ᶜaql, al- ᶜāqil, al-maᶜaqūl* to God's omnipotence because he talks about God's power separately. However, being the only being who can apply this formula shows his great power. Yaḥya's formulation moves beyond the roles of the *Aqanīm* to the reason behind the existence of each *Uqnūm*. The existence of the intellect cognizing itself necessitates the existence of *al- ᶜāqil* (the intellectually cognizing subject) and *al-maᶜaqūl* (the intellectually cognized object). The existence of the Father necessitates the existence of the Son and the Spirit. No other being can accomplish this formula because all other beings need external beings to serve as the subject and the object. The Trinity is the only model that shows God not needing otherness outside his being in order to be able to conceive. As the intellect cognizes itself and becomes the cause of the meaning of the intellectually cognizing subject and the intellectually cognized object, the Father is the cause of begetting the Son and the procession of the Spirit. He does not need any other being to be able to achieve this formula.

The last attribute that is related to the doctrine of the Trinity is the immutability of God. This attribute means that God does not change in his character or nature, unlike his creation. Unlike God, a human father was not a father before having his son. In fact, he became a father when he had a son. The heavenly Father has always been a Father because there was no time when the Father was not a Father and the Son did not exist. The relationship between the Father and the Son is mutual, simultaneous, and has no beginning or end; therefore, it is unchanging. Furthermore, John brings to the attention of his readers that the Son of God is God's word. God is not wordless, and he has never been without his word at any point in history. Thus, it is correct to think of God being the communicator. His word was always with him and in him; and later on, it was revealed to humanity. What makes his word different from our language, is that our words are perishable and changeable, whereas he is unchanging and eternal. The Trinity works as a great model to potentially present the unchanging nature of God. If God's nature is subject to change, then God can improve and develop. At one point, he cannot do something and at another point, he can do it. The changing nature of God connotes progressive development within the divine essence; therefore, it is rejected totally in Christianity.

4

Western Contemporary Explanations of the Trinity

THE PREVIOUS CHAPTER PRESENTED the Arabic explanation of the Trinity among three Arab scholars who lived in the eighth, ninth, and tenth centuries. This chapter will discuss contemporary explanations of the doctrine of the Trinity in the West by engaging with many influential contemporary Christian scholars. The chapter will examine two types of explanations: the philosophical and the theological. While the philosophical Trinity is presented by Richard Swinburne, William Lane Craig, Brian Leftow, and Peter van Inwagen, the theological Trinity is presented by Paul Molnar, Kevin Giles, Bruce Ware, and others. More consideration and space will be given to the philosophical Trinity because of its apologetics value and contribution to non-Christians who are trying to understand the Trinity and Christians who are trying to learn how to defend it. This chapter is not intended to be a comprehensive study of all Western trinitarian thought. The purpose is to inform the reader of the most important trinitarian models and advance the dialogue between the monotheistic religions. This chapter will also inform the reader of the differences between the Arabic and Western explanations of the Trinity.

A Summarized Historical Background

Throughout history, Western theologians advanced their theological and philosophical studies more than Arab theologians. Many reasons contributed to this fact, but the main reason remains obvious. No studies can be developed without freedom of expression and government support. Shortly after the invasion of Islam, Arab Christian theologians, unfortunately, lost the freedom to study, debate, and publish, whereas Western scholarship was progressing and flourishing.

Trinitarian theology was always important to Western Scholasticism, but it was not the only important topic that Western scholars discussed. Western Scholasticism developed and debated several topics and theological doctrines, such as different views on soteriology, eschatology, bibliology, and many more. Consequently, several types of theological discussions emerged after the patristic era. In the early history of the church, Christians had to fight against many heresies, such as Arianism, Sabellianism, Nestorianism, and others. In the fourth century, the Nicene Creed was created as a standard of faith for the purpose of defining what is orthodoxy and what is heterodoxy.

In medieval times, Scholasticism flourished in the Latin church. Great names, such as Thomas Aquinas, Peter Lombard, and John Duns Scotus (and many more theologians and scholars) never neglected the doctrine of the Trinity; on the contrary, it was at the heart of medieval theology. While the patristic period witnessed major debates on the nature of the person of Christ, medieval theology was drawn more toward soteriological questions.[1] Many scholars during the thirteenth and fourteenth centuries treated the subject of the Trinity as if it was related to questions of theological epistemology; therefore, they were cautious about what role reason might play in order to help human beings learn about God and his nature.[2]

Despite the importance that the doctrine of the Trinity enjoyed in the patristic and medieval eras, some modern philosophers saw no practical benefit to it. Whether people understood it or not was not an important issue to them. Immanuel Kant, for instance, states,

> [The] doctrine of the Trinity, taken literally, has no practical relevance at all, even if we think we understand it; and it is even more clearly irrelevant if we realize that it transcends all our concepts. Whether we are to worship three

[1]Rik Van Nieuwenhove, *An Introduction to Medieval Theology* (Cambridge: Cambridge University Press, 2012), 2.

[2]John T. Slotemaker, *Trinitarian Theology in Medieval and Reformation Thought* (Switzerland: Palgrave Macmillan, 2020), 25.

> or ten persons in the Divinity makes no difference: the pupil will implicitly accept one as readily as the other because he has no concept at all of a number of persons in one God (hypostases), and still more so because this distinction can make no difference in his rules of conduct. On the other hand, if we read a moral meaning into this article of faith (as I have tried to do in Religion within the Limits etc.), it would no longer contain an inconsequential belief but an intelligible one that refers to our moral vocation.[3]

This thought is echoed by Friedrich Schleiermacher, who also did not see any practical and ethical benefit of this doctrine to the practical life of human beings. He states, "This doctrine itself, as ecclesiastically framed, is not an immediate utterance concerning the Christian self-consciousness, but only a combination of several such utterances."[4] Kant and Schleiermacher were interested not in the doctrine of God per se, but in the moral argument for God's existence. It is sad to read their claims about the Trinity because it is not true that this doctrine has no benefits to the moral argument. On the contrary, the doctrine of the Trinity is the foundation of objective moral truth. Theism entails a loving perfect God who makes commands; therefore, He is the standard for human moral obligations. When Christians neglect the doctrine of the Trinity, they will neglect to learn about God and his nature. Consequently, this will affect their moral conduct. Unlike Arab theologians and philosophers—who dealt constantly with Muslims and had to develop convincing answers to defend the legitimacy of this doctrine—some Western scholars, unfortunately, saw no benefits of the doctrine of the Trinity.

Between patristic theology and medieval theology, two types of trinitarian models emerged in the West: the philosophical Trinity and the theological Trinity. These are not two trinities, but scholars developed different models based on their educational background (philosophical or theological), the opponents' opinions during their times, and the need to answer those objections. The view that starts with natural theology will be called the philosophical Trinity. The view that starts with the nature of God,

---

[3]Immanuel Kant, *The Conflict of the Faculties (Der Streit der Fakultäten)*, trans. Mary J. Gregor (Lincoln: University of Nebraska Press, 1979), 65-67.

[4]Friedrich Schleiermacher, *The Christian Faith*, trans. H. R. Mackintosh and J. S. Stewart (Edinburgh: T&T Clark, 1989), 738.

the Nicene definition, and the subordination of the Son will be called the theological Trinity.

Philosophical Trinity

In the West, two types of philosophical Trinity were developed, the social Trinity and the Latin Trinity. The social Trinity can be traced back to the Cappadocian Fathers: Basil the Great, Gregory of Nyssa, and Gregory of Nazianzus. They were the first ones to formulate the distinctions between Father, Son, and Spirit, as defined by Christian orthodoxy. Their purpose was to preserve the distinctiveness and the coexistence of the three persons in the Godhead without jeopardizing the unity of the divine Being.

Gregory of Nazianzus offers a way of distinguishing the three Persons of the Trinity while maintaining their oneness. He states, "The very fact of being Unbegotten or Begotten, or Proceeding has given the name of Father to the First, of the Son to the Second, and [to] the Third . . . of the Holy Ghost, that the distinction of the Three Persons may be preserved in the one nature and dignity of the Godhead. . . . The Three are One in Godhead, and the One three in properties."[5] In a similar fashion, Gregory of Nyssa holds that the divine essence is common to the three persons.[6] He goes a step further with the human analogy, which he applies in a strict fashion when he compares the inner life of the Trinity with three human persons sharing the one, indivisible human nature. He states, "Their nature is one, at union in itself, and an absolutely indivisible unit, not capable of increase by addition or of diminution by subtraction, but in its essence being and continually remaining one, inseparable even though it appears plurality, continuous, complete, and not divided with the individuals who participate in it."[7] After three centuries, the Nicene and post-Nicene fathers have come up with creedal confessions to preserve orthodoxy.

Some Western theologians did not find the Cappadocian fathers' methodologies compatible with orthodoxy. They preferred to follow Augustine, who rejects the view that there is any sort of substrate in God,

[5]St. Gregory Nazianzen, *The Sacred Writings of Gregory Nazianzen*, trans. Charles Gordon Browne (Altenmunster, Germany: Jazzybee Verlag, 2017), 121.

[6]Richard Cross, "Two Models of the Trinity?," *The Heythrop Journal* 43 (2002): 280.

[7]St. Gregory Nyssen, *The Sacred Writings of Gregory of Nyssa*, trans. Henry Austin Wilson (Altenmunster: Jazzybee Verlag, 2017), 232.

claiming the equality of the Father and the Son's substance and function. To Augustine, God is just his nature, and the essence is somehow shared by the persons, and the essence of the Son is identical with the essence of the Father.[8] The distinction that Augustine makes is in relation to "what relates to the form of God, in which He is equal to the Father, and what to the form of a servant which He took, in which He is less than the Father . . . for both the Son and the Holy Spirit, according to the form of God, are equal to the Father, because neither of them is a creature."[9] The distinction that is made between Father-Son is necessary to say that the Son is the one who was sent and the Father is the one who sent Jesus, "According to the form of God, He and the Father are one; according to the form of a servant, He came not to do His own will, but the will of Him that sent Him."[10]

Social trinitarianism in recent times. Ever since the formulation of the Nicene Creed, philosophers and analytic theologians have never stopped developing or reflecting on the mystery of the Trinity. Within the last few decades, responses to the logical problem of the Trinity have emerged in three main ways: The first one is known as social trinitarianism, which starts with explaining the three persons of the Trinity, then moves to the one-being theology (threeness to oneness). As McCall and Rea state, "The divine persons are numerically distinct, and that the unity of the Trinity can be understood by way of a 'social analogy': the divine persons are relevantly like a family, a supremely unified community of monarchs, or three human persons whose interpersonal relationships are so strong as to be unbreakable."[11] This school purports to present the teachings of the Cappadocian fathers of the fourth century and emphasizes its starting point in the works of the economic Trinity—the economy of salvation.[12] Its primary aim is to secure an adequate distinction between the three persons within

[8]Augustine, *On the Trinity* 7.2.3. www.newadvent.org/fathers/130107.htm. Augustine, *On the Trinity* 6.10.12. www.newadvent.org/fathers/130106.htm.

[9]Augustine of Hippo, "On the Trinity," in *St. Augustin: On the Holy Trinity, Doctrinal Treatises, Moral Treatises*, ed. Philip Schaff, trans. Arthur West Haddan (Buffalo, NY: Christian Literature Company, 1887), 3:29-30.

[10]Augustine, *On the Trinity* 1.11.22.

[11]Thomas H. McCall and Michael C. Rea, "Introduction," in *Philosophical and Theological Essays on the Trinity* (Oxford: Oxford University Press, 2009), 5.

[12]Michal Valčo et al., "Ecumenical Trinitarian Reflections and the 'De Régnon Paradigm': A Probe into Recovering the Social-Trinitarian Emphases of the Cappadocian Fathers," *Constantine's Letters / Konštantínove Listy* 12, no. 1 (2019): 79.

the Godhead. This chapter will use Richard Swinburne and William Lane Craig as examples of the social Trinity.

Latin trinitarianism in recent times. The second school is called the Latin Trinity, which goes back to the psychological trinitarian triads of Augustine of Hippo (such as intellect, memory, and will). Augustine was not comfortable with the concept of persons within the Godhead; therefore, he emphasized God's unity over his diversity. This school starts with the one indivisible essence of God's being subsisting in three persons. Latin trinitarians focus on one divine being or substance, and they tend to think of God as oneself, one "I"—(one-person perspective of God)—as relates to others. They also believe that God constitutes three persons. After starting with one being, they move from this oneness to explain the three persons of the Trinity.

Western scholars such as Michal Valčo rejected the Cappadocian fathers' attempt because they tend to lose the distinction and coexistence of the three persons in the Godhead in the attempt to preserve the unity of the divine being, "either by speaking of chronologically distinct manifestations of God's beings in three consecutive modes as the Father, Son, and Spirit; or to relegate the Son to an 'adopted' son of God (ontologically different from the Father) and the Spirit to an impersonal force."[13] Latin trinitarianism, therefore, emerged in the West, focusing on the single center of God's power and will. Latin trinitarians need not believe that each person has his own intellectual power in order to use mental tokens that include terms such as *I* and *me*.

Latin trinitarians tend to believe that the numerical unity of God is secure, and the persons are distinct but not discrete.[14] The divine persons do not share a common divine part among them, but each of them is God, whole and entire.[15] The Latin trinitarians rarely express the relations among the three persons of the Godhead. Rather, they assert that some relation of numerical sameness holds between each of the persons and the Godhead. As Allan Coppedge states, "In the West an examination of the existence and the being of the one God is foundational. The discussion of the triuneness

[13]Valčo, "Ecumenical Trinitarian Reflections," 77.

[14]Brian Leftow, "Anti Social Trinitarianism," *Faith and Philosophy: Journal of the Society of Christian Philosophers* 21, no. 3 (2004): 53.

[15]Patrick Miron, *Catholic & Christian: A Book of Essential Catholic Catechesis* (UK: Trafford Publishing, 2016), 253.

of God is secondary."[16] For the purposes of this discussion, it would be helpful to take Brian Leftow's model as an example of the Latin Trinity.

Relative identity trinitarianism. In recent times, since approximately the 1980s, a third school has emerged, known as relative identity trinitarianism. It has its roots in a recent analysis of the relative identity theory. This approach is an attempt to reformulate the concept of numerical sameness without limiting it by absolute identity relations. Leibniz's principle of the indiscernibility of identical states explains that if *a* is numerically identical with *b*, then *a* and *b* are indiscernible because every property of *a* is a property of *b* and vice versa.[17] In other words, if *a* and *b* have exactly the same properties, including spatiotemporal properties, then they must be numerically identical. But the theory of relative identity tries to show that there are other properties that are not identical between *a* and *b*, and they try to apply this principle to the doctrine of the Trinity.

Using philosophical language, the logical problem of the Trinity (LPT) can be summarized as follows: "If there are x and y such that x is a God, x is not identical to y, and y is consubstantial with x, then it is not the case that there is exactly one God."[18] According to McCall and Rea, what sometimes goes unnoticed is that (LPT) is true only if (P) "x and y are not identical, then x and y are not numerically the same substance is true."[19] If (P) is false, "then it is possible that x and y are numerically the same but not identical. Thus, it is possible that the divine persons are genuinely distinct but yet, by virtue of their consubstantiality, one and the same God."[20]

According to some philosophers, the (LPT) can be solved and the Trinity can be understood with the help of relative identity theory. According to this theory, "it is possible for objects x and y to be the same F but not the same G—where F and G are sortals, and x and y are Gs as well as Fs."[21] In other words, sameness implies identity and identity is sortal-relative. Sortal means terms or quantifiable nouns, such as dog, table, man, and so on. So

---

[16]Allan Coppedge, *The God Who Is Triune: Revisioning the Christian Doctrine of God* (Downers Grove, IL: IVP Academic, 2007), 108.

[17]*Bloomsbury Guide to Human Thought*, s.v. "Identity."

[18]McCall and Rea, "Introduction," 9.

[19]McCall and Rea, "Introduction," 9.

[20]McCall and Rea, "Introduction," 10.

[21]H. E. Baber, "The Trinity: Relative Identity Redux," *Faith and Philosophy: Journal of the Society of Christian Philosophers* 32, no. 2 (2015): 161.

the philosophical concept of the sortal-relative of identity theory says, "Identity statements might be true relative to one sortal but false relative to another."[22] Relative identity theory denies classical identity, which says that every relative identity predicate dominates classical identity: that is to say, "for all sortals F, if x is the same F as y, then x = y." According to relative identity theory, some R1 predicates do not dominate classical identity.

To better illustrate this concept, I will borrow an example from Harriet Baber about air travel, which best explains the relative identity theory. However, I will tweak this example to fit my agenda. I will use two terms: *passenger* and *person*. Supposedly, a traveler with dual citizenship is making two trips while using two passports with two names spelled differently. The first trip is between Germany and the United States. The traveler is going from the Dallas airport directly to Frankfurt, Germany (trip 1). The second trip takes place within the European continent. The traveler is going from Frankfurt to Athens, Greece (trip 2). The question under investigation is this: can the airline know that this passenger is the same person? From the airline's point of view, they have two different passengers. It is very hard for the airline to know that the trips are done by the same person because he is using two different passports with two different names. But from the person's point of view, he is the same person with dual citizenship. In this case, we have two passengers but one person who is taking two trips.

The Christian doctrine of the Trinity is committed to the idea that there is one God and three Persons—Father, Son, and Holy Spirit who are all God but are not identical. The Father is God, the Son is God, and the Spirit is God, but the Father is not the Son or the Spirit. The Father is the same nature as the Son, but the Father is not the same Person as the Son. To solve the puzzle, philosophers who follow the relative identity theory suggest that being is not identical to person—hence Father, Son, and Holy Spirit are the same being but not the same person. A later section of the chapter will explore Peter van Inwagen's model of relative identity and the Trinity.

Richard Swinburne

The British scholar Richard Swinburne served as a visiting professor and lecturer in many British, American, and international universities, such as

[22]McCall and Rea, "Introduction," 10.

the University of Hull and the University of Keele.[23] His expertise lies in the connection between science and philosophical theories. Swinburne seeks to demonstrate how scientific theories show how the universe operates in an orderly manner and metaphysical theories show the meaningfulness and justification of Christian theology. He has published several books on different philosophical topics, such as *Space and Time* (1968), *The Concept of Miracles* (1971), *The Coherence of Theism* (1997) (which he revised in 2016), *The Existence of God* (1979), *Faith and Reason* (1981), and many more.

A priori argument. Swinburne follows the Nicene Creed by stating that "God's nature is three persons in one substance."[24] To explain this concept, Swinburne investigates this question: can there be two divine individuals? Then he explores the possibility of the Godhead having more than three divine individuals. He builds his argument on the basic assumption that "being divine should be understood as entailing and being entailed by being necessarily perfectly free, omniscient, omnipotent, and existing of metaphysical necessity."[25] However, could there be two or more individuals who are necessarily perfectly free, omniscient, and omnipotent? Swinburne explains that an omniscient and perfectly free individual will always be perfectly good. Such an individual might act according to his perfect goodness (act of essence) or according to his will (act of will). As Swinburne states, "A divine individual's compatibilist power is his omnipotence, the power to do anything logically possible, if he so chooses; his absolute power is the power to choose and do, and that is limited not merely by logical possibility but by perfect goodness."[26] Each individual will be bringing about many goods, both within himself and in relation to the other individual.

If this analysis is true, could there be two omnipotent individuals bringing frustration to each other? Swinburne suggests that since each would recognize the other as having divine properties, it is plausible that each would

---

[23]Richard Swinburne, "Richard Swinburne—Short Intellectual Autobiography," *Faculty of Philosophy: University of Oxford.* Accessed June 24, 2023. https://users.ox.ac.uk/~orie0087/.

[24]Richard Swinburne, *The Christian God* (New York: Oxford University Press, 1994), 170.

[25]Richard Swinburne, "The Trinity," in *Philosophical and Theological Essays on the Trinity,* eds. Thomas H. McCall and Michael C. Rea (Oxford: Oxford University Press, 2009).

[26]Swinburne, "The Trinity," 171.

now prevent or frustrate the acts of the other. For instance, if the first individual decides to create something, he is sure that the second individual will not object, and it would be good for the second individual to give it his backing.[27]

Swinburne imagines that the only possible conflict that might arise between the two individuals is when one decides to create something according to his own goodness that is in some way incompatible with an act the second individual is simultaneously trying to accomplish. However, within the essence of the Christian God and the relationship between the Father and the Son, this is not an option. Swinburne states,

> Such unity of action could be secured if the first individual solemnly vows to the second individual in causing his existence that he will not initiate any act (of will) in a certain sphere of activity that he allocates to him, while at the same time the first individual requests the second individual not to initiate any such act outside that sphere.[28]

Since the two divine individuals are perfectly good, then the vow among them necessitates that no one initiates any act of will within the other individual's allocated sphere of activity. The vow necessitates that they act according to their perfect goodness, which does not frustrate or even disagree with the other divine individual. In this case, their omnipotence is limited by their perfectly good nature.

Swinburne concludes that there can be more than one divine individual if it is necessary for the first one to bring about the existence of the second, but this can be only when the first divine individual has an overriding reason to bring about the existence of a second individual as an act of essence.[29] In the same sense, there can be a third divine individual if the first and the second divine individuals have an overriding reason to bring about the third individual with the divine understanding not to initiate acts of will in a certain sphere and to confine his acts of will to the first and second divine individuals. This means the Father is the first divine individual. He actively causes the second and the third divine individuals to cooperate and relate to each other in love. Jesus, the second divine individual, causes the third

---

[27]Swinburne, "The Trinity," 172.
[28]Swinburne, "The Trinity," 174.
[29]Swinburne, "The Trinity," 175.

divine individual. The third divine individual is the active cause of the existence of no other individuals.[30]

The overriding reason for the first divine individual to bring about the second or the third is the nature of God himself. God is love. Swinburne believes that "Love involves sharing, giving to the other what of one's own is good for him and receiving from the other what of his is good for one; and love involves cooperating with another to benefit third parties."[31] Love must share and cooperate in sharing, otherwise, it is not the best love. If there is only one divine individual, then there will be none other with whom to share. "So the love of a first divine individual G1 would be manifested first in bringing about another divine individual G2 with whom to share his life, and the love of G1 or G2 would be manifested in bringing about another divine individual G3 with whom G1 and G2 cooperatively could share their lives."[32] For love to be perfect, G2 and G3 would then cooperate in allowing G1 to continue in being.

Swinburne knows that his explanation might be limited by his human ability. So he does not neglect to suggest that the limitation he ascribes to the individual being is a matter of human limitation. He states, "I have presented a highly fallible human judgment as to what the best such mechanism (and so the one which would be adopted) would be . . . The 'limit' is a limit on the application of a human word to God; it is not to be understood as a constraint within a divine individual."[33] God cannot be limited because he is omnipotent. But there is a good chance that Swinburne is limited in his explanation, and this is why he calls his argument fallible.

The traditional doctrine. Swinburne concludes, "If there is at least one divine individual, and if it is logically possible that there be more than one divine individual, then there are three and only three divine individuals."[34] The Counsel of Nicaea confirmed the belief in one God and three persons but denied that there are three independent divine beings, any of which could exist without the other or act independently of each other. Swinburne agrees with the Nicene Creed that the three divine individuals should be

[30]Swinburne, "The Trinity," 177.
[31]Swinburne, "The Trinity," 177.
[32]Swinburne, "The Trinity," 177.
[33]Swinburne, "The Trinity," 174.
[34]Swinburne, "The Trinity," 179.

taken together as a collective source of being of all other things. The members of the Godhead are mutually dependent and necessarily jointly behind each other's acts. The collective source is indivisible in its action because each member would back the causal action of the others. The collective source is causeless, and the members are not dependent for existence on anything outside the Godhead.[35] The members of the collective have the divine properties of omnipotence, omniscience, and so forth. If all the members of the group know something, then the group itself is knowledgeable and aware of that thing. So the one God is to be read as the source of being of all other things; a collective source of being that has in it an indivisible unity.

Examining the claim that each of the individuals is God. Swinburne believes that there are differences among the divine individuals, both in respect to which depends on which and in respect of function. The divine names help us distinguish between them. "Father seems a name appropriate to the original source."[36] The Son is the only member who is incarnated, and the Spirit takes a primary role in sanctification. The Son is called by this name because the Father is the one who begets, and the Son is the one who was begotten. The Spirit does not beget nor is begotten, but he proceeds from the Father and the Son. Swinburne interprets the creed saying,

> The Council may be saying this: the Godhead is not just three individuals, each with its thisness, who have common essential properties. Rather, it is exactly the instantiation of the same essence of divinity which makes the Father God, as makes the Son God, as makes the Spirit God. They would be the same individual but for the relational properties which are distinct from the divine essence and which distinguish them.[37]

Swinburne admits that this part of his argument is not in the area of reason and does not go beyond any ecclesiastical tradition.

William Lane Craig

William Lane Craig is named by the Best Schools as one of the fifty most influential living philosophers. He is notable for his work on the kalām

[35]Swinburne, "The Trinity," 181.
[36]Swinburne, "The Trinity," 182.
[37]Swinburne, "The Trinity," 189.

argument and the existence of God, philosophy of time, and the historical Jesus. He has authored and edited over thirty books, including *Assessing the New Testament Evidence for the Historicity of the Resurrection of Jesus* (1989), *Divine Foreknowledge and Human Freedom* (1990), *Theism, Atheism and Big Bang Cosmology* (1995), *The Kalām Cosmological Argument* (2000), *Time and Eternity: Exploring God's Relationship to Time* (2001), and *What Does God Know? Reconciling Divine Foreknowledge and Human Freedom* (2023). Craig has also published over a hundred academic articles in different philosophical journals.[38]

Craig is a strong advocate of social trinitarianism. He provides a model that captures the central commitment of this view. Usually, social trinitarians believe that "in God, there are three distinct centers of self-consciousness, each with its proper intellect and will."[39] In contrast, the central commitment of anti-social trinitarianism is that "there is only one God, whose unicity of intellect and will is not compromised by the diversity of persons."[40] Craig's trinitarian model supports social trinitarianism because it focuses on the persons of the Trinity rather than the unity within the Godhead. It is worth mentioning that Craig believes there is no reason to think there is a perfect analogy to the Trinity among created things or among ideas related to creation. The analogies might be helpful as a springboard for philosophical reaction and formulation, but they are not to be taken literally and in exact similarity to the divine concept.

To expound on the Trinity, Craig borrows a mythical creature from Greco-Roman mythology who guarded the gates of Hades, the three-headed dog named Cerberus. Craig supposes that Cerberus has three brains, three distinct states of consciousness, and three wills. While Cerberus is a sentient being, he does not have a unified consciousness. The three heads are three centers of consciousness, and they are even named Rover, Bowser, and Spike. Since they are discrete, they might come into conflict with one another. One wants to move in one direction, but the other wants to move in

[38]William Lane Craig, "Biographical Sketch," *Reasonable Faith* (website). Accessed June 28, 2023. www.reasonablefaith.org/william-lane-craig.

[39]William Lane Craig, "Toward a Tenable Social Trinitarianism," in *Philosophical and Theological Essays on the Trinity*, eds. Thomas McCall and Michael Rea (Oxford: Oxford University Press, 2009), 89.

[40]Craig, "Tenable Social Trinitarianism."

a different one. One wants to sit while the other wants to stand or sleep; however, for Cerberus to make a move or to stand, the three have to agree on the decision. The three must cooperate in order to function. If Rover wants to sleep and Bowser and Spike to walk, then Cerberus will not be able to move or guard the gate as he was designed to. As Craig puts it, there must be a considerable degree of cooperation among Rover, Bowser, and Spike for them to work properly.

Despite the diversity of his mental states, Cerberus clearly is one dog. As Craig explains, "He is a single biological organism exemplifying a canine nature. Rover, Bowser, and Spike may be said to be canine, too, though they are not three dogs, but parts of the one dog Cerberus. If Hercules were attempting to enter Hades, and Spike snarled at him or bit his leg, he might well report, 'Cerberus snarled at me' or 'Cerberus attacked me.'"[41] What makes Cerberus one being is that he has a single body, and what makes him multiple is that he has triple heads.

The question of what makes several parts constitute a single object rather than distinct objects is a difficult one, but Craig wants to study the nature of the soul to get some insights. The souls of human beings and animals are immaterial substances. Craig explains that souls come in different variations of capacities and faculties. The human soul is the highest on the spectrum because what makes the human soul a person is that it is "equipped with rational faculties of intellect and volition which enable it to be a self-reactive agent capable of self-determination."[42]

Craig believes that God is a soul; he does not have a body. Normally, the human soul is equated with rational faculties, and it is considered an individual person because each soul is equipped with one set of rational faculties sufficient for being a person.

> Suppose, then, that God is a soul which is endowed with three complete sets of rational cognitive faculties, each sufficient for personhood. Then God, though one soul, would not be one person but three, for God would have three centers of self-consciousness, intentionality, and volition, as Social Trinitarians maintain. God would clearly not be three discrete souls because the cognitive faculties in question are all faculties belonging to just one soul,

---

[41]Craig, "Tenable Social Trinitarianism."

[42]Craig, "Tenable Social Trinitarianism," 99.

> one immaterial substance. If this is true, then God would be one being which supports three persons, just as our individual beings each support one person.[43]

Craig's way of explaining the formula of the three persons in one substance is related to the soul of that being (animal, human being, or divine being) and how well-developed this being is on the spectrum of creation. This is to say, the soul might have several faculties that are related to the being, and there is no reason that might prevent us from thinking that the divine soul is not so richly endowed, as they possess three sets of cognitive faculties sufficient for personhood. If the being is an animal, then his soul is primitive on the spectrum of abilities and faculties. Human beings have more advanced souls that allow them to become rational persons, and God's soul is at the top of the spectrum. It possesses three sets of cognitive faculties sufficient for personhood.[44]

Brian Leftow

Leftow is an American philosopher who specializes in the philosophy of religion, medieval philosophy, and metaphysics. He has many academic honors, such as the Brackenridge Distinguished Resident in Philosophy from the University of Texas/San Antonio and Distinguished Scholar Fellowship from the Center for Philosophy of Religion, University of Notre Dame. Leftow has authored and edited many books, three of which are published by Oxford University Press: *Anselm's God, Anselm's Proofs,* and *God and Necessity*. He wrote *Aquinas: Questions on God*, and *The Cambridge Companion to Anselm,* both of which are published by Cambridge University Press. He also has published and reviewed more than hundreds of academic articles, including "Time-Travel and the Trinity," "On Hasker on Leftow on Hasker on Leftow," and "A Latin Trinity," which were published in the *Faith and Philosophy Journal*.[45]

---

[43]Craig, "Tenable Social Trinitarianism," 99.

[44]William Lane Craig, "Another Glance at Trinity Monotheism," in *Philosophical and Theological Essays on the Trinity*, eds. Thomas McCall and Michael Rea (Oxford: Oxford University Press, 2009), 126.

[45]Brian Leftow "Curriculum Vitae," *Rutgers School of Arts and Sciences*. Accessed July 1, 2023. https://philosophy.rutgers.edu/people/regular-faculty/regular-faculty-profile/182-regular-faculty-full-time/954-leftow-brian.

Unlike Swinburne and Craig, Leftow follows the Latin Trinity model of the doctrine of the Trinity. He prefers this model because it has fewer difficulties explaining the Trinity, especially since the three persons are not discrete. In a nutshell, Latin Trinity can be defined in the following way: "There is just one divine being (or substance), God. God constitutes three Persons. But all three are at bottom just God. They contain no constituent distinct from God. The Persons are somehow God three times over."[46] Within this view, God is one divine substance, not three centers of consciousness as in the social Trinity. Monotheism is preserved because the life of God is composed of "three event-based persons who exist simultaneously."[47] The doctrine of the Trinity is likewise preserved because the three-persons view is similarly retained.

To explain his model of the Trinity, Leftow makes sure he stays within the limits of orthodoxy. Therefore, he lays his arguments on two foundations. (1) The Athanasian Creed, which acknowledges the three persons of the Trinity and their divinity. It states, "We are compelled by the Christian verity to acknowledge every Person by Himself to be both God and Lord."[48] (2) The Latin Trinity model of Thomas Aquinas, which concentrates on the divine nature, not the three persons of the Trinity. Aquinas states, "Among creatures, the nature the one generated receives is not numerically identical with the nature the one generating has. . . . But God begotten receives numerically the same nature God begetting has."[49] These two concepts will be the foundation of Leftow's model of the Trinity.

Leftow introduces a new term, *trope*, to explain the doctrine of the Trinity. This word means "an individualized case of an attribute."[50] To explain this concept, Leftow gives the example of Abel and Cain. Even though they were both human, they were different. Cain's humanity was not identical to Abel's because each had distinct tropes of human nature. The same concept pertains to the Trinity: "while Father and Son instance the divine nature (deity),

[46]Brian Leftow, "Anti Social Trinitarianism," in *Philosophical and Theological Essays on the Trinity*, eds. Thomas McCall and Michael Rea (Oxford: Oxford University Press, 2009), 52.

[47]Leftow, "Anti Social Trinitarianism."

[48]James Sullivan, "The Athanasian Creed," in *The Catholic Encyclopedia: New Advent*. Accessed July 4, 2023. www.newadvent.org/cathen/02033b.htm.

[49]S. Thomae de Aquino, *Summa Theologiae* (Ottawa: Studii Generalis, 1941), 39, 5 *ad* 2, 245a. Edmund Hill, *The Mystery of the Trinity* (London: Geoffrey Chapman, 1985), 103.

[50]Leftow, "Anti Social Trinitarianism," 53.

they have but one trope of deity between them, which is God's. While Abel's humanity ≠ Cain's humanity, the Father's deity = the Son's deity = God's deity. But bearers individuate tropes. If the Father's deity is God's, this is because the Father just is God: which last is what Aquinas wants to say."[51] By this same reasoning, Aquinas did not believe that the Father alone is God, but the Son and the Holy Spirit are God as well.

Time-travel model. Leftow invites his readers to imagine themselves watching a musical play in which Jane is dancing on the stage. Jane can time travel. She goes to the stage on the left side, performs her dance, and then time travels to the past and appears on the right side of the stage to perform another dance. Jane appears both on the left and right side of the stage simultaneously. She moves between the two points in a straight line. She appears to be in different places at the same point in our lives, but not at the same point in hers. From the audience's perspective, Jane appears in different places on the stage at the same time; but from Jane's perspective, she is not in many places at the same time; instead, she is in different events.

In this story, there is one *trope* of human nature, which is Jane's *trope*. Leftow admits that this might sound like an odd example, but he hopes readers will concentrate on the dance or many dances of one substance. Each dancer is Jane, but these are many events; and Jane is there many times over.[52] In this example, Jane has genuine personal interaction. "She leans on herself for support, smiles to herself, talks (and talks back) to herself. The talk may even be dialogue in the fullest sense. . . . The Wells-o-matic [the time travel machine] lets the one Jane be present at one time many times over, in many ways, as the leftmost Rockette, the rightmost, etc. It gives us one Jane in many *personae*."[53] Leftow believes the analogy makes sense in a metaphysically possible world containing backward time travel.

When we apply this example to the Trinity, we find both similarities and differences. In terms of similarities and the way this model applies to God, Leftow states,

---

[51]Leftow, "Anti Social Trinitarianism," 53.

[52]Brian Leftow, "A Latin Trinity," *Faith and Philosophy: Journal of the Society of Christian Philosophers* 21, no. 3 (2004): 307-8.

[53]Leftow, "Latin Trinity," 308.

> God's life has the following peculiar structure: at any point in our lives, three discrete parts of God's life are present. But this is not because one life's successive parts appear at once. Rather, it is because God always lives His life in three discrete strands at once, no event of His life occurring in more than one strand and no strand succeeding another. In one strand God lives the Father's life, in one the Son's, and in one the Spirit's. The events of each strand add up to the life of a Person. The lives of the Persons add up to the life God lives as the three Persons. There is one God, but He is many in the events of His life, as Jane was in the chorus line: being the Son is a bit like being the leftmost Rockette.[54]

However, along with these similarities, there are also differences between the doctrine of the Trinity and the time-travel model. While the life of God is represented in the successive appearances of Jane, with the divine, those appearances are not successive multiple lives. They are three discrete parts of God's singular life. God always lives his life in three discrete strands at once. One strand is the Father's life, the second strand is the Son's life, and the third strand is the Holy Spirit's life. These strands are not many (only three), and they do not appear after each other. God is one, but he is many in the events of his life.

Every event in God's life is part of the Father, the Son, and the Spirit. In the example, it appears as the chorus line. God does not live as Father, Son, and Holy Spirit. He is not the Father in one life and the Son or the Spirit in another. Jane has just one life, with consecutive episodes. The Father, Son, and Spirit are not consecutive episodes in the divine life. This example does not include the entire life of Jane; whereas, God's life consists of three other things which count as an entire, ongoing life. In other words, God's life runs in three streams. Jane is limited in her movements and time. She dances in one spot, runs to the machine, and then dances in another spot. Not so for God: God always lives in all three streams. "God's life always consists of three non-overlapping lives going on at once, none after the other, as the series of positive numbers consists of two non-overlapping series . . . 'going on at once' within the series, neither after the other."[55] As expected, the doctrine of the Trinity is hard to illustrate; therefore, many might find this example hard to understand.

---

[54]Leftow, "Latin Trinity," 312.

[55]Leftow, "Latin Trinity," 312.

Toward Latin Trinity. Leftow is against the social Trinity because, in his opinion, numbers matter, and the Latin Trinity secures the numerical unity of God. In the Old Testament, God said, "Hear, O Israel: The Lord our God, the Lord is one" (Deut 6:4). The unity of God should be understood in a numerical sense, and this cannot happen under the social Trinity. When it comes to divine actions, Leftow believes that "if the Persons are discrete, and only the Son died for our sins, then however much the Father and Spirit helped out, it seems that the Son did more for us than the other two, who neither bled nor suffered."[56] In the social Trinity, where the three persons are three discrete substances, it would be hard to explain the reason behind loving or being loyal to the Father as much as to the Son or the Spirit, especially since human beings did not see the Father working the human redemption, but only the Son who died for humanity's sins. The Latin Trinity does not face such a problem because "there is just one substance to whom we owe anything for our salvation, God. There can be a question of unequal loyalty or debt to two discrete divine substances. There cannot be a question of unequal loyalty or debt to one and the same substance."[57]

Leftow believes that there are four ways to consider how the three discrete persons might participate in one divine action if a person does not wish to assign the persons fields of sole agency. (1) One of the three persons makes the largest contribution of the act, and the other two persons support him or cooperate with the act. (2) All three persons contribute partially but equally to the action. (3) The three persons overdetermine the divine action by each of them contributing on his own to fully account for the divine effect. (4) It could be, as Leftow states,

> The three Persons together just are one agent, in the sense they make not three distinct contributions, however related, but just one contribution among them. So to say: the Father acts, the Son acts, and the Spirit acts, and yet there are not in any sense three acts, but one act. Any act-token which is the Father's is equally and fully the Son's and Spirit's, without overdetermination, partial contribution, etc.[58]

[56]Leftow, "Anti Social Trinitarianism," 79.
[57]Leftow, "Anti Social Trinitarianism," 79.
[58]Leftow, "Anti Social Trinitarianism," 79.

According to Leftow, the third and fourth options should be rejected because any equal or unequal partial action that each person performs will cause an equal or unequal part of the effect. If one of the persons rules one action, it seems to follow that that person is the ruler of the action and maybe the God of that action. Or it could mean that while no part of the effect is assignable to any one person alone, the three persons together participated in a single effect. This means no one individual has caused the action to succeed, and all together succeed to cause it.

Leftow is against the group-mind theory, in which the persons of the Trinity have fully submerged, composing a fully integrated mind, which accounts for mental acts. Within this theory, the mind of God (or the mind of the Trinity) is understood as a single human mind. Leftow believes that if every person of the Trinity makes a less-than-full contribution to any mental act, then no person accounts fully for the act; therefore, no person of the Trinity could be fully divine or fully perfect. In the Latin Trinity, the Son is not discrete from the other persons. Leftow explains, "For the Son to be in the forefront of an act is just for God to be more prominent in one role (or state, etc.) than he is in others. So thanking the Son is thanking the same individual God who is Father and Spirit. We cannot owe God more thanks than we owe God."[59] Leftow gives the example of parting the sea. It is not as if each person of the Trinity contributes one-third of the force needed to split the sea. God divides the sea by deciding that it shall be divided. The acts of God in the Latin Trinity model are just acts of God.

Peter van Inwagen

Peter van Inwagen is an American analytic philosopher and the leading figure in contemporary metaphysics, philosophy of religion, and philosophy of action.[60] While he works in a wide variety of areas of philosophy, his expertise lies in metaphysics, the philosophy of action, and the philosophy of religion. Van Inwagen published several books with academic publishers, such as *Being, Freedom, and Method: Themes from the Philosophy of Peter*

---

[59]Leftow, "Anti Social Trinitarianism," 79.

[60]Peter van Inwagen, "Biography," *University of Notre Dame*. Accessed July 14, 2023. https://philosophy.nd.edu/people/emeritus/peter-van-inwagen/.

van Inwagen from Oxford University Press; *God, Knowledge, and Mystery: Essays in Philosophical Theology* from Cornell University Press; and *Thinking About Free Will* from Cambridge University Press.

Van Inwagen admits that the Trinity is a mystery; however, he strives to provide a philosophical answer to refute the charges that Christians are either simple polytheists or that polytheism and monotheism are the same things. Van Inwagen is preoccupied with the divine love concept. He starts with this question: is salvation individual? He admits that maybe it is the case, but there is something more. The beatific vision of the saints enjoying their relationship with God is not just individual but corporate. He states, "The love we have for each other will be a restored image of the love that the Persons of the Trinity have for one another."[61] If salvation is restoring the image of God that has been distorted by sin, loving one another is part of that restored image. This idea of love motivates van Inwagen to come up with a sophisticated philosophical explanation of the doctrine of the Trinity. His main concern is the minimal Trinity—the belief that God being one in being and three in persons is logical.

After van Inwagen explains the relative identity theory, he turns the doctrine of the Trinity into philosophical equations to test its logical credibility. He starts by denying the classical identity theory (explained earlier in this chapter) and the expression "x is the same apple as y." He also denies the expression "z is a horse & z = w." This is the classical image of "z is the same horse as w." The two horses might have similar descriptions, but they are two different horses. Generally speaking, relative identity is different from relative identity logic+, which is relative identity with extra data. Relative identity logic+ includes extra information that makes sense in one way and no contradictions can be deduced from it if all the set of data were examined.

Van Inwagen relies on the concept of dominance in philosophy, which can be explained this way: "$I\alpha\beta \rightarrow$ (F . . . α . . . ↔ F . . . β . . .) where F . . . α . . . is a sentence in which β does not occur, and F . . . β . . . is like F . . . α . . . except for having free occurrences of β at some or all places at which F . . .

[61] Peter van Inwagen, "And Yet They are Not Three Gods but One God," in *Philosophical and Theological Essays on the Trinity*, eds. Thomas McCall and Michael Rea (Oxford: Oxford University Press, 2009), 218.

α . . . has free occurrences of a."[62] A relative identity predicate dominates predicate F if all sentences of the form "Iaβ → (F . . . a ← → F . . . β)" are true. If relative identity predicates dominate all relative identity predicates, then being the same H entails being the same F for all sortals F. However, some of the relative identity predicates are not dominant. Van Inwagen gives the example of two men, one of whom is called John Locke and the other Don Locke. Clearly, they have the same surname, but they are not the same person because surname fails to dominate a great variety of predicates, such as "'is alive in the twentieth century,' 'has never heard of Kant,' 'is the same man as,' and so on."[63] When this principle is applied to the Trinity, there are two undenied relative identity predicates—*being* and *person*. Is being the same as person? Van Inwagen does not assume that either of these predicates dominates the other, and neither of them is eliminable in favor of dominant relative identity predicates and ordinary predicates.[64]

Van Inwagen believes that "being" has causal powers. Being can be a person because "A being is a person (something that is the same being as something is also the same person as something) if it is self-aware and has beliefs and plans and acts on the basis of those beliefs to execute those plans. (As Boethius says, a person is an individual substance of a rational nature.)."[65] Absolute identity provides us with definitions of "x is the same being as x" and "x is the same person as x," but allows us to deny that "x is the same being as y" or "x is the same person as y." For instance, we can deny that "x has causal power." Van Inwagen explains that if there is such a relation as classical or absolute identity, and this relation was subdominant, then we should believe that all relative identity predicates entail the conditional x is the same being as y → x=y. Trinitarians must either deny classical-absolute identity theory, or—if it exists—recognize that it is not dominated by "is the same being as."[66]

Van Inwagen takes the route of examining each predicate of the Christian belief of the doctrine of the Trinity to prove that if all the predicates are logical, then being is not the same as person, and it is possible to have one

---

[62]van Inwagen, "Not Three Gods," 229.
[63]van Inwagen, "Not Three Gods," 231.
[64]van Inwagen, "Not Three Gods," 236.
[65]van Inwagen, "Not Three Gods," 238.
[66]van Inwagen, "Not Three Gods," 238.

being and three persons without logical contradiction. Van Inwagen tests the predicate "x is divine," explaining,

> x is necessarily existent; essentially almighty, all-knowing, and perfect in love and wisdom; essentially such that nothing contingent would exist unless x willed it . . . CT1 Ⱥx (x is divine →x is a being & x is a person).
>
> This is redundant to the consequent phrase, since any person is, necessarily, a being.
>
> CT2 Ⱥx (x is a person → x is a being).
>
> It follows from CT1 that something is a divine Person if and only if it is a divine Being:
>
> CT3 Ⱥx (x is a person & x is divine ↔ x is a being & x is divine).[67]

Van Inwagen assumes that "is the same being as" dominates "is divine." He also assumes that CT4 ȺxȺy (x is the same being as y → [x is divine ↔ y is divine]).[68] The most important consequence of CT4 is that if a being is divine, then any being who is the same being as that being is divine. Van Inwagen does not assume, however, that the same person dominates "divine" because the "'same person' is not dominated by such predicates as 'is a man' and 'was born in the world. It follows from CT1 and CT4 that if x is a divine Person and y is the same being as x, then y is a person. It does not follow that y is the *same* person as x."[69] If this is true, then something is a divine person if and only if it is a divine being (CT3), which consequently is consistent with there is one divine being and three divine persons.

The example that van Inwagen uses to illustrate his idea is related to three dogs who are each a purebred dachshund for sale at different prices. This information about the dogs is not relative identity predicates. It should be taken as absolute identity, "is the same breed as" and "is the same price as." All these sentences are examples of absolute identity, not relative identity. Therefore, they are not good examples to illustrate the Trinity regarding relative identity theory. As stated earlier, in metaphysics, absolute identity needs to be rejected to avoid asserting that there are three divine beings and three divine persons.

---

[67]van Inwagen, "Not Three Gods," 239.
[68]van Inwagen, "Not Three Gods," 239.
[69]van Inwagen, "Not Three Gods," 239.

Van Inwagen wants to show that because of relative identity theory, we cannot deduce formal inconsistency or contradiction from S in relative identity logic. S is considered the set of sentences containing various information about three dogs. There are three dogs: A, B, and C. Dog C prances from A to B and does no other prancing, and nothing besides C prances. Suppose that Dog A is barking at B and at nothing else, and nothing else barks besides Dog A. Given these assumptions and the earlier ones about prices and breeds, it is easy to verify by inspection that all the members of S are true on the proposed reinterpretation. Van Inwagen believes that we can apply the same set of S to the trinitarian belief, and no formal contradiction can be deduced in that logic from a set of trinitarian set of sentences that are true on some interpretation, such as: God is the same being as the Father, God is a person, God is the same person as the Father, God is the same person as the Son, the Son is not the same person as the Father, and God is begotten.

Theological Trinity

The immanent versus the economic view. The previous scholars can all be classified under the philosophical Trinity. These scholars use natural theology as their starting point (and many other methods) to understand the Trinity. However, theologians prefer to argue historically and biblically to explain the Trinity because they see the above models as speculative, historically untested, and deviating from Nicene trinitarianism. For instance, Paul Molnar, who based his model on Thomas Torrance and Karl Barth's theology, emphasizes the distinction between the immanent Trinity and the economic Trinity. There are not two Trinities here, but one. Understanding the difference between the immanent and the economic is related to God in himself, his relation to creation, and how we understand him through his revelation.

The immanent Trinity, which is also called the ontological Trinity, uses terms that explore the internal relationship among the three persons of the Trinity. The language gives attention to the inexpressible mystery of what God is like within himself apart from reference to his works with creation. Thus, "the immanent Trinity is God-as-God-is throughout eternity."[70] It

[70]Stanley Grenz, David Guretzki, and Cherith Fee Nordling, *Pocket Dictionary of Theological Terms* (Downers Grove, IL: InterVarsity Press, 1999).

denotes the personal properties of the three persons of the Trinity: The Father begets the Son, the Son is begotten, and the Holy Spirit proceeds.[71]

The economic Trinity, on the other hand, refers to "the manifestations of the three persons of the Trinity in relationship to the world, particularly in regard to the outworking of God's plan (economy) of salvation and redemption."[72] It is the Father who sent the Son for our redemption, the Son who acquires the redemption, and the Holy Spirit who applies the redemption to us. Thus, the economic Trinity denotes the activities of God and the role of the persons of the Trinity regarding creation, salvation, and redemption.

Some theologians, such as Karl Rahner, Jürgen Moltmann, and Eberhard Jüngel, believe that the immanent Trinity is the economic Trinity and vice versa. They see God's threefold presence in the history of salvation as identical to God's own inner triunity. Moltmann, for example, states, "In order to grasp the death of the Son in its significance for God himself, I found myself bound to surrender the traditional distinction between the immanent and the ontological Trinity."[73] For Moltmann, the event of the crucifixion is not only an event of the economic Trinity but also an event within the eternal Trinity.

Other theologians see the previous view as ambiguous and open to misunderstanding. Therefore they do not separate the immanent from the economic Trinity, but they make a distinction between them. Such theologians believe that we know the triune God through God's relationship with his creation; however, this does not mean God became triune in his relation with the world. God himself was and is a triune God even before creating the universe. Hence, God reveals himself as a triune God through his economy because he is a triune God. As Seung Goo Lee explains, "We can recognize that God is the triune God in the process of examining God's creation and redemption through Christ, especially, while examining the coming of Christ, his self-disclosure, the coming of the Holy Spirit to the New Testament church on Pentecost, the works of the Holy Spirit in the

---

[71]Some scholars believe that the Holy Spirit proceeds from the Father and the Son together, and others believe that the Holy Spirit proceeds from the Father through the Son.

[72]Grenz, Guretzki, and Nordling, *Pocket Dictionary*.

[73]Jürgen Moltmann, *The Trinity and the Kingdom: The Doctrine of God*, trans. Margaret Kohl (London: SCM Press, 1981), 160.

church, and the response of the church to the Holy Spirit (esp., Acts 5:1-16)."[74] In other words, the trinitarian nature of God precedes his revelation and our knowledge of him.

One of the reasons these theologians rejected Rahner and Moltmann's model is because it starts with human experience and moves up to understand God. As Paul Molnar explains:

> The immanent trinity and the economic trinity could not be identified or confused but distinguished and united in a way analogous to the Incarnate Logos. Since the relation between God and creatures was irreversible, it could neither be seen nor described by looking at history as such; any such attempt would project our experience into the inner life of God, and re-define the immanent trinity by reason and not revelation.[75]

In Molnar's opinion, theology cannot begin with human experience and redefine God's antecedent existence if the criterion is the human Jesus.

Molnar emphasizes the unity of the immanent and the economic Trinity to avoid stripping God of his freedom in creating human beings. God is God with or without creation; in contrast, Moltmann's panentheism starts from human experience and reconstructs theology in a way that does not allow God to be God without the love that communicates salvation. God constituted the salvation plan not because he had to (forced by his love), but because of who he is as immanent Trinity out of pure freedom. As Torrance states, "God is therefore no blind fate, no immanent force acting under the compulsion of some *prius* or unknown law within his being."[76] There is no determinism in God's being, but God was free to break the bondage of sin and start a personal relationship with human beings. This way of explaining the Trinity shifted the argument to issues related to the obedience, humiliation, and subordination experiences of the human Jesus to the divine Father and whether these actions were experienced by God the Son in his divine nature as well.[77]

---

[74]Seung Goo Lee, "The Relationship between the Ontological Trinity and the Economic Trinity," *Journal of Reformed Theology* 3 (2009): 90-107.

[75]Paul Molnar, "The Function of the Immanent Trinity in the Theology of Karl Barth: Implications for Today," *Scottish Journal of Theology* 42 (1989): 370.

[76]Thomas Torrance, "Predestination in Christ," *Evangelical Quarterly* 13 (1941): 116.

[77]Readers who are interested in studying this topic further can read George Hunsinger, Paul Molnar, and their reply to Bruce McCormack.

The gradational vs. the equivalence views. The eternal generation of the Son also led theologians to argue two different views about the Trinity, the gradational view and the equivalence view.[78] The proponents of the gradational view argue that there is an eternal hierarchy of authority among the three persons of the Trinity. The Father is the supreme member of the Trinity with the highest authority. The Son and the Spirit are subordinate and submit to this authority. This gradational relationship has been in eternity past, during the earthly ministry of Jesus, and in the present ministry of the Holy Spirit in the life of the church. It will also be the same in the eternity future. Despite the gradational authority, there is equality of the being or essence among the three persons of the Trinity.

Bruce Ware is one of the proponents of this view. He believes in "functional hierarchy." Quoting Philippians 2:9 he explains that "clearly, if the Father is the one who exalts the Son, and if the Father gives to the Son his all-surpassing name, then the Father has supremacy over the Son."[79] Any biblical reference to the Father's superiority to the Son is to be referred to this temporary functional and missional subordination. Regarding the relationship between the Father and the Son, "the Son in fact is the eternal Son of the eternal Father, and hence, the Son stands in a relationship of eternal submission under the authority of his Father."[80] He adds, "Surely, they are not distinct in essence, for each share fully the identically same divine nature. Their distinction, rather, is constituted, in part, by *taxis*—the ordering of Father, Son, and Holy Spirit within the Godhead."[81] Ware believes that there is an order in the Godhead and it is reflected in creation and human relationships. This order is a built-in structure of authority and submission.[82]

The equivalence view holds that the Father, Son, and Holy Spirit are eternally equal in authority. The subordination of the Son and the Holy Spirit is temporary and functional. "The temporary functional subordination of the Son and the Holy Spirit to the Father has been established for the purpose

[78] I am following Millard Erickson's titles and definitions of these views that he mentions in his book *Who's Tampering with the Trinity? An Assessment of the Subordination Debate* (Grand Rapids, MI: Kregel Academic & Professional, 2009).

[79] Bruce A. Ware, *Father, Son, and Holy Spirit: Relationships, Roles, and Relevance* (Wheaton, IL: Crossway, 2005), 37.

[80] Ware, *Father, Son, and Holy Spirit*, 51.

[81] Ware, *Father, Son, and Holy Spirit*, 51.

[82] Ware, *Father, Son, and Holy Spirit*, 51.

of carrying out a particular mission. But when that mission is completed, the three Persons' full equality of authority will resume."[83] In other words, the submission of the Son is not eternal, but temporal for a particular purpose and a particular time. Once that purpose is accomplished everything goes back to its original status.

Stanley Grenz, with coauthor Denise Kjesbo, gave the major exposition of his view of the relationship between the three persons of the Trinity in a book on the role of women in the church. In this book, he explains the mutual dependence of the Son and the Father upon one another, stating,

> Finally, the argument from Christ's example often overlooks the deeper dynamic of mutual dependence within the Trinity. Jesus willingly submitted himself to the One he called "Abba." Thereby he reveals that the Son is subordinate to the Father within the eternal Trinity. At the same time the Father is dependent on the Son for his deity. In sending his Son into the world, the Father entrusted his own reign—indeed his own deity—to the Son (for example, LK 10:22). Likewise, the Father is dependent on the Son for his title as the Father. As Irenaeus pointed out in the second century, without the Son the Father is not the Father of the Son. Hence the subordination of the Son to the Father must be balanced by the subordination of the Father to the Son.[84]

Because of the equivalence view, Grenz believes in mutual dependence between the Father and the Son and he puts the traditional view in a linear way between the persons of the Trinity. There is no authority of the Father over the Son because the Father also is dependent on the Son.

Kevin Giles is a proponent of the equivalence view as well. He believes that the Son and the Holy Spirit have a functional submission to the Father for a certain period of time, or until the purpose of God is accomplished. Millard Erickson captures Giles's position well, explaining that the three persons of the Trinity are

> equal in their eternal authority. For a period of time and for a specific purpose within the redemptive economy of God, the Son and then the Spirit

[83]Kevin N. Giles, *Jesus and the Father: Modern Evangelicals Reinvent the Doctrine of the Trinity* (Grand Rapids, MI: HarperCollins, 2006), 18.

[84]Stanley Grenz and Denise Muir Kjesbo, *Women in the Church: A Biblical Theology of Women in Ministry* (Downers Grove, IL: InterVarsity Press, 1995), 114.

> voluntarily assumed a position of functional subordination to the Father, and in the case of the Spirit, to the Son as well. At the completion of these respective redemptive tasks, however, the equal authority possessed in eternity past is reassumed and will continue to be possessed and exercised through all eternity future.[85]

The proponents of this view believe in the equal and eternal authority of the three persons of the Trinity. They believe that on the gradation view, where the Son is necessarily subordinate to the Father (which means he cannot but be subordinate), the love of Jesus to humanity is distorted. If under all circumstances, the Father has authority and the Son is subordinate to the Father, then love is not real because it does not come from a free will decision. Jesus had to come to the world and sacrifice himself because of his subordination, not because of his love to humanity.

The followers of the equivalence view also believe that on the equivalence model, the quality of being subordinate is an accidental quality. It does not change the nature of the Son and who he is. On the other hand, to the gradationists, authority and subordination are essential properties. "If they were not possessed, the Father would not be the Father and the Son would not be the Son. . . . Authority is part of the Father's essence, and subordination is part of the Son's essence, and each attribute is not part of the essence of the other person."[86] Erickson introduces a philosophical distinction: what something is, is different from what something does. On the gradation view, subordination is part of the divine essence, whereas, on the equivalence view, subordination is part of the divine work. If we say subordination is part of the divine essence, then Jesus cannot but be subordinate and this makes him inferior. If we say subordination is part of the divine work, then subordination is linked to the divine will and any subsequent act belongs to the will of God, not to his essence.

In the West, scholars are free to choose and develop whatever model they think is biblical. There are no limitations, prohibitions, or restrictions to how scholars understand and think about God, except for the limitations they choose to apply (historical, creedal, or biblical). There is no scholar that will be persecuted because of her views. Moreover, criticism is not

---

[85]Erickson, *Who's Tampering?*, 79.
[86]Erickson, *Who's Tampering?*, 172.

considered personal, and despite the differences among scholars and the many views explained earlier, I have not come across a scholar calling his opponent a heretic. Scholars understand that where there is freedom, there are differences. It is good to agree to disagree.

The most important note to add here is that despite all the differences among these views, none of them make a separation between the three persons of the Trinity within the Godhead. Instead, they all believe that the three persons share the same divine essence and they are distinguished in role. Theologians are not suggesting that the Son is inferior to the Father because of his eternal subordination, but he is equal in nature and distinct in role. In a similar fashion, philosophers are not trying to redefine the Trinity, claiming to be infallible, and insisting that their model is the right one. On the contrary, they all admit fallibility. What is more important is that all Christians around the world believe that the Trinity is a mystery. Those who claim to understand God fully are indirectly claiming to be gods.

Conclusion

Though some Western philosophers were not interested in the doctrine of the Trinity because they did not see any value in it for their studies, many other Western philosophers delved into this doctrine to answer their opponents' objections, especially the claim that the Trinity is not logical. Moreover, explaining this doctrine in the West took a different turn than in the Middle East for different reasons. First, the nature of Western objections was different from Islamic objections. Muslims thought that the Trinity is not logical, but only a few of them provided philosophical reasons for their objections. The majority of them thought the Qur'an provides a different explanation of the Trinity than what Christians are thinking. Early Western Christians, on the other hand, faced philosophical objections to the Trinity, but they did not have to deal with different accounts of the Trinity. All they needed to do was to follow, expand, and defend the patristic creeds.

Modern Western Christians have always enjoyed the freedom of thinking, studying, and debating, a dynamic that has contributed to the development of many arguments. Christians in the Middle East, however, have historically lacked such freedom. Many of them wrote defenses that could not be published for the public. Yaḥya Ibn ᶜAdī, for instance, is not well known in the Middle East among layman Christians, even though he is a well-known philosopher. Most of his writings are circulated in academia among philosophy students, but churches do not discuss his works for different reasons.

This chapter presented different models of the Trinity in the West that scholars think share the idea of orthodoxy. I divided them into philosophical and theological models. The philosophical models are not an attempt to redefine the doctrine of the Trinity. Instead, philosophers exhibit their defense using metaphysical concepts. The scholars claimed fallible and limited knowledge when they spoke about God, but their purpose was to test and expand the orthodox Christian creeds and help others understand the God they worship. These scholars published many other academic papers in Christian journals evaluating and critiquing each other's models, which gave them the opportunity to strengthen and clarify their arguments even more.

The theological Trinity got tangled with the doctrine of the eternal subordination of the Son; however, it is an attempt to explain the different views about how theologians can understand the relation between the three persons of the Trinity in relation to other doctrines, especially salvation and redemption. Despite the importance of these attempts, I believe the theological Trinity does not have a great apologetic value. Christians may benefit from the dialogue among the different views; however, the differences among the views might confuse non-Christians.

The development of the doctrine of the Trinity in the West has some similarities to the Arabic theological development, but it also has many differences, which makes it hard to classify Arab theologians under one or another model of Western trinitarianism. Many Arab theologians follow the gradational view. They would agree with certain aspects of social trinitarianism, such as starting with threeness before moving to oneness. They are preoccupied with discussing the relationship among the three persons of the Trinity and the unity of the Godhead. They understand the oneness of God to mean one divine being, one Godhead, one virtue, one will, one operation, one principality, one power, one domination, and one kingdom. This explanation seems to be closer to Latin trinitarianism.

Social trinitarians Swinburne and Craig develop their arguments with a contemporary touch. Swinburne focuses on the number of the divine persons and explores the reason behind them being three, no more or less. Craig focuses on the three centers of consciousness in the divine Godhead. Swinburne's model might be accepted more among Arab scholars than Craig's model of the mythical creature Cerberus. The main reason is culture. In Arabic culture, Christians do not prefer using myths to refer to God or to metaphysical concepts related to God because Muslims accuse them of being polytheists, reducing Greco-Roman gods to just three. Using a mythical example to refer to any idea related to God will risk the concept of the Trinity and reinforce misconceptions Muslims already have.

The relative identity model, especially van Inwagen's version, seems to be very promising because first, it is an informative, crosscultural, and highly philosophical example. If readers do not like the example of three dogs in relation to the Trinity (because it might be perceived as demeaning), they can change it to something else or keep the philosophical equations because they are academically neutral. Moreover, the philosophical part of van Inwagen's model is highly informative. Lay people might fall into the trap of classical identity and think that similarities entail absolute identity. However, explaining that this is not the only option available is a plus. The example that van Inwagen gives about the two people with the same last names but who are two different persons is very helpful. It shows that despite the highly philosophical approach of this argument, minimal Trinity can be illustrated with simple examples of the relative identity theory to prove that having one divine being and three divine persons is not a contradiction.

Numerical identity concerned Latin trinitarians; but Yaḥya, who is hard to classify as one, was concerned with *wāḥid* in his trinitarian argument as well. However, he took the numerical identity to the route of relative identity. I think he is one of the first philosophers to talk about the relative identity of the Trinity because he was one of the first to suggest that God is one in one sense and multiple in a different sense. Because of his philosophical background, he was able to understand and show that the concept of unity and multiplicity in different senses is not a contradiction.

Understanding this distinction and the different theological approaches is important; however, it is beyond the purpose of this book and the space dedicated in this chapter to explain all the views and mention all the Western theologians and methods. This chapter does not deal with the doctrine of the Trinity in relation to the Catholic church. Most of the scholars mentioned here belong to the evangelical school. If readers would like to learn more about the development of the doctrine of the Trinity, including among Catholics, they can research works by R. P. C. Hanson, Lewis Ayres, Matthew Levering, Gilles Emery, and Johannes Zachhuber.

5

A Contemporary Christian Answer to Islamic Objections Against the Trinity

NOW THAT THE STUDY HAS OFFERED background on the medieval period in the Middle East and three major Arab theologians and their defenses of the Trinity, it will move to present a modern defense of the doctrine of the Trinity against Islamic objections, especially the doctrine of *tawḥīd*. During the medieval period, Arab Christian scholars were preoccupied with proving the oneness of God over discussing the importance of God being manifested in three persons. They moved from the three *Aqānīm* to the one divine being. Western scholars, on the other hand, were influenced by Neoplatonism, in which "the presentation of Christian theology began from the one God and then went on to the God triune."[1] Therefore, they were preoccupied with the relational aspect of the three persons of the Trinity over proving the oneness of God.

To defend the Trinity, Christian Middle Eastern scholars discussed God's attributes. John of Damascus, for instance, listed them to explain what kind of God Christians believe in; whereas Theodore Abū Qurrah and Yaḥya ibn ᶜAdī expanded the explanation and used God's attributes in their illustrations to define the Trinity and prove God's oneness. Western scholars, on the other hand, did not neglect the discussion of divine attributes, but they included significant reorientations and revisions. Therefore, this current

[1]Veli-Matti Karkkainen, *Trinity and Revelation: A Constructive Christian Theology for the Pluralistic World*, vol. 2 (Grand Rapids, MI: Eerdmans, 2014), 71.

chapter serves as a bridge between the East and West to present a comprehensive, but not an exhaustive, trinitarian model showing God as the greatest conceived being.

The Greatest Conceived Being: A Summary

Christian scholars always pursue ways to understand God. Throughout church history, they formed several creeds in order to fight heresies and defend orthodoxy. In similar fashion, Muslim scholars have always sought ways to talk about Allah. They call theology the science of kalām,[2] which is used, not for the purpose of understanding Allah—Allah is supremely transcendent, and no one can understand him—but for the purpose of speaking about Allah as the Qur'an reveals him.

In both religious disciplines, Christian and Muslim scholars proceed with caution, especially in using terms that describe the essence of God. They believe that using *absent terms*—terms that have no fixed meanings—leads to people speaking about abstract concepts because no one knows what an author means by these terms. Christian theologians such as John of Damascus and Theodore Abū Qurrah realized this fact and encouraged their audience to seek comparisons between the attributes of God and the nature of man to discover the differences. Abū Qurrah argues that people can learn about God's attributes by observing Adam's virtues, acknowledging his defects, and affirming the gap between the human and the divine natures.[3] If some ideas or experiences do not match or map onto the divine essence, then people know nothing about God and his perfection. As medieval Christian scholar John Duns Scotus puts it, "If things were really this bad, we would have no better reason to call God wise than a rock."[4] He adds,

> Every metaphysical inquiry about God proceeds in this fashion: the formal notion of something is considered; the imperfection associated with this

---

[2]According to Tim Winter, "For most of this 'classical' period [tenth to thirteenth centuries] the *kalām*, literally 'discourse,' that is to say, the formal academic discipline which one scholar aptly calls 'Islamic doctrinal theology.'" Tim Winter, ed., "Introduction," in *The Cambridge Companion to Classical Islamic Theology* (Cambridge: Cambridge University Press, 2008), 2.

[3]Qusṭanṭine Bashā, *Mayamir Theodore Abū Qurrah Usquf Ḥārān: Aqdam Ta'lif Arabi Nasrani* [The Articles of Theodore Abū Qurrah the Bishop of Ḥārān: The Oldest Arabic Christian Writings] (Beirut: Al-Fou'ad Printing Press, 1904), 27.

[4]Alexander Hall, "Scotus: Knowledge of God," *Internet Encyclopedia of Philosophy*. Accessed January 22, 2022. https://iep.utm.edu/scotuskg/.

> notion in creatures is removed, and then, retaining the same formal notion, we ascribe to it the ultimate degree of perfection and then attribute it to God. . . . Consequently, every inquiry regarding God is based upon the supposition that the intellect has the same univocal concept which it obtained from creatures.[5]

When Christian scholars say God is the seer, the hearer, and the communicator, they know what vision, hearing, and communication are; however, they ascribe the ultimate and the perfect ability to see, hear, and speak with all creation to God who is omnipotent.

While this method of inquiry followed Christian theologians throughout church history, Muslim theologians resisted such comparison, acknowledging a wide chasm between Allah and humanity. As Islamic theology evolved, many Muslim traditionalists in the early years of kalām followed the principle of "*man ṭalaba al-dīn bi'l kalām tazandaqa* (whoever seeks religion through kalām becomes a heretic)."[6] This slogan did not refer to the whole project of theology as represented by *Usūl al-Dīn* (the origin of religion), but to the investigation of the basic features of the nature of Allah, especially his attributes, which some early Muslim thinkers engaged in. Later generations of Muslim scholars accused other theologians of assuming too much about the knowability of the divine nature, so they created the doctrine of *bila kayfa* (without asking how). It means believing in certain attributes (Allah's ninety-nine beautiful names) without attempting to understand them beyond their description in the Qur'an and traditions. The discussion of Allah's attributes continued afterward in a very limited way.

Both Christian and Muslim theologians confess the perfect-divine theology. Divine perfection relates to a state of completeness or absolute wholeness. As stated in chapter one, the greatest conceived being has no ontological deficiencies, has no flaws, or depends on anything else. There is no greater being that can be thought of that deserves human worship except the greatest conceived being. This concept can be demonstrated with the following equation: maximally good + maximally perfect = maximally great. This is the definition of the greatest conceived being. In other

[5]Hall, "Scotus: Knowledge of God."

[6]Oliver Leaman, "The Developed Kalām Tradition," in *The Cambridge Companion to Classical Islamic Theology*, ed. Tim Winter (Cambridge: Cambridge University Press, 2008), 81.

words, God is maximally good and maximally perfect; therefore, he is the greatest conceived being.

Maximal divine goodness means God cannot be morally better; there is no room for him to obtain more moral skills. His goodness is maximal and full. If there is anything in the world that can contribute to or increase his goodness, then he is a minor God. In like manner, maximal divine perfection means he lacks no thing (e.g., skill, ability, attributes, etc.). There is nothing in creation that can add or subtract from him. God did not create the world because he must or ought to, nor because he needs to. God is self-sufficient; he does not need the world to be unsurpassably great. He is perfect with or without the world. Divine maximal goodness and aseity (self-sufficiency) make theists (both Christian and Muslim) believe that God/Allah is the greatest conceived being, and therefore, he deserves human worship.

Theists, however, follow two different models for divine perfection—Trinity and *tawḥīd*. The study advocates for the divine trinitarian model because it demonstrates divine perfection in an unsurpassable way. As Kallistos Ware states, "The doctrine of the Trinity is not just one possible way of thinking about God. It is the only way. The one God of the Christian church cannot be conceived except as Trinity."[7] Other nontrinitarian models of theism (especially *tawḥīd*) do not reveal God as unsurpassably perfect. Their presentation of the divine essence portrays God as contingently relational, especially before creation. Allah was alone with no other person to communicate with. All his divine communicative attributes were dysfunctional before the existence of creation because there was no one to practice these attributes with—for example, Al-Baṣīr (the Seer), As-Samīᶜ (the Hearer), Ar-Razzāq (the Sustainer), Ash-Sahkūr (the Thankful), al-Ḥāfiẓ (the Preserver), al-Muqīt (the Nourisher), Ar-Raqīb (the Watcher), al-Karīm (the Generous), al-Mujīb (the One who Responds to Those Who Ask), and so on.[8] Consequently, the Islamic presentation of *tawḥīd* shows that Allah

[7]Kallistos Ware, "The Holy Trinity: Model for Personhood-in-Relation," in *The Trinity and an Entangled World: Relationality in Physical Science and Theology*, ed. John Polkinghorne (Grand Rapids, MI: Eerdmans, 2010), 107.

[8]This list of Allah's attributes is taken from Al-Gazālī, *Ninety-Nine Names of God in Islam: A Translation of the Major Portion of Al-Gazālī's al-Maqsad and al-Asnā*, trans. Robert Stade (Ibadan, Nigeria: Daystar Press, 1970).

is contingent upon his creation in order to communicate. This shortcoming in the divine nature affects the greatness of the divine and runs the risk of misperceiving the greatest conceived being.

The argument goes this way:

P1: One aspect of divine perfection is relationality—the greatest conceived being should be a relational being in order to be perfect and good (the greatest).

P2: The trinitarian model shows God as an eternally relational divine being (intrarelational and interrelational).

C: God as a Trinity is the greatest conceived being.

The Greatest Conceived Being Is Relational in Nature

Many theologians appeal to the concept of divine attributes in an attempt to discover the mystery of the divine essence. One of the ways to understand the greatest conceived being is by studying his attributes to ensure that none of them is in conflict with other attributes. The attribute that this chapter will focus on is the relational nature of God—God in relationship. It is rare to see the relationality of God discussed in theology proper as an attribute; however, the relationality of God in the sense of interconnectedness is undeniable in any theistic worldview. God communicates and connects with his creation. He hears his people's prayers, answers their inquiries, and reveals his will. If God does not possess the ability to relate, then he is a lesser God. If he is nonrelational, then he cannot communicate with his creation. He cannot hear the prayers of believers and cannot communicate his divine revelation and will. In the theistic worldview, the greatest conceived being does not miss any attributes, which might make him imperfect. Therefore, within theism, God must be relational.

Relationality: An essential trait of divine personality. *Relationality is essential in the theistic worldview.* All theistic worldviews (Judaism, Christianity, and Islam) believe that God connects with his creation in one way or another. God gave his revelation (the Bible and the Qur'an). He spoke directly with his prophets (Ex 31:18; Dan 5:25) and he communicated his message to human beings through angels and apostles. Today, the written revelation is completed, but God still communicates with his people. He listens to their prayers and answers their needs (Ps 4:3; Jn 9:31; 1 Jn 5:14; Surah 21:48, 76; 35:22). In other words, within a theistic worldview, God is still involved in his creation by communicating with his followers. He did not leave the world alone to wrestle with its challenges, as in a deistic worldview.

Relationality is essential to personhood. Relationality requires personal agency—an agent who can hear/listen and speak/talk. The form of communication is not important at this point, and it will not be addressed. The significant point, however, that this study conveys is that no relationship of any sort (such as father-son or master-slave) can be done without the ability to connect. The minimum requirement for starting a relationship is the ability to see, hear, and communicate. Objects, such as newspapers, televisions, and computers are all transmitters rather than ends in themselves. They do not represent or reflect themselves, but they point to a variety of things, such as the flux, flow, and changing circumstances around the world.[9] They are unable to create or maintain a relationship, unless there is a personal agency behind them.

Relationality rules out indifference. Usually, objects are indifferent to what is around them. Scotus states, "Something with passive power is indifferent to contrary states of affairs, like how logs are indifferent to being hot or not being hot. After all, a log does not care, so to speak, whether it is one or the other, for there is nothing about a log that requires that it be hot, or that it not be hot."[10] On the contrary, an agency of a person who cares about the status of the log can interact with it by heating it up and causing it to receive heat. In the same sense, an active power, such as the sun, is indifferent to the many effects it can bring about to creation; however, an agency of a person (who has some control over the effects of the sun) is not indifferent to its effects. A personal agency is intentional about its effects on the creation because it seeks to emphasize virtue and minimize harm.

Relationality requires otherness—another agency to connect with. The communicative ability of a personal agency cannot be completed without another personal agency to receive, convey, and impart the information being transmitted. Relationships require at least two agents for meaningful

---

[9]Robert Cooper, "Peripheral Vision: Relationality," *Organization Studies* 26, no. 11 (November 2005): 1691.

[10]J. T. Paasch, *Divine Production in Late Medieval Trinitarian Theology: Henry of Ghent, Duns Scotus, and William Ockham* (Oxford: Oxford University Press, 2012), 139.

interaction. It is pointless for someone to make a relationship with himself, or to be satisfied seeing the dirt or listening to the wind. Pure individualism or selfishness is not perceived as a virtue. Even psychologists, while they emphasize the traits of self-awareness for the sake of furthering and improving interpersonal relationships, do not recommend it for the sake of furthering individualism.[11]

Relationality is essential for human flourishing. Relationality is fundamental for human flourishing. God does not only ask people to worship him, but he also promises to bless them if they believe and obey him. Those who are not believers will not receive his blessings, and those who believe will receive their deserved awards. In other words, the results of the divine relationality should lead to human flourishing (at least for those who are obeying the divine communication/revelation). Those who do not want to have a relationship with God might not enjoy human flourishing, but those who want to establish a relationship with God are promised a thriving life. If this is true, then God ought to communicate to establish a relationship with his creation. If he is unable to convey his message or listen to prayers, then his greatness is disputable.

Humanly speaking, some people are better than others in their relatedness and communication with other people. Some can make friends so easily—it comes naturally to them—whereas others struggle with making friends and relating to people. No matter how hard connecting with others is, the ability to communicate and relate is essential to any person, otherwise the individuals would be stripped of their humanity. Needless to say, human relationships are different from God's relationship to the world. God is transcendent and does not need humanity to flourish (Eccles 5:2; Is 6:1; Surah 87:1; 2:255; 42:12). While this is true, there is a need to note that God is omnipotent (able to do all possible things; Rom 4:21: 2 Cor 9:8; 2 Tim 1:12; Surah 17:99; 23:17; 36:81; 46:33); therefore, being unable to establish a relationship with his creation (especially human beings) would not be a virtue, but a defect.

In a nutshell, relationality is a fundamental attribute to divine agency. Most theistic religions believe that God created human beings to worship

---

[11]Helen C. Boucher, Serena Chen, and Molly Parker Tapias, "The Relational Self Revealed: Integrative Conceptualization and Implications for Interpersonal Life," *Psychological Bulletin* (2006): 151-79. Erik H. Erikson, *Identity: Youth and Crisis* (New York: Norton, 1968).

him. Relationship with the divine started through the divine agency (God) who communicated to human beings their need and duty to worship him. Intuitively speaking, if the divine agency is unable to communicate this requirement, then he is to blame, not the human. In other words, the first step in relationality starts with the divine, who is communicated to be the supreme, the creator, and the omnipotent; subsequently, he deserves to be worshiped. God's inability to communicate with his creation at any point in history would be considered a flaw, not a perfection.

The fundamental factor of relationality. *Relationality: Intrarelational nature of the divine.* Intrarelationality is essential to the divine agency because it shows God not only as relational but also as eternally relational. Christians and Muslims perceive God as an eternal divine being, which indicates that God has no beginning and no end. He was not born, does not have a starting point, and will not die (Rom 1:20, 16:26; 1 Tim 1:17; Surah 28:88; 55:27). As Stanley Grenz states, "To refer to God as spirit means to understand God as the Living One."[12] Living in this case implies the idea of always/eternally living.

Since creation has a starting point (at one time in history there was no creation), then scholars can think of divine relationality in two ways: the relationality of God before the creation and after it. The divine intrarelationality is related to God's unity, and it refers to his sociality within the Godhead—God as a community and the way he perceives himself. This criterion helps thinkers understand God's nature inwardly—whether he is alone (as one agent) or a communion of persons—and whether his relational nature is consistent with his eternality.

Relationality: Interrelational nature of the divine. Interrelationality is another type of divine relationality related to the communication between God and his creation. God is integrally involved with his creation. He is not static, but active and affected by the events of the world. Any relationship requires at least two agents: one speaks while the other listens, one loves while another receives the love, and so on. This criterion is important because it provides answers about the nature of the relationship of God with his creation. How does God relate/act with his creation and what does he require/

---

[12]Stanley J. Grenz, *Theology for the Community of God* (Grand Rapids, MI: Eerdmans, 1994), 83.

expect from his creatures? After the fall, what did he do to save humanity? This criterion helps thinkers understand God's nature outwardly through his actions.

Allah and Relationality

The main Islamic theological schools: A historical overview. As stated in chapter three, during the Islamic formation of theology (kalām), theological and philosophical conflicts arose between two major Arabic schools of thought: the traditional and the rational. The traditional school, led by the Ashᶜarites, stressed the idea that revelation should precede reason. They viewed inspired writings as superior to human reasoning and believed that faith and surrender were therefore required. Consequently, "interpretation of the text was to be either limited or forbidden, and ignorance must be admitted."[13] On the other hand, the rational school, represented by the Muᶜtazilites, recognized the necessity of reason. They placed reason above revelation. Faith was not complete without understanding. When a discrepancy between the mind and revelation occurs, interpretation is required. In the eleventh century, after a long dispute, the Muᶜtazilites were accursed and the Ashᶜarites were recognized as the orthodox party.[14] Based on this distinction, both Ashᶜarites and Muᶜtazilites presented different perceptions of the divine attributes. While they both were intent on saving God's unity, they became preoccupied with God's power over God's relationality.

Islamic overview of divine attributes. The two Sunni groups disputed the topic of Allah's names/attributes. In the Qur'an, Mohammad states that "to Allah alone belong all perfect attributes. So call on Him by these" (Surah 7:180 Islam International Publications, 2015; 17:110; 20:8; 59:24).[15] Following Mohammad's commands, Muslims believe that they should not look to nature

---

[13]Kamal Al-Yazaji, *Ma'alim al-Fikir al-'Arabi fi al-'Asar al-Wasit* [Highlights of the Arab Thought in the Middle Ages] (Beirut: Dar Al-ᶜIm Lilmalayīn, 1979), 151-57. Imad N. Shehadeh, *God with Us and Without Us, Volumes One and Two: The Beauty and Power of Oneness in Trinity versus Absolute Oneness* (Carlisle: Langham Creative Projects, 2020), 109.

[14]William Thomson, "Al-Ashᶜari and His Al-Ibanah," *The Muslim World: A Quarterly Review of History, Culture, Religions & The Christian Mission in Islamdom* 32, no. 3 (1942): 253.

[15]Bukharī, *Ṣaḥīḥ Bukharī*, Hadīth nos. 6410, 2736, and 7392. Accessed January 8, 2022. https://sunnah.com/bukhari:6410. Sunan ibn Majah, Hadīth no. 3861. Accessed January 8, 2022. https://sunnah.com/ibnmajah:3861. Jamiᶜ At-Tirmidhī, Hadīth 3507. Accessed January 8, 2022. https://sunnah.com/tirmidhi/48.

or the virtues that human beings enjoy in order to extract God's attributes. Instead, they should only use the names that Allah and Mohammad used in the Qur'an. The dispute was over what names to include and what are the meanings of these names.

Using different methods of interpretation, the Ashᶜarites' understanding of Allah's attributes resulted in different interpretations from the Muᶜtazilites. The most famous scholar the Ashᶜarites followed was Aḥmad ibn Ḥanbal (AD 855), who rejected the Muᶜtazilites' rationalism and gave precedence to divine revelation. Ibn Ḥanbal believed that the attributes of God, according to the teachings of the Qur'an, are not subject to human reasoning, and thus must be accepted without qualification.[16] Asking whether God's attributes are part of his essence (in him) or part of his will (without him) was an unacceptable religious innovation.[17]

The ongoing issues between the Ashᶜarites and Muᶜtazilites culminated in the question of anthropomorphism (*tashbīh*). The Qur'an speaks of God's hands (Surah 38:75), eyes (Surah 54:14), and face (Surah 55:27). It also describes him as hearing (Surah 2:127; 17:1; 22:61), seeing (Surah 4:58, 134; 5:71; 17:30), and seating himself on his throne (Surah 20:5), apparently implying that he has a body. Many Ashᶜarite scholars, such as al-Bāqillānī, al-Juwaynī, and al-Ghazālī, argue that these verses must be understood metaphorically. As al-Juwaynī states, "What is correct, in our view, is that the hands [of God] should be construed as power, the eyes as vision, and the face as existence."[18] Ashᶜarites were eager to avoid anything that might be construed as anthropomorphism (*tashbīh*).[19]

Dar al-Ifta al-Missriyyah, which is the highest religious authority in Egypt, issued a mandate on their website, commending Sunnis to

> Believe in them [Allah's attributes] and to receive them with acceptance and resignation. And to not engage in its interpretation, its refutation, likening

---

[16] H. Laoust, "Ahmad b. Hanbal," in P. J. Bearman et al., eds., *Encyclopaedia of Islam Online*, 12 vols. (Leiden, Netherlands: Brill, 2004). www.encislam.brill.nl. This idea is related to the doctrine of *bila kayfa* ("without asking how").

[17] Abdullah Saeed, *Islamic Thought: An Introduction* (Florence: Taylor & Francis Group, 2006), 65.

[18] Al-Juwaynī, *A Guide to the Conclusive Proofs for the Principles of Belief: Al-Irshad*, trans. Paul E. Walker (Reading, UK: Garnet Publishing: 2001), 86.

[19] Jerry R. Halverson, *Theology and Creed in Sunni Islam: The Muslim Brotherhood, Ash'arism, and Political Sunnism* (New York: Palgrave Macmillan, 2010), 19.

> the attribute to something tangible, and other problematic methodologies. It is incumbent to establish the attribute as it came and to leave interpreting its meaning and to resign its meaning to the One who spoke of it in accordance with the way of those who are firmly established in the faith . . . He [Allah] has castigated those who innovate in interpretation "But those in whose hearts is perversity follow the part thereof that is allegorical, seeking discord, and searching for its hidden meanings, but no one knows its hidden meanings except God."[20]

Dar al-Ifta al-Missriyyah also quotes Imam Aḥmad ibn Ḥanbal, who, regarding Allah descending to the sky of this earth and the scene on the day of resurrection, has stated that "we believe in these texts and we verify their truth without asking how, or without seeking a meaning and we desire nothing of this. We believe that what the Messenger of God brought is truth and we do not respond to him nor do we describe God with more than what He has described of Himself, 'there is none like unto Him and He is the all seeing, all hearing.'"[21] This statement affirms the attributes of Allah, and if any of them are ambiguous or equivocal, then Sunnis should accept them as is without further question.

What is important to our study is that the Ashᶜarites affirmed Allah's attributes (*sifat*), divided them into two groups, and emphasized seven essential ones. The first group is the essential *sifat*. They are called *Al-sifat al-dhatīya* (attributes in essence): namely power, knowledge, life, will, speech, hearing, and sight, which eternally subsist in God's essence. From eternity, Allah is omnipotent, omniscient, living, willing, speaking, all-hearing, and all-seeing. The second group is called *Al-sifat al-fiᶜlya* (attributes in actions), such as mercy, love, wrath, and so on. These attributes exist only as Allah acts with his creation. The Ashᶜarites' semantics regarding the attributes of actions is ambiguous. Some scholars say, "These attributes [attributes in actions] are therefore not eternal and do not subsist in His [Allah] Essence."[22] Other scholars say that these attributes are eternal, but they are not related to the essence of God but to his will.[23]

---

[20]Dar Al-Ifta Al-Missriyyah, "Who are the Ash'arites?" Accessed January 8, 2022. www.dar-alifta.org/Foreign/ViewFatwa.aspx?ID=8001.

[21]Dar Al-Ifta Al-Missriyyah, "Who are the Ash'arites?"

[22]Halverson, *Theology and Creed*, 21. The issue of the attributes of acts is complicated.

[23]Shehadeh, *God with Us and Without Us*, 112.

Mu^ctazilites, on the other hand, contributed to the attribute debate by presenting different views from the Ash^carites. According to John Renard, the Mu^ctazilites' views "flow from the first principle: since God is simply and irreducibly one, his 'essential' attributes (power, knowledge, existence) are identical with God's being. But since God also acts in time, his speaking, hearing, seeing, and willing are separate from God's essence and subject to change."[24] Mu^ctazilites attempted to save a strict concept of monotheism, which, in their opinion, requires an uncompromized observance of the transcendence and the absolute unity of God. In their view, Allah should be pure in essence and has no attributes because assigning attributes implies multiplicity.[25] If the attributes are identical with God, then they would have to be identical among themselves. God's knowledge would thus be the same as God's omnipotence.

The Mu^ctazilites maintained the attributes of essence; however, they insisted that it would be blasphemous to acknowledge the attributes of action as defining what God is like.[26] According to Shehadeh, "Mu^ctazilites maintained that the attributes of action are not eternal, but created, and therefore, contingent, unnecessary and changing."[27] Allah's attributes in actions are the abstract meanings, human semantics, and knowledge that were created to know Allah. Thus, it is easy to imagine a time when Allah did not have these attributes because they only came into being when he acted with his creation. As a result of this claim, Mu^ctazilites made Allah mutable and subject to change.[28]

The intrarelationality of Allah. Neither the Ash^carite nor the Mu^ctazilite understanding of Allah's attributes show him as relational before creation. Mu^ctazilites do not believe that Allah's attributes, such as seeing, hearing, and speaking, are eternal. Most of the Islamic dispute happened over God's speech, in which Mu^ctazilites view Allah's speaking as an attribute of action; therefore, it is not eternal. Moreover, Mu^ctazilites have different interpretations for Allah being the seer and the hearer. Al-Shahrastānī mentions

---

[24]John Renard, *Islam and Christianity: Theological Themes in Comparative Perspective* (Berkeley: University of California Press, 2011), 105.

[25]Saeed, *Islamic Thought*, 65.

[26]Al-Yazaji, *Ma'alim al-Fikir*, 17.

[27]Shehadeh, *God with Us and Without Us*, 111.

[28]Shehadeh, *God with Us and Without Us*, 112.

several Muᶜtazilite views on this topic. Al-Kaᶜbī, for instance, believes that Allah being the seer and the hearer means "he is aware of what is being said and seen."[29] Other scholars, like Al-Jibāʾī, understood Allah (the seer and the hearer) as *al-Ḥay* (the living, who is not dead, full of life, and the existent).[30] In other words, Muᶜtazilites do not affirm the attributes of Allah as part of his essence; subsequently, they are not eternal. They interpret Allah being the seer and the hearer by alluding either to his life or his knowledge of the objects of seeing and hearing. To protect Allah's unity, Muᶜtazilites end up presenting a mutilated concept of the divine by making him unable to see or hear from eternity.

The Ashᶜarites, on the other hand, acknowledge that Allah sees and hears because it is written in the Qur'an that "He is the Hearing, the Seeing" (Surah 42:11, Shakir). The problem with this view lies in the idea that Allah could hear and see eternally before creating the world because these attributes are part of his essence. But here's the question that Ashᶜarites never asked: Whom did Allah see or hear before the creation of the world? If he did not see or hear anyone, he only started seeing and hearing after the creation; consequently, his nature changed. Perhaps he had the potential ability to see and hear, but his attributes were dysfunctional until he created the world.

The eternal divine communication problem in Islam, which is mentioned in chapter three, extends to Allah's speech. Remember, the Ashᶜarites' view about Allah's speech is understood by his perpetual state of being, as a substance (*maᶜna*), not in the sense of a set of temporal ideas or representations, but as an eternal divine attribute. This understanding raises the same problem of seeing and hearing: Allah had no one to communicate with before the creation of the world. His ability to communicate was contingent on his creation.

The conflict between the Muᶜtazilites and the Ashᶜarites regarding the relationality of Allah exposes the weakness of absolute oneness. Muslims encounter a dilemma with their concepts of *tawḥīd* based on their descriptions of Allah's attributes. Those who affirm the eternality of the attributes—especially speaking, seeing, and hearing—mutilate their concept of the

[29]Al-Shahrastānī, *Nihāyat Al-Iqdām fī ᶜIlm al-Kalām* [The End of the Process of Kalam Science] (Cairo, Egypt: Maktabat al-Thaqafa al-Diniya, 2009), 341.

[30]Al-Shahrastānī, *Nihāyat Al-Iqdām*, 341.

divine because Allah needs another agent to speak, see, and hear. Otherwise, Allah would be speaking, seeing, and hearing with himself, and that would be meaningless. Those who do not affirm the eternality of the attributes, on the other hand, end up presenting a minor image of the divine who could not communicate—speak, hear, or see—until after the creation came into existence because there was no subject of communication to fulfill his attributes with.

To answer this dilemma, later Muslim scholars suggested that Allah did not form creation *ex-nihilo* (out of nothing), but instead by emanation. The concept of emanation means that all created things are derived from something else in the sense that secondary things proceed or flow from the primary.[31] Abū Sulaymān al-Sijistānī (AD 1001) believed in eternal creation. Time does not have beginning or end. According to Joel Kraemer, al-Sijistānī maintains that God's power is "spread throughout the world permanently" and saw creation as "a non-temporal, eternal process."[32] This means God did not create out of nothing nor in six literal days as the Qur'an states. Instead, creation is perpetually existent with God. Ibn Taymīyya (AD 1328), who was regarded as a kalām theologian and not a philosopher, argues for the idea of continuous creation from eternity. Commenting on a *Ḥadīth* in *Ṣaḥīḥ Bukhārī* and a Quranic verse, he argues that Allah created this world while his throne was already in existence.[33] It is written in the Qur'an that Allah "is Who created the heavens and the earth in six Days—and His Throne was upon the water" (Surah 11:7 Pickthall). This verse connotes the idea that water and Allah's throne were already in existence when Allah created the world in six days. Jon Hoover notes,

> God's creative activity had a beginning. They correctly see that reason dictates that God could have become an agent after not having been one unless a prior cause originated to necessitate the change. That is, it is impossible that God arbitrarily started creating at some point in the past after never having created before. Here ibn Taymiyya endorses the philosophers' axiom of efficient

[31] *The New Encyclopedia of Judaism*, s.v. "Emanation." Accessed March 24, 2024. www.jewishvirtuallibrary.org/emanation.

[32] Joel Kraemer, *Philosophy in the Renaissance of Islam: Abu Sulaymān Al-Sijistānī and His Circle (Studies in Islamic Culture and History)*, vol. 8 (Leiden: Brill Academic, 1987), 197, 219-22, 224.

[33] The exact wording of this *Ḥadīth* as ibn Taymiyya relates it does not appear in the standard collections of *Ṣaḥīḥ Bukhārī*, but his text is close to that found in 3190 and 3191.

> causality—every event requires a cause—and he rejects the Kalām view that it is in the nature of God's will to decide without prior cause.[34]

Despite ibn Taymīyya's suggestion about the eternality of the world, the dilemma of the relationality of Allah remains unanswered. For even if water and Allah's throne (or just basic atoms) is all that existed at the beginning (from eternity), Allah's attributes as the hearer and communicator were not perfected until the creation of human beings. Allah was still unable to communicate in a relational way or demonstrate his relational nature until the creation of human beings. Allah's inability to see, hear, and speak limits his power and perfection. Additionally, the idea of the eternal nature of water and God's throne is problematic. For only Allah is eternal, and all that is eternal is Allah.[35] If water or Allah's throne was eternal, as ibn Taymiyyah claims, then other things were Allah or associating with Allah from eternity. This idea is completely rejected in Islam because it is inconsistent with the doctrine of *tawḥīd*—only the divine is eternal. In other words, the eternality of the universe limits the divinity of Allah because it presents something else as eternal, and this idea refutes the concept of *tawḥīd*.

The interrelationality of Allah. Allah's attributes describe him communicating with his creation, which raises the question of the interrelationality of Allah. The Qur'an describes Allah speaking to angels, teaching them mysteries about the future, and ordering them to bow to Adam (Surah 2:30-34). The Qur'an also depicts Allah hearing the pleading of woman regarding her husband (Surah 58:1), seeing everything (Surah 17:1; 26:218; 96:14), and hearing everything (Surah 5:76; 6:13; 21:4). Perhaps most importantly, the Qur'an itself is the speech of Allah to his servant via the angel Jibril Mohammad (Surah 6:19).

Most theistic scholars believe that God is a person/agent.[36] He is not a person as human beings are, but he is a person in a unique, divine way. The

---

[34]Jon Hoover, "Perpetual Creativity in the Perfection of God: Ibn Taymiyya's Hadith Commentary on God's Creation of This World," *Journal of Islamic Studies* 15, no. 3 (2004): 294.

[35]According to the Sunni Creed, Al-Aqīdah al-Tahāwiyyah, Allah is "the eternal without a beginning and enduring without end. . . . He has existed with His timeless attributes before His creation, which added nothing to His essence that was not already among His attributes. As His attributes were before creation, so will they continue forever." Abū Jaʿfar al-Ṭaḥāwī, *Al-Aqīdah al-Tahāwiyyah*, trans., Abū Amīna Elias, accessed March 3, 2024, www.abuaminaelias.com/aqeedah-tahawiyyah/.

[36]Islamic scholars use different ways/words to refer to Allah, such as *Creator*, *Aḥad*, *Wāḥid*, and so on. However, they rarely use the word *person*. Therefore, they do not agree whether *person*

divine person, for instance, is eternal, having no beginning or end. He is not born, and he cannot die.[37] The divine person is not a secondary but a primary and absolute notion in existence. As John Zizioulas states, "Nothing is more sacred than the person since it constitutes the 'way of being' of God himself."[38] Christians and Muslims, however, differ on the idea of whether God (as a person) exists in communion or alone. Christians believe that if God is a person, then he cannot exist in isolation or alone; whereas Muslims have no problem with God being alone and lonely. They believe that there is no plurality in him because his essential characteristic is that of unity. Nevertheless, his lack of plurality means he is not in relationship throughout eternity, for there is no other with whom he might relate.

The reason behind this difference is that Christians relate the idea of personhood to the idea of identity. Being a person means being unique and unrepeatable. Even if a person dies, she will still be remembered for who she was. Her skills, traits, characteristics (good and bad) will always be remembered. However, animals, who are not persons, are replaceable, and their traits and characteristics are repeatable. "They can be similar; they can be composed and decomposed; they can be combined with others in order to produce results or even new species; they can be used to serve purposes—sacred or not, this does not matter."[39] On the contrary, persons cannot be replaced, reproduced, combined, or used the same way animals are used—even the most sacred ones. Whosoever treats persons in such a way automatically turns them into a thing. When people die, they perish physically, but they bring into existence their personal particularity. As Zizioulas explains,

> Death dissolves us all into one indistinguishable nature, turning us into "substance," or things. What gives us an identity that does not die is not our nature but our personal relationship with God's undying personal identity. Only when nature is hypostatic or personal, as is the case with God, does it exist

should be used to describe God. Those who call Allah a person quote Sahih Muslim Ḥadīth no.1499a, "No person is more jealous of his honour than Allah, and no persons, is more fond of accepting an excuse than Allah, . . . and no one is more fond of praise than Allah . . ." https://sunnah.com/muslim:1499a.

[37]Frederic H. Chase, trans., "The Orthodox Faith," in *Saint John of Damascus Writings* (New York: Fathers of the church, 1958), 178, 183. Al-Ṭaḥāwī, *Al-Aqīdah al-Tahāwiyyah.*

[38]John D. Zizioulas, *Communion and Otherness: Further Studies in Personhood and the Church* (London: Bloomsbury Publishing, 2007), 166-67.

[39]Zizioulas, *Communion and Otherness*, 167.

> truly and eternally. For it is only then that it acquires uniqueness and becomes an unrepeatable and irreplaceable particularity in the "mode of being" which we find in the Trinity.[40]

Some Muslims might partially agree with this explanation; however, those who reject the idea that God is a person are trying to avoid the term because of its anthropomorphic connotation. Such Muslims prefer to use other titles and names of Allah, such as *rabb* (*lord*; Surah 40:28; 43:64), a word used to refer to the God of Mohammad or the God of al-Kaᶜba. *Ilāh* (*a god*—pl. *āliha*), a word of considerably lower incidence in the Qur'anic text, is used often to refer generically to the false gods of others, including Jesus and Mary (Surah 5:116, 16:51; 20:88).[41]

Whether Allah is defined as a person or a divine agent, his relationality to the world is essential. The Islamic presentation of divine attributes can be opaque because absolute oneness focuses on the power of Allah and the freedom of his will. A revealed action of God "deals with the will of Allah and not Allah himself."[42] Shehadeh thinks that "the emphasis was placed upon the phenomenon that there is never a promise given by God in the Qur'an that is not accompanied by a statement stressing his freedom and power to act according to how he chooses."[43] This is mainly because in Islam, human beings are created primarily to worship Allah rather than to have a relationship with him. Ida Glaser states, "The ultimate in relationship is willing submission rather than interaction."[44] Glaser adds, "God's love may cause him to have mercy on his creatures, even to the extent of communicating with them; but it is a love that condescends in beneficence rather than a love that shares in relationship."[45] Relational love includes both benefits and relationship.

If the previous analysis is true, then God's absolute power and authority over the whole universe constitute a master-slave relationship instead of a father-child relationship. It is his right alone to enforce the affairs of men as

---

[40]Zizioulas, *Communion and Otherness*, 167.

[41]Aziz Al-Azmeh, *The Emergence of Islam in Late Antiquity: Allah and His People* (Cambridge: Cambridge University Press, 2014), 285.

[42]Arne Rudvin, "Islam: An Absolutely Different Ethos?," *International Review of Mission* 71 (1982): 59.

[43]For more elaboration on this idea, please see Shehadeh, *God with Us and Without Us*, 114-16.

[44]Ida Glaser, "The Concept of Relationship as a Key to the Comparative Understanding of Christianity and Islam," *Themelios*, vol. 11, no. 2 (January 1986): 59.

[45]Glaser, "Concept of Relationship," 58.

he wills, and it is the duty of the slave to obey and worship his master without questioning. Al-Shahristānī openly affirms this kind of relationship between Allah and everything in his creation (including human beings) by indicating that "Ar-Raḥmān [another one of Allah's names] should not have a son because he is exalted. He did not become, nor was caused to exist; he did not beget, nor was begotten; but everything to him is as slavery to masterdom. All who existed in heavens and on earth become slaves to Ar-Raḥmān, and he is the master of everything and its [the world's] creator, and the God of all that exists . . ."[46]

The super-transcendence of Allah in Islamic theology presents him as above his creation because there are no signs of personal interaction with human beings. When Allah wanted to interact with his created beings, he sent them several prophets, such as Abraham, Moses, Jonah, and many others. When the age of maturity, or the age of reason approached, Allah sent prophet Mohammad to his people as the Seal of the prophets (Surah 33:40). He did not simply reveal the continuation of the Judeo-Christian faith, but he claimed to be the culmination of all previous revelations.[47] Up to this point, Allah did not leave himself without a witness. He was still communicating with his people. He saw the conditions of humanity, heard their agony, and taught them what they need to know about his majesty. He corresponded with them by speaking, and he spoke by revealing. He communicated by sending a messenger, whom he gave supreme authority to reveal his will (Qur'an 42:51). After this point, Allah stopped communicating with human beings. He stopped sending prophets and revealing more messages. It seems that Allah gave humanity the moral law and taught them the ethical codes that they should apply, but he then left them on their own to struggle and fight. This part of Allah's relationality is missing from Islamic theology. Allah seems to distance himself from the creation.

The original equation of God's perfection + God's moral goodness does not seem compatible with the Islamic presentation of the divine. For Allah to be the greatest, he must be maximally good and maximally perfect. Maximally good means God cannot morally improve. He cannot be nonrelational at one point of history, then become relational, and later stop

[46]Ash-Shahristānī, *Nihāyat al-Iqdā fī cilm al-Kalām* (Baghdad: Muthanah), 179.

[47]David Waines, *An Introduction to Islam*, 2nd ed. (Cambridge: Cambridge University Press, 2014), 27.

being relational again. Being nonrelational at any point in history makes him a minor god. Similarly, God being maximally perfect means he lacks nothing. If he does not exhibit the feature of relationality necessarily, then he is a contingent being. He needs his creation in order to be relational. Before the creation of human beings, there was no one to hear, see, or speak to. The doctrine of *tawhīd* rejects the idea of relationship within the divine community and emphasizes the idea of oneness—Allah is *Wāhid*, *Aḥd*, and *Samad*. He is not a community of external persons who need no creation to communicate with, but he is contingently reliant on his creation to be relational.

Despite all the attempts to protect God's transcendence and perfection, being morally contingent does not make the Islamic divine being necessarily perfect. Allah is either essentially morally perfect or essentially morally defective. For the greatness of Allah to occur, his goodness and perfection should match. Just as we understand God's omnipotence to be threatened by God not being able to make water H_2O, we need to take God's greatness to be threatened by the fact that he cannot exhibit the attribute of relationality necessarily. The concept of God existing eternally independent of the world must here be judged as being strictly incoherent. By logical necessity, the concept of Allah's self-sufficient sociality must be rejected.

The Trinitarian God and Relationality

As is commonly known, Christians believe in the Trinity. The Trinity to Christians is not just a doctrine or a concept. It is more than that. It is God himself. God is unique; he is totally unlike anything else. So, to define the Trinity is to define God. Is it possible to define the undefinable? Human language fails theologians in two ways: first, it is based upon time. While God is not limited to time, human beings speak of the past, the present, and the future. Thus, when they speak about God, they are forced to place misleading limitations upon his being. Second, words often carry with them "baggage," which is to say that specific words might conjure up a particular mental image.[48] The most obvious example is using the word *person* when we are describing the deity—the persons of the Trinity. Like Muslims,

[48]James White, *The Forgotten Trinity* (Grand Rapids, MI: Bethany House Publishers, 1998), 14.

Christian theologians are aware that human beings (as persons) are unlike God. To avoid any confusion, Arab and Syriac theologians invented a special theological term and called it *Aqānīm* (sg. *Uqnūm*) to refer to the persons of the Trinity. The three Arab Christian scholars that were discussed in the previous chapter followed this pattern, and this study will follow the same pattern. Arab Christians who were conversing with their Muslim peers knew about the problem of anthropomorphism and its Islamic rejection. They saw the necessity of inventing theological terminology that helps clarify the meaning of the divine persons while honoring the distinction.

It has been argued in the previous chapter that most Chalcedonian Christians follow the definition of the Trinity of the Apostles' Creed. God is one divine being manifested in three *Aqānīm.* Like Muslims theologians, Arab Christian theologians explained the doctrine of God by discussing his attributes. However, they did not classify the attributes into two categories (the attributes of essence and the attributes of actions); instead, they emphasized that the knowledge of God is possible through studying God's actions and through observing humanity's virtues while keeping the distinction between the divine and human virtues clear.

Most of these Arab Christian theologians did not include the relationality of God in their discussions. This attribute is closely related to the omnipotence, omnibenevolence, and the immutability of God. If God is not eternally relational, then he is a minor God who is an abstract concept, and not a being that deserves worship. If God is not relational in essence, then he is not maximally good because relationality is superior to nonrelationality, and lacking relationality indicates lacking ability, which makes God nonomnipotent. Finally, if God was not relational, but he became relational after he created human beings, then his nature changed. He was not perfect at one point in history because he was not able to practice all his virtues, but at another point in history, he became able to. This change in God's nature indicates inferiority.

The next sections discuss in further detail how the relationality of God is important to show the perfection of his nature. In Christianity, God is eternally relational because the three persons of the Trinity are eternal in nature. The trinitarian model is the only way to show God as intrarelational within himself and interrelational with his creation, without compromising his omnipotence, omnibenevolence, and immutability—all of which reflect his perfection. For to construe God's sociality as being world-dependent rather than self-sufficient presents weakness in the divine essence.

The trinitarian God is intrarelational. Christian theologians emphasize God in his revelation. God's own eternal being and the salvific actions of the three divine *Aqanīm* in history reflect the intratrinitarian relations in the eternal Godhead. For all the attributes of the Father are beheld in the Son, and all the attributes of the Son belong to the Father, insomuch as the Son abides wholly in the Father and in turn has the Father wholly in Himself. Thus, the *Uqnūm* (person or hypostasis) of the Son becomes, as it were, the form and countenance by which the Father is made known, and the *Uqnūm* of the Father is made known in the form of the Son.[49] Basil of Caesarea points out that the Son beholds the attributes of the Father, and the Son's attributes belong to the Father, "in so much as the Son abides wholly in the Father and in turn has the Father wholly in Himself."[50] The Father and the Son interdwell with one another in an intimate relationship in which each fully knows and beholds the other.

John of Damascus was one of the prominent theologians who spoke about the intrarelationality of God. He developed what was later called the doctrine of perichoresis—the mutual indwelling of the Father and the Son and the Holy Spirit within the blessed Trinity.[51] This doctrine grasps the circulatory character of the triune God in which the persons exist in one another. Perichoresis is seen in the mutual cleaving of the *Aqanīm*, in which

> the abiding and resting of the Persons in one another is not in such a manner that they coalesce or become confused, but, rather, so that they adhere to one another, for they are without interval between them and inseparable and their mutual indwelling is without confusion. For the Son is in the Father and the Spirit, and the Spirit is in the Father and the Son, and the Father is in the Son and the Spirit, and there is no merging or blending or confusion.[52]

[49]St. Basil of Caesarea, *Letters* 38, 8. Accessed January 21, 2022. www.newadvent.org/fathers/3202038.htm.

[50]St. Basil, *Letters* 38, 229.

[51]It is called in the twelfth century *perichoresis* (Greek) and *circumincession* (Latin).

[52]Chase, "Orthodox Faith," 202.

Each *Uqnūm* of the Trinity is vitally existing in the other two without losing his own identity. Miroslav Volf calls such a construct reciprocal interiority.[53] We find this type of thinking predominantly in the Johannine writings in the New Testament. John sees the Father in the Son and the Son in the Father (Jn 14:11). Divine unity is an act of interiority; it is an expression of divine intrarelationality.

The doctrine of perichoresis provides a proper ground for claiming that God is not contingently relational, but that God is eternally relational because he is relational within himself. God is fundamentally a community of divine *Aqānīm* who displays love and functions in harmony within himself. Since God is triune in nature, perichoresis promotes the idea that God is never "alone." According to Bruce Ware, God "never experiences, whether with or without the world he has made, a sense of individual isolation and 'loneliness.' He never has been lonely or alone, in this sense, nor could he ever be, even in principle. The one God is three! He is by very nature both a unity of Being while also existing eternally as a society of Persons."[54] God is a relational being. He is social within himself and in relationship with his creation. Ware adds:

> In this tri-Personal relationship the three Persons love one another, support one another, assist one another, team with one another, honor one another, communicate with one another, and in everything respect and enjoy one another. They are in need of nothing but each other throughout all eternity. Such is the richness and the fullness and the completion of the social relationship that exists in the Trinity.[55]

Perichoresis reveals that God is not a distant, alone, or lonely deity who foregoes intimate interaction with persons; rather, God is intrinsically personal and therefore reaches out in love and offers humans what they most desperately need—a personal relationship with him.

Against the Islamic understanding (especially al-Warrāq's claim), the Trinity is not a contradiction but a paradox. According to *Bloomsbury Guide*

---

[53]Miroslav Volf, *After Our Likeness: The Church as the Image of the Trinity* (United Kingdom: Eerdmans, 1998), 209.

[54]Bruce A. Ware, *Father, Son, and Holy Spirit: Relationship, Roles, and Relevance* (Wheaton, IL: Crossway, 2005), 16.

[55]Ware, *Father, Son, and Holy Spirit*, 16.

to Human Thought, a paradox is a Greek word that means "Against expectation, in mathematics, is a pair of mutually contradictory statements, or apparently contradictory statements, which are both deductions from statements which are accepted as true."[56] The Trinity is an apparent contradiction to those who do not understand the progression of divine revelation. Christians believe that the Trinity is not a contradiction, because if it is, then God is one and not one at the same time and in the same sense and relationship. However, the Trinity is one divine being in one sense and three *Aqanīm* in another sense. In God, we find the eternal and singular being existing and expressing himself in the three *Aqanīm* of the Father, (who is not the Son or the Spirit), the Son (who is not the Father or the Spirit), and the Spirit (who is not the Father or the Son). The three members of the Godhead work together in harmony and in complementary roles. They are not three and one in the same sense—otherwise the Trinity would be a logical contradiction (*A* and *not A* at the same time).

Many Christian scholars like to offer illustrations from life and creation to explain the Trinity, as Abū Qurrah and ibn ᶜAdī did in the previous chapter. I personally do not like to use this method because, as stated earlier, the Trinity is not a mere concept: it is the being of God, and nothing in creation can be similar or equivalent to God. However, Ware's musical illustration might be useful to explain the concept of perichoresis, which is a philosophical concept about the relationship between the three *Aqanīm*, and does not define the divine being.[57] The perichoretic relationship between the *Aqanīm* might be illustrated as a musical band. There are different voices singing in different pitches. One carries the melody and others carry the strains of harmony to fill out and complement the melody. The one who carry the melody is important, but not alone, for all voices are important to

[56]*Bloomsbury Guide to Human Thought*, s.v. "Paradoxes," ed. Kenneth McLeish (Bloomsbury: 1993).

[57]Millard Erickson explains, "In Latin, the term came to be translated by two words, which represent two different understandings of the nature of persons, and which together capture the full meaning of the Greek. The word, *circuminsessio*, means literally 'to be seated in.' It conveys the more static conception of being located within one another. The word, *circumincessio*, is a more dynamic concept. It comes from a word meaning to permeate or interpenetrate. Together, these ideas as found in perichoresis, mean both permanence of location with respect to another and ongoing interchange or sharing." Millard Erickson, *God in Three Persons: A Contemporary Interpretation of the Trinity* (Grand Rapids, MI: Baker Books, 1995), 230. Ware, *Father, Son, and Holy Spirit*, 31.

achieve harmony. In order for this to happen, each part must be an expression of the same score and the same composition, expressing the mind of the composer.[58] The concept of perichoresis is similar: "God's unified nature expressed richly and beautifully in the three equal and full possessions and manifestations of that one nature, with each 'voice' contributing variously, yet with complete unity and identity of nature or essence."[59] As stated earlier, the three divine *Aqanīm* are not identical divine persons, but they are harmonious and complementarian in their roles of accomplishing God's one purpose, goal, and salvific work, since they each possess fully the one, undivided divine essence.

The trinitarian God is interrelational. In Christianity, God is not only intrarelational but also interrelational. The relational structure of the concept of divine relationality also includes God's relations with the world. Being relational means living in relationship with others and recognizing the interconnectedness with them. In a human sense, relationship with others means being engaged, centered, grounded, clear, generous, humble, and kind. A positive relationship with another person is always valued and hoped for. In Christianity, the triune God desires to have a personal, encountering relationship with his people and enter into a relationship with his creation. He is even willing to do more than that: he is willing to enter his creation to facilitate that relationship.

From beginning to end, and in virtually every chapter in between, the relational presence of God unifies and advances the biblical story. The Bible begins with God's presence relating to his people in Genesis and ends with God's presence relating to his people in Revelation. In the Old Testament, God enters into a covenantal relationship with Abraham and promises to bless him and his descendants. God's powerful presence appears to Moses in the burning bush and on Mount Sinai and is seen in the tabernacle and later in the temple. God's deliverance of his people from Egypt, protection through their journey in the wilderness, and direction into the Promised Land all point to God's presence and his desired relationship with his people. Throughout much of the Old Testament, God's covenantal relationship with Israel is revealed by an often repeated, three-part statement: "I will be your

---

[58]Ware, *Father, Son, and Holy Spirit*, 31.

[59]Ware, *Father, Son, and Holy Spirit*, 31.

God" (Ex 6:7; Jer 11:4), "you will be my people" (Jer 7:23), and "I will dwell in your midst" (Ezek 43:7, 9; Zech 2:11). This indicates that the concept of God dwelling among his people is foundational to his covenant with Israel; yet as a result of their continuous sin and disobedience, Israel was expelled from God's presence and sent into exile.

The restoration of God's presence promised throughout the Old Testament (Zech 2:10-13) is fulfilled in the New Testament when Jesus, Immanuel (God with us), appears. As Duvall and Hays state, "The incarnation brings to a climax the relational presence of God, the theme that drove the entire OT story."[60] The apostle John presents Christ as the Logos in two senses. The first refers to ordinary speech among people: "my word" (Jn 8:37) and "the word of the woman" (Jn 4:39). The second refers to a theological title of a historical person: the Word (Jn 1:1-2, 14), the Word of life (1 Jn 1:1), and the Word of God (Rev 19:13). John introduces the Word as being always in a relationship with the Father, who came to the world (through incarnation) to disclose God and his nature to us. He came to reveal that the transcendent God, who is above humanity, draws near to be in relationship with human beings. The doctrine of the incarnation reveals that the Son became a human person at a specific point in time, being born as a baby and living life on earth as the God-man. Jesus, as "the radiance of the glory of God and the exact imprint of his nature," further reveals the deeply personal nature of the triune God (Heb 1:3 ESV).

As Shehadeh declares, God, upon his presence in the incarnation, "did not stop at giving humanity revelations to understand with their minds; he himself came to guide each individual personally. He did not stop at giving humanity laws to try to obey in their own efforts; he himself came to grant power to each individual personally."[61] While revelation stresses Jesus' exalted and glorified status, it also affirms his incarnation as a significant aspect of God's relational presence.

God's relationality culminates in the crucifixion and the resurrection of Jesus. While God longs for a relationship with humanity, their sins prevent that relationship. God is holy, and human beings are sinful. The only

---

[60]J. Scott Duvall and J. Daniel Hays, *God's Relational Presence: The Cohesive Center of Biblical Theology* (Grand Rapids, MI: Baker Academic, 2019), 22.

[61]Shehadeh, *God with Us and Without Us*, 465-66.

solution was for God to take upon himself the initiative to draw humanity closer through the death and the resurrection of Jesus. The end goal is to establish God's kingdom, where he will dwell among his people forever.

The relational story of God and humanity does not end with Jesus' death or resurrection; the last revelation of God does not end with Jesus nor with an eschatological hope for the future. In the book of Acts, after Jesus' ascension, the Holy Spirit comes to dwell within each believer. Just as the holy presence of God in the Old Testament dwelled in the temple, the promised Spirit comes on the day of Pentecost in fulfillment of God's promise to live within and among God's people (e.g., Acts 2 fulfilling the promise of Joel 2:28). Jesus refers to the Spirit as another (of the same kind) "advocate" or "helper" (Jn 14:16), who testifies about Jesus, reminds the disciples of his teachings, guides them into all truth, and discloses what is to come (Jn 14:26; 15:26; 16:13). One of the primary roles of the Holy Spirit is to assure believers of God's presence in their lives (1 Jn 3:24).[62] God's relational presence drives the story line from beginning to end, consistently unifying the biblical metanarrative and moving the divine plot toward the ultimate goal of God living with his people in the new creation.

Conclusion

The Qur'an reveals Allah as contingently relational. Because of the doctrine of *tawḥīd*, the extent to which Allah is a relational deity is debatable. Islamic scholars view Allah as the "One and Indivisible" (Surah 112:1) agent who created this world; therefore, he is highly transcendent above it. Islamic scholar Seyyed Hossein Nasr affirms that "the Quran continuously emphasizes the Unity and the oneness of God, and it can be said that the very raison d'être of Islam is to assert in a final and categorical manner the oneness of God and the nothingness of all before the Majesty of that One."[63] This view, consequently, makes Allah alone before the creation of the universe. At that time, there was no one to see, hear, or speak to—especially before the creation of human beings. Arguably, without the concept of the Trinity, one cannot hold an eternally relational conception of God because many attributes of personality are expressed within the

[62]Duvall and Hays, *God's Relational Presence*, 254.

[63]Seyyed Hossein Nasr, *Islam: Religion, History, and Civilization* (New York: HarperOne, 2002), 3, 6.

context of a relationship—in addition to things like seeing, hearing, and speaking there are things like love, communication, empathy, and self-giving. The functionality of such attributes before the world came into being is open to challenge, making it impossible to see as Allah intrinsically and eternally relational. If Allah is truly the seer, the hearer, and the communicator, one must presume that these attributes were dysfunctional until Allah created the world. In that case, Allah would be dependent on creation, which appears to be at odds with what Surah 112:2 says: "Allah—the Sustainer needed by all." A dependent deity would be merely a minor deity because he needs his creation to be able to speak, see, and hear.

The Bible reveals God as eternally relational. The Christian view of the divine (one God who exists in three *Aqanīm*) seems to present God as eternally relational and independent of his creation. The three *Aqanīm* within the Godhead, (distinct, yet not separate) who exist in a relationship with one another, present the personal and loving nature of God. Their interpenetrating relationship exists at the center of the universe. Because of this special relationship within the Godhead (via the three divine *Aqanīm*), God does not need the creation to see, hear, communicate, or be compassionate. All his acts/attributes were functional before the creation of the world within the Godhead. All of God's actions in history are expressions of this intimate, personal relationship that exists at the very heart of ultimate reality.

The reciprocal and mutual relationship between the three *Aqanīm* demonstrates the nature of God's relationship with the world, which is the key to knowing God as well. The way God relates to himself and to creation helps human beings realize that the world arose not as a self-unfolding divine subject, but through the will of God, who as a free being brought forth a world out of an overflow of love. The world is the product of the mutual activity of the Father, the Son, and the Holy Spirit, not just a product of his power. God is relational—with the world or without it. He does not need the world to be social. He has accomplished his relationality within himself through the *Aqanīm*. Thus, God is not dependent on other agents to activate his attributes as the seer, the hearer, and the communicator.

The assumption is that Christians and Muslims agree when it comes to the perfect being theology because God already has specified his perfection in the Bible and the Qur'an. No improvement in respect to power, morals, duration, presence, or anything of the kind is possible for him. If whatever is divine is perfect, then it would be better to be necessarily perfect than to be contingently perfect. Therefore, being necessary relational is better than being contingently relational.

Being perfect does not allow an attribute that is incompatible with perfection to exist. If being relational in all respects is a perfection, then it is better to have it necessarily than contingently. If whatever is divine is perfect, then it is necessary that whatever is securely and permanently divine is securely and permanently perfect.[64] "If it is possible to be securely and permanently divine, it is possible to be securely and permanently perfect."[65] Therefore, an omniscient, omnipotent, and perfectly relational being who can maintain his relationality is more perfect than the one who cannot maintain his rationality (even if he chooses to). Therefore, an omnipotent God is the one who is able to secure things (e.g., seeing, hearing, and having a relationship) permanently So his rationality renders his choice permanent.[66] The maximum of security and permanence in perfection would be having relationality of God necessarily. If an eternally relational divine being is better than a contingently divine being, and his relationality is compatible with the rest of his attributes, then perfect-being theology lies within the court of Christianity, and the doctrine of the Trinity, not the doctrine of *tawhīd*, is the only model that shows God eternally relational.

---

[64]Brian Leftow, *God and Necessity* (Oxford: Oxford University Press, 2012), 195-97.

[65]Leftow, *God and Necessity*, 195-97. Leftow explains that it is possible to be more or less permanently perfect—if both A and B are perfect at all points in their lives, but A has a longer life, A is more permanently perfect than B. It is also possible to be more or less securely so. And by the same token, plausibly it is better to be more rather than less securely and permanently perfect. So perfection must be had with the maximum security and permanence with which it can be had.

[66]Leftow, *God and Necessity*, 197.

Conclusion

CHRISTIAN-MUSLIM RELATIONS in the eighth, ninth, and tenth centuries resulted in the rise of Islamic theology (kalām). The House of Wisdom established by Hārūn al-Rashīd, the translation work that was carried out by the Syriac scholars, and the debates between Muslims and Christians in the presence of the caliphs paved the way for the development of Islamic theology. Christians (Chalcedonians, Jacobites, and the Church of the East) were already known for being multilingual and profoundly rooted in Greek philosophy, and they spent centuries developing their theology against various heresies—especially in relation to the Trinity and Christology. During this time, many learned, wrote, and preached in the Arabic language because Muslims were not willing to learn the local languages, but they spread Arabic, the language of the Qur'an, in schools and public systems. As a result, the first part of the Abbasid century saw an unprecedented rise in Arabic Christian apologetic writings directed against Islam.

Various Islamic schools of thought started emerging during this time of history, forming many standard belief systems (e.g., Qadarites, Jabrites, Ashᶜarites, Muᶜtazilites, Murjiᶜites, Kharijites, and Shiᶜites). Muᶜtazilites enjoyed a golden period of theological and political dominance during al-Ma'mūn's reign, which had implications for the nature of the Christian-Muslim debates during this period. The discussion about Allah's speech, the nature of the Qur'an, and Allah's attributes started in this period and carried on until the Ashᶜarites became the majority view in the eleventh century, in addition to many Christian apologies that were devised to defend Christian beliefs against Islamic objections.

During this time, the doctrine of the Trinity was widely accepted in most Christian communities. By the end of the fourth century, the expression "one ousia and three hypostases" was settled within the Christian tradition. However, the historical discussion of the doctrine of the Trinity is completely ignored in the Qur'an. The Qur'anic understating of the Trinity includes Mary as a divine person within the Godhead. This perspective was never part of orthodox Christianity throughout its history; however, it seems that Mohammad perhaps inferred the divinity of Mary from another source. Many studies written on this topic suggest that Mohammad learned about the nonconventional Trinity (God the Father, God the Mother, and God the Son) from cultic Christians or nonorthodox communities who lived in the Arabian Peninsula during the seventh century. This research shows that while the previous studies are possible, there is no sufficient Islamic historical information that suggests that Mohammad was in contact with such communities. The Christian information about cultic Christianity in Arabia is scarce, and the historical Islamic records suggest that Mohammad was in contact with Christians who had decorated churches. During that time of history, holy icon veneration was rejected by the Western church, but venerating icons was flourishing in the East. The *Theotokos* icon and many other icons were widely spreading and decorating the Eastern churches. Mohammad probably developed a nonorthodox understanding of the Trinity by observing Christian icons, especially the *Theotokos* icon.

The first objection this study addresses is classified as nonhistorical because the Qur'an ignores the historical development of the doctrine of the Trinity, especially the Nicene Creed. While Mohammad was in contact with Christians in the Levant, Arabia (Makkah and Medina), and Africa (through his wives), he heard and most likely saw the Christian icons—the most famous of which is the *Theotokos* icon. His contact with this icon probably happened in the Levant when he was a young man, in Makkah inside al-Ka^{c}aba, or from his wife who went to Ethiopia at the beginning of his calling and came back reporting about a magnificent icon of Mary she had seen in Africa. Since there is no historical evidence—from Islamic or Christian sources—that suggests that Mohammad learned about the divinity of Mary from orthodox or cultic Christians, it is reasonable to think that his understanding of Mary and her divine role was acquired by inference rather than by cultic teachings. In other words, knowing that

Christians believe in the Trinity and seeing them venerating the icons—especially the *Theotokos* icon—might have played a major role in Mohammad's misunderstanding of the Trinity, which he then conveyed in the Qur'an.

The second group of objections is semantic in nature and related to the three *Aqanīm*. The titles "Father" and "Son" are understood in both literal and anthropomorphic senses. The Father had a wife who bore him a son, and they called him Isa. The Father, Son, and Spirit are three deities who resemble the polytheistic nature of the Christian worldview. Theodore Abū Qurrah, who was attentive to this objection, argues that every perfection apparent in creation must also be a prediction of the creator. He based his argument on Surah 3:59: "Surely the likeness of Isa is with Allah as the likeness of Adam." If Adam did not beget a son, then he would be the head and the representative of animals, such as pigs, asses, and worms, who have a paltry nature compared to humans. In this way, Adam would be just a representative of what is below him in nature. Begetting a son makes Adam the head and the representative of all humanity. In the same sense, those who say God does not beget attribute deprivation to his divinity by making him ruler over what is less than he is and unable to rule over what resembles him.

In relation to this objection, Abū Qurrah distinguishes between logical and nonlogical names. He explains that logical names indicate persons, such as Peter, Paul, and John, and nonlogical names indicate natures, such as man. While logical names can be many, nonlogical names are collective in nature and singular in form. The number three does not apply to the names because it indicates human nature. While it is correct to say Peter, Paul, and John are three men, it is not correct to say Peter is mankind. In the same sense, God is a name that indicates divine nature; whereas Father, Son, and Holy Spirit are names that indicate three divine *Aqanīm*. The essence of God cannot be plural, and the titles Father, Son, and Holy Spirit attribute plurality to the Godhead, not to his essence.

The third group of objections is called the nonrational objections, which are agreed upon by most ancient, medieval, and contemporary Muslim scholars who accuse Christians of being nonlogical in their explanation of the Trinity. The idea of believing in three persons and calling them one God is illogical to the Muslim mind. Yaḥya Ibn Adī takes the rational route and provides answers that might be applied to the semantic and the nonlogical objections. Using philosophy, he discusses the concept of *al-wāḥid*. Muslims call Allah *al-wāḥid* to convey that he is one (divine being) in a numerical sense. Yaḥya, who was attentive to this objection, was the first Arab Christian philosopher to argue that the creator is one in one sense and multiple in another sense. Being one is one aspect of the meaning of *al-wāḥid*, not the full meaning, because *wāḥid* can be understood in many different senses. God is one as a divine person, but he cannot be one in genus, species, relation, or continuum because all these types of essences require either the existence of others or a causal connection to exist. However, God is the uncaused cause of everything. While he causes other things to exist, he cannot be caused by anything/anyone else. Moreover, it is semantically and philosophically wrong to understand *wāḥid* in one sense, which is the numerical, because *wāḥid* does not refer only to quantity but also to quality, such as qualitative names referring to color and taste. Restricting the meaning of *wāḥid* to the numerical sense is a mistake because the word has several meanings and can be understood in different senses. Some of them can be applied to God, while others cannot.

While Muslims follow the doctrine of *bila kayfa* in regard to Allah's attributes, they refuse to compare Allah to any of his creation. They believe that Allah is transcendent and that it is demeaning to the divine nature to be compared with human nature, for there are no similarities that can be discovered. John of Damascus, Abū Qurrah, and Yaḥya, on the other hand, base the doctrine of God's attributes on the concept that every perfection apparent in creation must also have precedence in the creator. Realizing that the attributes of perfection in God are unrestricted and eternal in contrast to those in man, Yaḥya explains that it is wrong to say that nothing is similar to God because similarity does not require complete matching identification. There are no two similar persons/things that are identical in all their attributes. If two persons/things are similar, it is necessary that they do not match. They are similar in one aspect, but they are different in many. They are not identical, and not all their attributes align. Yaḥya's explanation answers the problem of anthropomorphism and logically explains that Christians are not wrong when they look at the virtues of human beings to extract the attributes of God.

The danger of separating God's actions from his nature is that it impairs a person's knowledge of what is real and objective about God as he is in himself. Separating the attributes of action from the attributes of essence deprives the essence of its content and meaning, for God is not a mere substance essentially separated from his attributes. Such a notion would reduce the divine essence to a barren concept, a hypothesis devoid of content and meaning. "God's being is not the bearer of the divine attributes; rather, God's essence and attributes are identical."[1] Thus, preventing reflection on the essence of God amounts to preventing God from revealing wonders about himself, and this robs humankind of understanding God's relationship with his creation and his purposes for it. This is a narrow but revealing point that can be identified at the end of the eighth and early ninth centuries as Muslims came to a greater awareness of Christian thoughts about the divine attributes, the *sifat* Allah. This encounter helped bring Islam to a greater theological and philosophical maturity, while Christians confronted the challenge of translating traditional doctrines into a new idiom.

While many Muslim scholars refuse to compare Allah to any of his creations to learn about his transcendence, Western philosophers use reason, philosophy, and metaphysics to learn about the nature of God. They believe there is no problem using human reason as long as they admit it is fallible. While Western philosophers know that learning the divine nature is almost impossible, they believe that learning something about it is possible and it should be done. It is better to try and fail, than not to try at all. Analytic theologians and philosophers can learn and improve each other's arguments by debating, conversing, and reviewing them, instead of just criticizing and declaring those who try as heretics.

The best example of this that I can think of is Brian Leftow's argument of the Latin Trinity and how it can form an excellent answer to the neo-orthodox theologian Karl Barth, who rejected the view of the divine persons and the distinct centers of consciousness and will. Barth explicitly believes that the numerical unity of the essence of the persons should be presumed. He also proposes the term "mode of being" as a replacement for the traditional term person/s. He cautions against thinking there is anything like an

[1]Carl F. H. Henry, *God, Revelation and Authority: God Who Stands and Stays*, vol. 5 (Wheaton, IL: Crossway, 1999), 130.

"I—Thou" relationship within the Trinity: "we are speaking not of three divine I's, but thrice of the one divine I."[2] Thus there are not

> three different personalities, three self-existent individuals with their own special self-consciousness, cognition, volition, activity, effects, revelation, and name. The one name of the one God is the threefold name of Father, Son and Holy Spirit. The one "personality" of God, the one active and speaking divine Ego, is Father, Son, and Holy Spirit. Otherwise we should obviously have to speak of three gods.[3]

If we do, then we will be speaking about mythology. Instead, Barth insists on understating the modes of being of God as God revealed three times in different senses. God the Son is God a second time in a different way. The divine name, "The name of the Father, Son and Spirit means that God is the one God in threefold repetition."[4] There is one divine "I," who subsists simultaneously in three different ways or three different modes of being. At the same time, Barth wanted to use the three-person account. He regularly speaks of the love and fellowship between the Father and the Son. But how can this love be manifested if there are no persons?

Brian Leftow's model becomes handy here because both Leftow and Barth resist the social-trinitarian model, they both insist on the numerical oneness of God in threefold repetitions, and they both want to avoid modalism and polytheism. But where Barth leaves the reader perplexed and confused, Leftow provides an analogy and set of claims that offer help to Barth's model. As McCall states, "If Leftow's model successfully avoids modalism, it might offer coherence to Barth's account—which otherwise remains puzzling at best and perhaps even internally unstable."[5] This is not to say that I believe in the Latin trinitarian model, but this is to illustrate the importance of discussions, debates, and collaborations that happen among scholars.

Building on the early Christian Arab and Western apologies on the Trinity, the topic of the relationality of God emerges as the most important

---

[2]Karl Barth, *Church Dogmatics I.1: The Doctrine of the Word of God*, trans. G. W. Bromiley (Edinburgh: T&T Clark, 1975), 351.

[3]Karl Barth, *Church Dogmatics IV.1: The Doctrine of Reconciliation*, trans. G. W. Bromiley (Edinburgh: T&T Clark, 1956), 205.

[4]Barth, *Church Dogmatics I.1*, 350.

[5]Thomas McCall, "Theologians, Philosophers, and the Doctrine of the Trinity," in *Philosophical and Theological Essays on the Trinity* (Oxford: Oxford University Press, 2009), 339.

aspect of this study. Relationality of God is an essential divine attribute that was not given much attention in Islamic and Christian Arab theologies. The trinitarian model of divinity demonstrates that God is eternally relational because he is intrarelational and interrelational. He is intrarelational within himself in the Godhead, as the three *Aqanīm* live in eternal harmonious relationship of love, honor, and respect. God is fundamentally a community of divine *Aqānīm,* who has never experienced loneliness and isolation, whether with or without the world. God is in need of nothing to practice his relationality. He is not dependent on his creation to be able to see, hear, communicate, and love. He is the seer, the hearer, the communicator from eternity to eternity. Such is the richness and the fullness and the completion of the social relationship that exists in the Trinity.

Although Muslims believe that Allah interacted and communicated with humanity, the nature of the interrelationality of God with creation is shown differently within Islam and Christianity. In Christianity, the triune God moves closer to human beings throughout history, further revealing the personal nature of the Godhead. In the Old Testament, God pursues human beings in the Garden. When the fall occurs, he offers help and guidance on how to live a holy life. In the New Testament, the second person of the Trinity, Jesus, takes on human flesh in order to dwell among human beings, ultimately repairing their personal relationship with God (Phil 2:6-11). Additionally, the third person of the Trinity—the Holy Spirit—following Jesus' ascension to heaven, is sent to dwell and live within believers. God pursues his creation through the incarnation of the Son and the indwelling of the Holy Spirit.

The divine Islamic concept of relationality, on the other hand, is not eternal. Because of absolute oneness, Allah is contingent in his relationship with creation. When there is no concept of plurality in the Godhead, his relational attributes seem to be dysfunctional, and therefore, God's essence is dependent on his creation. In Islamic theology, Allah is attributed as the seer (the one who sees everything) and the hearer (the one who hears everything); however, based on the absolute oneness model, he was not always able to see or hear everything because before creation there was nothing to see or hear. This presentation of the divine makes some aspects of the deity contingent on creation.

The Islamic view differs from the Christian view in two aspects: (1) the creation of human beings is not Allah's priority. (2) The most important goal in creating the world is to show Allah's power and magnificence. The Islamic understanding of creation implies that the created world has more value than human beings. Mohammad states, "Certainly the creation of the heavens and the earth is greater than the creation of the men, but most people do not know" (Surah 40:57). Man is not the greatest creative act of Allah, and the universe is far more complex and magnificent than man. The ultimate purpose, however, for creating human beings is for them to worship Allah (Surah 51:56). In other words, Allah created human beings to show his glory and majesty, not to start a relationship with them. Ibn Kathīr explains in his commentary that "worship Allah" means "I [Allah] created them to command them to worship me, not because I need them."[6] Despite the fact that God's relationality does not necessarily mean that he needs his creation, in the Islamic view, creation is the natural consequence of the creator who cares about showing his power and dominion more than expressing his love toward his creatures. The concept of the ultimate power of the divine is the most important aspect in Islamic belief; however, it ignores the relationality of the divine.

If Allah is the greatest, how can human beings know, acknowledge, and worship his greatness without having a relationship with him? Relationality is what teaches humanity about the divine. It implies that the value the world has for God is in expressing, not in constituting. Moreover, the eternal relationality of God increases the value of the world before God—precisely because God does not need it to be God. The world, therefore, takes on the beauty of grace and free love that is greater than the necessity of power and domination. God saves because he loves and has mercy, not only because he is free. His love is based on a decision he made long before the world was created.

Worshiping the divine for his absolute power and magnificence without having a relationship with him makes human beings slaves. In this scenario, their relationship with the divine is to acknowledge his grandeur and majesty without being able to closely open up to him. He is like a master receiving

[6]Abū al-fidā Ismaʿīl Ibn Kathīr, *The Explanation of the Great Qur'an* (Beirut: Dar Ibn Ḥazm, 2000), 1768.

honor rather than a father who cares about the well-being of his sons and daughters. While the slave-master relationship is based on command and obedience, the father-son relationship is about respect, nourishment, and protection. Slaves seek to please their masters because they fear punishment, whereas sons and daughters seek to please and honor their father because they love him and he loves them. Love, respect, and sustenance are the foundational elements of this relationship, not fear and trembling.

Unfortunately, when twenty-first century Christians think about the word *God*, they do not think about the Trinity. Like in the Islamic view, people think of God as the most powerful, eternal spiritual being who is the creator of the universe. In most people's understanding, God is also a moral judge who will ultimately decide who gets to spend eternity in heaven or in hell. The hope of this study is to encourage Christians to think of God as the Trinity first before contemplating his majesty, expectation, and commands. The eternal existence of God as Father, Son, and Holy Spirit was the central affirmation of the ancient church and the fundamental truth from which all other theological understanding flowed, and I hope this notion continues and does not fade into obscurity.

Finally, it is significant for the purposes of Christian-Islamic discussion that the parties involved in such debates and apologetical writings understand themselves to be seeking a common end—a clearer expression of true statements about God and all of creation. The purpose of this study is directed toward this goal. It is not the writer's intention to offend the Islamic presentation of the divine but to push the conversation toward a more reformed view that honors God. A successful participation in such dialogue means not simply that one has convinced one's opponent, but hopefully that the discussion is furthered toward a better end.

The status of Christianity in Arabia is a fascinating topic that deserves more attention and research. Few scholars have attempted to write on this topic because of political reasons. For more than fifty years, Saudi Arabia was a closed country ruled by Shari^{c}a law. However, recent changes have introduced more liberties in the kingdom that might usher in educational opportunities that need to be taken advantage of. Excavation was banned in Saudi Arabia; therefore, most of the historical arguments about cultic Christianity were either arguments from silence or based on the limited testimonies of early church fathers. Mohammad's connection with these cults cannot be historically confirmed, such as the case with the Collyridians/Marian cults. Hopefully, such research will be allowed soon in the Arabian Peninsula, which might reveal more information regarding Christianity in that community, the Syriac community in the Arabian gulf, and the Christian community in Najran.

The project of commending Christian doctrine in an Islamic environment is an area that should be further explored for three distinct reasons. First, learning the source of Mohammad's understanding of the Trinity would help with further discoveries about other topics, such as Jesus' nature and his miracles in the Qur'an. Further findings about Christian doctrine in an Islamic environment will help apologists immensely today. Second, learning about the history of Christianity in the Arabian Peninsula would help with the study of historical Mohammad. Many European scholars are advocating for the nonhistorical view of the Islamic prophet, pushing the origination of Islam to the Levant under the Umayyad dynasty. Excavation works in the Arabian Peninsula would help reveal whether their arguments are factual or false. Third, excavations in general have an unpredictable nature regarding what scholars might find. Sometimes excavations affirm their predictions, and sometimes they surprise them completely with new discoveries. Scholars might be able to find additional biblical manuscripts, apocryphal literature, and hymnals that early Arab Christians used in their masses and prayer times.

There are several Arab Christian theologians and philosophers that are not known in the West. This study has shed some light on Theodore Abū Qurrah's theology and Yaḥya Ibn ᶜAdī's philosophy, especially related to their defense of the Trinity. Grasping their works and presenting their ideas to the public arena of Western thought is one of the unfinished projects of this study. Abū Qurrah left a great inventory of literature in Greek and Arabic that has not yet been translated into English. There are potential studies to be written about Abū Qurrah's theological and apologetical methodology, his defense against iconoclasm, and his theory of human free will, among other things.

Like Abū Qurrah, Yaḥya's Christian philosophical works are not translated into English and deserve considerable attention. In fact, what makes his apologetics unique is his Aristotelian philosophical background. He was one of those who translated the works of Aristotle into Arabic. He also was a student of the famous Islamic philosopher al-Fārābī. His discussion of *al-waḥid* is unique because he took most of his ideas from his Muslim professor and applied it to his understanding of the divine. The most important book he left is about morality, called *Tahdhīb al-Akhlāq* [Refining Ethics]. According to Nadine Abbas, it is one of the most important books about the philosophy of ethics in the Arabic world.[7] Translating this book into English will contribute profoundly to the fields of ethics and theology.

Among the points most relevant and most worthy of further consideration is the doctrine of creation in Islam in relation to the doctrine of *tawḥīd*. The multiple views of the doctrine of creation and the schism between traditionalists and philosophers would lead to multiple understandings of *tawḥīd* and potentially to a misunderstanding of the doctrine of Allah. Traditionalists deny the philosophers' suggestions regarding the creation of the world. As briefly presented in this study, some medieval philosophers believed in the eternality of time, and others believed in creation by emanation. Their beliefs threaten the doctrine of *tawḥīd* because they assume an eternal nature of the universe is necessary. However, creating another eternal reality alongside Allah is inconsistent with the nature of absolute oneness because it makes Muslims binitarian monotheists, not unitarians as they claim.

The same problem might be applied to the Qur'an when scholars assume its eternal nature. The eternal nature of the Qur'an makes Muslims binitarian as well, requiring them to clarify how the Qur'an relates to Allah's absolute oneness. The Qur'an's purpose is to deliver a divine message that has a dialogic character. If this is true, how can the Qur'an (the eternal) communicate with human beings (the noneternal)—especially since the Qur'an is written for people, not for angels? To speak of the Qur'an as a distinct eternal reality to Allah is similar to speaking of the *Logos* as a distinct eternal reality to the Father. Muslims reject such belief and consider it a *shirk* (association). Therefore, further illumination is required as to the double standard of allowing the Qur'an and the creation to have distinct eternal realities from

[7]Nadine Abbas, "al-Falsafa wa al-Lahoot was al-Akhlaq 'ind Yaḥya ibn ᶜAdī" [The Philosophy, Theology, and Ethics of Yaḥya ibn ᶜAdī], *Tafahum Magazine* (2015): 137. Retrieved from https://tafahom.mara.gov.om/storage/al-tafahom/ar/2015/048/pdf/07.pdf.

Allah, but not granting this liberty to the *Logos*. Why is otherness allowed to be predicated in Allah by Muslims and not considered *shirk*, whereas Christians are not allowed such concept in their theology?

Moving from Islam's foundational era to more modern theological developments, the topic of the relationality of God has an apologetic potential against process theology. To classify the relationality of God as an attribute of essence is to make God a personal being. Process theologians, such as Paul Tillich, advocate for the concept of "God as Being." In Tillich's view, God is not a Being, because that would describe God as one "being" among other beings. Rather, "God is being itself"—or "the ground of being."[8] If God as the ground of being infinitely transcends everything, then whatever one knows about a finite thing one knows about God, because it is rooted in him as its ground. At the same time, anything one knows about a finite thing cannot be applied to God, because he is, as Tillich says, "ecstatically experienced and symbolically expressed."[9]

Another topic Tillich talks about is the distinction between a "sign" and a "symbol." "Signs" (like letters and written words) have no essential connection to what they represent but are merely used to point to their referent. "Symbols," on the other hand, have a stronger similarity or "participation" with the thing to which they refer. Religious symbols negate themselves in their literal meanings but still have something to say about God, including his qualities, actions, and manifestations. They have a symbolic character, but the meaning of "God" is completely missed if one takes the symbolic language literally. God's "fatherhood" for instance is a symbol because of the fatherly qualities that God and other fathers share. The letters *G-O-D* share nothing essential with God and are therefore only a "sign" for God. Process theology turns God from a personal being into an idea; therefore, by focusing on the relational aspect of God, conservative theologians have an argument to turn God into a Being in a personal way, not just as a symbol. While someone might suggest that all "Godtalk" is symbolic and does not exhaust the mystery of God's being, the analogy of personal encounter and the use of person as a theological model have distinct advantages over impersonal approaches to the problem.

---

[8]Paul Tillich, *Systematic Theology*, vol. 1 (Chicago: University of Chicago Press, 1967), 84.
[9]Tillich, *Systematic Theology*, 148-49.

To Christians, the centrality of the doctrine of the Trinity cannot be denied. To them, the Trinity is not a problem to be solved but rather a beauty to be discovered, a mystery to be clarified, and a Being to have a relationship with. Their readiness to receive God's revelation of himself, like a beauty and a mystery, provides growing knowledge with no end. The Trinity is not a contradiction or a barrier to belief; rather, it is the being of God, whose discovery is an unending worship.

Bibliography

Abbas, Nadine. "al-Falsafa wa al-Lahoot was al-Akhlaq ʻind Yaḥya ibn ᶜAdī" [The Philosophy, Theology, and Ethics of Yaḥya ibn ᶜAdī]." *Tafahum Magazine* (2015): 138-68. Retrieved from https://tafahom.mara.gov.om/storage/al-tafahom/ar/2015/048/pdf/07.pdf.

———. "Mafhoom al-Ulohiya ʻind Yaḥya ibn Adi in the Book of Maqala fi al Mawjoodat [Yaḥya's concept of divinity in the book "the Reply to al-Waraq and the Article of the Findings"]," *Dar Al-Machreq Magazine* 87, no. 1 (2013): Kindle.

———. *Nathariyat al-Tawhid wa al-Tathleeth of Yaḥya Ibn Adi fi Kitabihi ʻal-Rad ʻAla al- Warrāq'* [Yaḥya Ibn ᶜAdī's Philosophical Theory of Monotheism and Tri-theism in his book The Reply to al-Warrāq']. Beirut, Lebanon: Centre de recherche et de publications de L'orient Chretien, 2014.

ʻabd al-Rahman, A'isha. *Nisa' al-Nabi* [The Prophet's Wives] (self-published).

Abrahamov, Binyamin. "Al-Ḳāsim Ibn Ibrāhīm's Theory of the Imamate." *Arabica* T. 34 (1987): 80-105.

Al-Azmeh, Aziz. *The Emergence of Islam in Late Antiquity: Allah and His People*. Cambridge: Cambridge University Press, 2014.

Al-Azraqī, Abī al-Tawlīd. *Akhbar Makkah wa ma ja'a fiha min Akhbar [The News of Makkah and Its Ruins]*. Edited and published by Abdula Dahīsh, 2003.

Al-Balādhurī, Abū al-ᶜabās. *Kitāb Futḥāt al-Buldān the Origins of the Islamic State*. Translated by P. K. Hitti. New York and London, 1916.

Al-Farābī, Abū Nasr. *The One and the Unity*. Casablanca: Dar Tobqal Publishing, 1990.

Al-Gazālī. *Ninety-Nine Names of God in Islam: A Translation of the Major Portion of Al-Gazālī's al-Maqsad and al-Asnā*. Translated by Robert Stade. Ibadan, Nigeria: Daystar Press, 1970.

Al-Ḥarīrī, Abu Musa, *Priest and Prophet*. Diar ʻAkil, Lebanon: Dar Li'ajl al-Ma'rifa, 2005.

Al-Juwaynī. *A Guide to the Conclusive Proofs for the Principles of Belief: Al-Irshad*. Translated by Paul E. Walker. Reading, UK: Garnet Publishing, 2001.

Allies, Mary H, trans. *John of Damascus on the Holy Images*. London, UK: Thomas Baker, 1898.

Al-Muqaddasī, Muḥammad Ibn Aḥmad. *Kitab Ahsan al-taqasim fi maʻrifat al-aqalinm*. Edited by M. J. de Goeje. Leiden: Brill, 1967.

Al-Qāsimī, Jamāl al-Dīn. *Maḥāsin al-taʼwīl*. Vol. 6. Cairo, Egypt: Dārihyāʼ al-kutub al-ʻarabiyya, 1957.

Al-Qortobi, Muhammad Iben Ahmad. "Tafsir Al-Qortobi." Ar-Riyadh, Saudi Arabia, 2003. Accessed December 13, 2020. https://quran.ksu.edu.sa/tafseer/qortobi/sura9-aya29.html #qortobi.

Al-Rassī, Al-Qāsim Ibn Ibrāhīm al-Husnī. *al-Rad ʻAla al-Nassara* [The Reply to the Christians]. Edited by Hanafi Abduallah. Cairo, Egypt: Dar al-Afaq al-Arabia, 2000.

Al-Shahrastānī. Al-Shahrastānī, *Nihāyat Al-Iqdām fī ᶜlm al-Kalām* [The End of the Process of Kalam Science]. Cairo, Egypt: Maktabat al-Thaqafa al-Diniya, 2009.

Al-Sharafī, ᶜabd al-Majīd. *The Islamic Thought about the Reply to the Christians: To the End of the Tenth Century*. Tunisia: al-Dar al-Tunisya LilNashir, 1986.

Al-Sijistānī, Abū Sulaymān. *Muntakhab Siwan al-Hikma*. ᶜAbd Arahman Badawī. Teheran: Foundation Cultilrelle de l'Iran. 1974.

Al-Ṭabarī, Muhammad Ibn Jarīr. *Tafsīr al-Tabarī*. Accessed December 12, 2020. https://quran.ksu.edu.sa/tafseer/tabary/sura5-aya72.html#tabary.

Al-Ṭaḥāwī, Abū Jaᶜfar. *Al-Aqīdah al-Tahāwiyyah*. Translated by Abū Amīna Elias. Accessed March 3, 2024. www.abuaminaelias.com/aqeedah-tahawiyyah.

Al-Waḥidī, Abī Ḥasan ᶜalī. *Asbāb al-Nuzūl* [The Reasons of Revelation]. Edited by ᶜiṣām al-Ḥmīdān, Dammam, Saudi Arabia: Dar al-Iṣlāḥ, 1992.

Al-Warrāq, Muḥammad ibn Hārūn Abū ᶜĪsā. *Anti-Christian Polemic in Early Islam: Abū ᶜĪsā al-Warrāq's "Against the Trinity."* Edited & translated by David Thomas. Cambridge: Cambridge University Press, 1992.

al-Yasu'ī, Samir Khalil. "Maqala fi al-Tawhid [An Article in Divine Oneness]." In *al-Turath al-Arabi al-Masiḥi* [the Arabic Christian Heritage]. Jounieh, Lebanon: Al-Maktaba al-Boulissiah, 1980.

Al-Yazaji, Kamal. *Youhana al-Dimishqi: Ara'oh al-Lahootiya wa Masael 'ilm al-Kalam* [John of Damascus: His Theological Opinions and the Issues of Theology]. Beirut, Lebanon: Manshūrat al-Nūr, 1984.

———. *Ma'alim al-Fikir al-'Arabi fi al-'Asar al-Wasit* [Highlights of the Arab Thought in the Middle Ages]. Beirut: Dar Al-ᶜlm Lilmalayīn, 1979.

Ash-Shahristānī. *Nihāyat al-Iqdā fī ᶜilm al-Kalām*. Baghdad, Iraq: Muthanah.

At-Tabriz, Imam Khatib. *Mishkat al-Masabih*. Vol. 22. Ḥadīth no. 195. Accessed February 20, 2021. https://sunnah.com/mishkat:4508.

Augustine. *On the Trinity* 6.10.12. www.newadvent.org/fathers/130106.htm.

———. *On the Trinity*. 7.2.3. www.newadvent.org/fathers/130107.htm.

———., "On the Trinity." In *St. Augustin: On the Holy Trinity, Doctrinal Treatises, Moral Treatises*, edited by Philip Schaff. Translated by Arthur West Haddan. Buffalo, NY: Christian Literature Company, 1887.

Awad, Najib George. *Orthodoxy in Arabic Terms: A Study of Theodore Abu Qurrah's Theology in Its Islamic Context*. Boston: De Gruyter, 2015.

Baber, H. E. "The Trinity: Relative Identity Redux." *Faith and Philosophy: Journal of the Society of Christian Philosophers* 32, no. 2 (2015): 161-71.

Baggett, David and Jerry Walls. *Good God: The Theistic Foundations of Morality*. Oxford: Oxford University Press, 2011.

Barasch, Moshe. *Icon: Studies in the History of an Idea*. New York: New York University Press, 1995.

Barış, Mustafa Necati. "First Translation Activities in Islamic Science History and their Contribution to Knowledge Production." *Cumhuriyet Ilahiyat Dergisi* 22. no. 1 (2018): 705-30.

Barth, Karl. *Church Dogmatics I.1: The Doctrine of the Word of God*. Translated by G. W. Bromiley. Edinburgh: T&T Clark, 1975.

———. *Church Dogmatics IV.1: The Doctrine of Reconciliation*. Translated by G. W. Bromiley. Edinburgh: T&T Clark, 1956.

Bashā, Qusṭanṭine. *Mayamir Theodore Abū Qurrah Usquf Ḥārān: Aqdam Ta'lif arabi Nasrani* [Mayamir Theodore Abū Qurrah Usquf Ḥārān: The Oldest Arabic Christian Writings]. Beirut: Al-Fou'ad Printing Press, 1904.

Bayet, Charles. *Byzantine Art*. New York: Parkstone International, 2008.

Beaumont, Mark. "Muslim Readings of John's Gospel in the ᶜAbbasid Period." *Islam and Christian-Muslim Relations* 19:2 (2008): 179-97.

Belting, Hans. *Likeness and Presence: A History of the Image before the Era of Art*. Translated by Edmund Jephcott. Chicago: The University of Chicago Press, 1996.

Benko, Stephen. *The Virgin Goddess: Studies in the Pagan and Christian Roots of Mariology*. Leiden, NY: Brill, 1993.

Bennison, Amira K. *The Great Caliphs: The Golden Age of the 'Abbasid Empire*. New Haven: Yale University Press, 2009.

Bertaina, David. "An Arabic Account of Theodore Abu Qurra in Debate at the Court of Caliph al-Ma'mun: A Study in Early Christian and Muslim Literary Dialogues." PhD diss., The Catholic University of America, 2007.

Bittar, Amina. *The History of the Abbasid Dynasty*. Damascus: Damascus University Press, 1997.

Block, C. Jonn. "Philoponian Monophysitism in South Arabia at the Advent of Islam with Implications for the English Translation of Thalātha' In Qur'ān 4. 171 And 5. 73." *Journal of Islamic Studies* 23, no. 1 (2012): 50-75.

Boss, Sarah Jane. "The Title Theotokos." In *Mary: The Complete Resource*. New York: Oxford University Press, 2007.

Boucher, Helen C., Serena Chen, and Molly Parker Tapias. "The Relational Self Revealed: Integrative Conceptualization and Implications for Interpersonal Life." *Psychological Bulletin* (2006): 151-79.

Boyd, Gregory A. "The Self-Sufficient Sociality of God: A Trinitarian Revision of Hartshorne's Metaphysics." In *Trinity in Process: A Relational Theology of God*. Edited by Joseph A. Bracken and Marjorie Hewitt Suchocki. London: Bloomsbury Academic, 1997.

Bradford, Brian C. "The Qur'anic Jesus: A Study of Parallels with Non-Biblical Texts." PhD diss., Western Michigan University, 2013.

Brock, Sebastian. *Holy Spirit in the Syrian Baptismal Tradition*. Vol. 9. Oxford: Oxford University Press, 1979.

Brock, Sebastian, and Susan Ashbrook Harvey. *Holy Women of the Syrian Orient*. Oakland, CA: University of California Press, 1998.

Brubaker, Leslie, and John Haldon. *Byzantium in the Iconoclast Era C. 680–850: A History*. Cambridge: Cambridge University Press, 2011.

Bukhārī, Muḥammad ibn Ismā'īl. *Ṣaḥīḥ Bukhārī*. Ḥadīth no. 7439. Accessed April 28, 2020. https://sunnah.com/bukhari/97.

Cameron, Averil. "The Theotokos in Sixth-Century Constantinople: A City Finds its Symbol." *The Journal of Theological Studies* 29, no. 1 (1978): 79-108.

Carroll, Michael P. *The Cult of the Virgin Mary: Psychological Origins*. Princeton, NJ: Princeton University Press, 1986.

Chase, Frederic H., trans. "On Heresies." In *John of Damascus: The Fathers of the Church Writings*. Vol. 37. Washington, DC: Ex Fontibus, 2012.

———, trans. *The Fathers of the Church: A New Translation*. Vol. 37. New York: Fathers of the Church, 1958.

———, trans. *John of Damascus: The Fathers of the Church Writings*. Vol. 37. Washington, DC: Ex Fontibus, 2012.

———, trans. "The Orthodox Faith." In *Saint John of Damascus Writings*. New York: Fathers of the Church, 1958.

———, trans. *Saint John of Damascus Writings*. New York: Fathers of the Church, 1958.

Childers, J. W. "Baradeus, Jacob (c. 500–578)." In *The Encyclopedia of Christian Civilization*. Edited by G. T. Kurian Wiley, 2012. Accessed December 7, 2020.

Cooper, Robert. "Peripheral Vision: Relationality." *Organization Studies* 26, no. 11 (November 2005): 1689-1710.

Coppedge, Allan. *The God Who Is Triune: Revisioning the Christian Doctrine of God*. Downers Grove, IL: IVP Academic, 2007.

The Council of Ephesus. s.v. "Counter-statements to Cyril's 12 Anathemas." *New Advent*. Accessed February 23, 2021. www.newadvent.org/fathers/2701.htm.

Craig, William Lane. "Another Glance at Trinity Monotheism." In *Philosophical and Theological Essays on the Trinity*, edited by Thomas McCall and Michael Rea. Oxford: Oxford University Press, 2009.

———. "Biographical Sketch." *Reasonable Faith* (website). Accessed June 28, 2023. www.reasonablefaith.org/william-lane-craig.

———. "Toward a Tenable Social Trinitarianism." In *Philosophical and Theological Essays on the Trinity*, edited by Thomas McCall and Michael Rea. Oxford: Oxford University Press, 2009.

Cross, F. L. and Elizabeth A. Livingstone, eds. *The Oxford Dictionary of the Christian Church*. Oxford: Oxford University Press, 2005.

Cross, Richard. "Two Models of the Trinity?" *The Heythrop Journal* 43 (2002): 275-94.

Dar Al-Ifta Al-Missriyyah. "Who are the Ash'arites?" Accessed January 8, 2022. www.dar-alifta.org/Foreign/ViewFatwa.aspx?ID=8001.

Deek, Ignatius "Maymar fi Wujud al-Khaliq wa al-Din al-Qawim [An Article about the Creator's Existence and the Right Religion]." In *al-Turath al-Arabī al-Masīḥī* Jouniey, Lebanon: al-Maktaba al-Boulisiya, 1982.

Dennison, James, ed. *Francis Turretin Institutes of Elenctic Theology*. Translated by George Musgrave Giger. Vol. 1. Phillipsburg, NJ: P&R, 1992.

Du Bourguet, Pierre. *L'art Copte*. Paris: Ministere D'Etat Affaires Culturelles, 1967.

Duvall, J. Scott and J. Daniel Hays. *God's Relational Presence: The Cohesive Center of Biblical Theology*. Grand Rapids, MI: Baker Academic, 2019.

Ebied, Rifaat, and David Thomas, eds. *The Polemical Works of ʿAlī al-Ṭabarī*. Boston: Brill, 2016.

Endress, Gerhard. "Theology as a Rational Science: Aristotelian Philosophy, the Christian Trinity and Islamic Monotheism in the Thought of Yaḥya Ibn ᶜAdī." In *Ideas in Motion in Baghdad and Beyond: Philosophical and Theological Exchanges between Christians and Muslims in the Third/Ninth and Fourth/Tenth Centuries*. Vol. 124. Edited by Damien Janos. Leiden, Netherlands: Brill, 2015.

———. *The Works of Yahya Ibn ᶜAdi: An Analytical Inventory*. Wiesbaden, West Germany: Dr. Ludwig Reichert Verlag, 1977.

Erickson, Millard. *God in Three Persons: A Contemporary Interpretation of the Trinity*. Grand Rapids, MI: Baker Books, 1995.

———. *Who's Tampering with the Trinity? An Assessment of the Subordination Debate*. Grand Rapids, MI: Kregel Academic & Professional, 2009.

Erikson, Erik H. *Identity: Youth and Crisis*. New York: Norton, 1968.

Esposito, John L. *Islam: The Straight Path*. 4th edition. New York: Oxford University Press, 2011.

Farah, Caesar. *Islam: Beliefs and Observances*. Hauppauge, NY: Barron's Educational Services, 2000.

Fretheim, Terence E., Michael J. Chan, and Brent A. Strawn. *What Kind of God? Collected Essays of Terence E. Fretheim*. Winona Lake, Indiana: Eisenbrauns, 2015.

Giles, Kevin N. *Jesus and the Father: Modern Evangelicals Reinvent the Doctrine of the Trinity*. Grand Rapids, MI: HarperCollins, 2006.

Goddard, Hugh. "Muslim and Christian Beliefs." In *Contemporary Muslim-Christian Encounters: Developments, Diversity, and Dialogues*. Edited by Paul Hedges. New York: Bloomsbury Academic, 2015.

Goldziher, Ignác. *Introduction to Islamic Theology and Law*. Princeton, NJ: Princeton University Press, 1981.

———. "Zum Islamischen Bilderverbot." *Zeitschrift der Deutschen Morgenländischen Gesellschaft* 74 (1920).

Gottheil, Richard. "A Christian Bahira Legend." *Zeitschrift für Assyriologie* 13 (1898): 189-210.

Glaser, Ida. "The concept of relationship as a key to the comparative understanding of Christianity and Islam." *Themelios*. Vol. 11. No. 2 (January 1986): 57-60.

Grabar, André. *Christian Iconography: A Study of its Origins*. London: Princeton University Press, 1980.

Grabar, Martyrium A. *Recherches sur le culte des reliques chretien antique*. Vol. 2. Paris: Collège de France, 1946.

Grenz, Stanley J. *Theology for the Community of God*. Grand Rapids, MI: Eerdmans, 1994.

Grenz, Stanley and Denise Muir Kjesbo. *Women in the Church: A Biblical Theology of Women in Ministry*. Downers Grove, IL: InterVarsity Press, 1995.

Grenz, Stanley, David Guretzki, and Cherith Fee Nordling. *Pocket Dictionary of Theological Terms* (Downers Grove, IL: InterVarsity Press, 1999).

Griffith, Sidney H. "Al-Naṣārā in the Qur᾽ān: A hermeneutical reflection." In *New Perspectives on the Qur'ān: The Qur᾽ān in Its Historical Context*. Edited by Gabriel Said Reynolds. London: Routledge Taylor & Francis, 2011.

———. "The Apologetic Treatise of Nonnus of Nisibis." *ARAM* 3 (1992): 115-38.

———. *The Church in the Shadow of the Mosque: Christians and Muslims in the World of Islam*. Princeton, NJ: Princeton University Press, 2008.

———. "Eutychius of Alexandria on the Emperor Theophilus and Iconoclasm in Byzantium: A Tenth Century Moment in Christian Apologetics in Arabic." *Byzantion* 52 (1982): 154-90.

———. "Images, Islam and Christian Icons: A Moment in the Christian-Muslim Encounter in Early Islamic Times." In *La Syrie de Byzance a l'Islam: VIIe-Ville siècles*, Colloque 1990. Edited by Pierre Canivet and Jean-Paul Rey-Coquais. Damascus: Institut Frangais de Damas, 1992.

———. "The Melkites and the Muslims: The Qur'ān, Christology, and Arab Orthodoxy." *Al-QanṬara* 33, no. 2 (2012): 413-43.

———. "Reflections on the Biography of Theodore Abu Qurrah." *Parole de l'Orient: revue semestrielle des études syriaques et arabes chrétiennes* 18 (1993): 143-70.

———. *Theodore Abū Qurrah: A Treatise on the Veneration of the Holy Icons*. Louvain, Belgique: Peeters, 1997.

Guillaume, A. *The Life of Muhammad: A Translation of Isḥāq's Sirat Rasūl Allah*. New York: Oxford University Press, 1998.

Gutas, Dimitri. *Greek Thought, Arabic Culture: The Graeco-Arabic Translation Movement in Baghdad and Early Abbasaid Society*. 2nd–4th/5th–10th C. London: Taylor & Francis Group, 1998.

Hall, Alexander. "Scotus: Knowledge of God." *Internet Encyclopedia of Philosophy*. Accessed January 22, 2022. https://iep.utm.edu/scotuskg/.

Halverson, Jerry R. *Theology and Creed in Sunni Islam: The Muslim Brotherhood, Ash'arism, and Political Sunnism*. New York: Palgrave Macmillan, 2010.

———. *Theology and Creed in Sunni Islam: The Muslim Brotherhood, Ash'arism, and Political Sunnism*. New York: Palgrave Macmillan, 2010.

Hamarneh, Sami K. *Encyclopedia of the History of Science, Technology, and Medicine in Non-Western Cultures*. Edited by H. Selin (Dordrecht: Springer, 2008), https://link.springer.com/referenceworkentry/10.1007/978-1-4020-4425-0_9188.

Hamidullah, Muhammad. "Aqdam Dustur Musajjal fi-l-ʿAlam." *Islamic Scholars Conference* 1 (1937): 98-123. Accessed February 14, 2021. Retrieved from https://abulhasanalinadwi.org/book/aqdam-dastoor-musajjal-fil-aa/.

Harvey, Susan Ashbrook. "Feminine Imagery for the Divine." *St Vladimir's Theological Quarterly 37 (1993): 111-39.*

Heintaler, Tereza. *al-Massiḥiyiin al-ʿarab Qabil al-Islam [The Arab Christians before Islam], trans. Lamis Fayed. Cairo: Dar al-Nashir al-Usqufiya, 2017*

Henry, Carl F. H. *God, Revelation and Authority: God Who Stands and Stays*. Vol. 5. Wheaton, IL: Crossway, 1999.

Higton, Mike, s.v. "Hypostasis." In *Cambridge Dictionary of Christian Theology*, edited by Ian A. McFarland, et al. Cambridge: Cambridge University Press, 2011.

Hill, Edmund. *The Mystery of the Trinity*. London: Geoffrey Chapman, 1985.

Hjälm, Miriam L., ed. *Senses of Scripture, Treasures of Tradition*. Vol. 5. Leiden, Netherlands: Brill, 2017.

Hoover, Jon. "Perpetual Creativity in the Perfection of God: Ibn Taymiyya's Hadith Commentary on God's Creation of This World." *Journal of Islamic Studies* 15, no. 3 (2004).

Husseini, Sara Leila. *Early Christian-Muslim Debate on the Unity of God : Three Christian Scholars and Their Engagement with Islamic Thought (9th Century c.e.)*. Leiden, Netherlands: Brill, 2014.

Ibn al-Nadīm,Muhammad ibn Isḥāq. *Fihrist*, edited by M. Riḍā-Tajaddud. Tehran: Dar al-Masirah, 1971.

———. *The Fihrist of Al-Nadīm: A Tenth-Century Survey of Muslim Culture*. Vol. 1. New York: Columbia University Press, 1970.

———. *The Fihrist of Al-Nadīm: A Tenth-Century Survey of Muslim Culture*. Vol. 2. New York: Columbia University Press, 1970.

Ibn Kathīr, Abū al-Fidā Ismaʿīl. *Tafsir Ibn Katheer*, accessed December 28, 2020. https://quran.ksu.edu.sa/tafseer/katheer/sura6-aya101.html#katheer.

———. Tafseer al-Qur'an al-Atheem [*The Explanation of the Great Qur'an*]. Beirut: Dar Ibn Ḥazm, 2000.

Ibn-al-Kalbī, Hishām. *The Book of Idols*. Translated by Nabih Amin Faris. Princeton, NJ: Princeton University Press, 1952.

Janosik, Daniel J. *John of Damascus: The First Apologist to the Muslims*. Eugene, OR: Pickwick, 2016.

John of Damascus. "The Discussion of a Christian and a Saracen." Translated by J. P. Migne. *Patrologia Graeca* 94 (1864): 266-73.

———. *Three Treatises on the Divine Images*. Translated by Andrew Louth. New York: St. Vladimir's Seminary Press, 2003.

Kalavrezou, Ioli. "Images of the Mother: When the Virgin Mary Became 'Meter Theou.'" *Dumbarton Oaks Papers* 44 (1990): 165-72.

Kalner, John. *Ishmael Instructs Isaac: An Introduction to the Qur'ān for Bible Readers*. Collegeville, MN: Liturgical Press, 1999.

Kant, Immanuel. *The Conflict of the Faculties (Der Streit der Fakultäten)*. Translated by Mary J. Gregor. Lincoln: University of Nebraska Press, 1979.

Karkkainen, Veli-Matti. *Trinity and Revelation: A Constructive Christian Theology for the Pluralistic World*. Vol. 2. Grand Rapids, MI: Eerdmans, 2014.

Kavvadas, Nestor. "Icon Veneration as a Stumbling Block: Theodore Abu Qurrah and Byzantine Orthodox Iconoclasts in the Early Abbasid Society." *Journal of Eastern Christian Studies* 72 (1-2) (2020).

Kennedy, Hugh. *When Baghdad Ruled the Muslim World: The Rise and Fall of Islam's Greatest Dynasty*. Cambridge, MA: Da Capo Press, 2004.

Khalek, Nancy. "Icons John the Baptist and Sanctified Spaces in Early Islamic Syria." In *Damascus after the Muslim Conquest: Text and Image in Early Islam*. Oxford: Oxford University Press, 2011.

Khalīl, Samīr. *Maqala fi al-Tawhid Lil Sheikh Yaḥya Ibn Adi (898-974)* [Treatise in Divine Unity to Sheikh Yaḥya Ibn Adi (898-974)]. Jounieh, Lebanon: Al-Maktaba al- Boulissiah, 1980.

King, Daniel, ed. *The Syriac World of the East*. New York: Routledge, Taylor & Francis Group, 2019.

King, G. R. D. "The Paintings of the Pre-Islamic Kaʿba." *Muqarnas* 21 (2004): 219-29.

Kitzinger, Ernst. "The Cult of Images in the Age before Iconoclasm." *Dumbarton Oaks Papers* 8 (1954): 83-150.

Kraemer, Joel. *Philosophy in the Renaissance of Islam: Abu Sulaymān Al-Sijistānī and His Circle (Studies in Islamic Culture and History)*. Vol. 8. Leiden: Brill Academic, 1987.

Lamoreaux, John C. "The Biography of Theodore Abi Qurrah Revisited." *Dumbarton Oaks Papers* 56 (2002): 25-40.

———. trans. *Theodore Abū Qurrah*. Provo, UT: Brigham Young University Press, 2005.

Laoust, H. "Ahmad b. Hanbal." In P. J. Bearman et al., eds. *Encyclopaedia of Islam Online*. 12 vols. Leiden, Netherlands: Brill, 2004. www.encislam.brill.nl.

Lapidus, Ira M. *A History of Islamic Societies*. 3rd ed. New York: Cambridge University Press, 2014.

Leaman, Oliver. "The Developed Kalām Tradition." In *The Cambridge Companion to Classical Islamic Theology*. Edited by Tim Winter. Cambridge: Cambridge University Press, 2008.

Lee, Seung Goo. "The Relationship between the Ontological Trinity and the Economic Trinity." *Journal of Reformed Theology* 3 (2009): 90-107.

Leftow, Brian. "Alston Chair of Religion." *Oxford University*. Accessed July 1, 2023. www.philosophy.ox.ac.uk/people/brian-leftow#tab-414476.

———. "Anti Social Trinitarianism." *Faith and Philosophy: Journal of the Society of Christian Philosophers* 21, no. 3 (2004).

———. "Anti Social Trinitarianism." In *Philosophical and Theological Essays on the Trinity*. Edited by Thomas McCall and Michael Rea. Oxford: Oxford University Press, 2009.

———. "Curriculum Vitae." *Rutgers School of Arts and Sciences*. Accessed July 1, 2023. https://philosophy.rutgers.edu/people/regular-faculty/regular-faculty-profile/182-regular-faculty-full-time/954-leftow-brian.

———. *God and Necessity*. Oxford: Oxford University Press, 2012.

———. "A Latin Trinity." *Faith and Philosophy: Journal of the Society of Christian Philosophers* 21, no. 3 (2004): 304-33.

Louth, Andrew. *St John Damascene: Tradition and Originality in Byzantine Theology*. Oxford: Oxford University Press: 2002.

Luce, A. A. *Monophysitism Past and Present: A Study in Christology*. Project Gutenberg, released December 2009. www.gutenberg.org/files/30219/30219-h/30219-h.htm.

Macdonald, Duncan Black. *Development of Muslim Theology, Jurisprudence, and Constitutional Theory*. New York: Charles Scribner's Sons, 1903.

Madelung, W. *Der Imam al-Qasim ibn Ibrdhim und die Glaubenslehre der Zaiditen*. Berlin: De Gruyter, 1966.

Makdisi, George. "Ashʿarī and the Ash'arites in Islamic Religious History I." *Studia Islamica* 17 (1962): 37-80.

Mālik Ibn Anas. *Al-Muwatta of Imam Malik ibn Anas: the first formulation of Islamic law*. Book 17. Ḥadīth no. 46. Accessed December 14, 2020. https://sunnah.com/urn/506220.

Mathews, Thomas, and Norman Muller. "Isis and Mary in Early Icons." In *Images of the Mother of God: Perceptions of the Theotokos in Byzantium*. Edited by Maria Vassilaki. New York: Taylor & Francis Group, 2005.

McCall, Thomas H. "Relational Trinity: Creedal Perspective." In *Two Views on The Doctrine of the Trinity*. Grand Rapids, MI: Zondervan, 2014.

———. "Theologians, Philosophers, and the Doctrine of the Trinity." In *Philosophical and Theological Essays on the Trinity*. Oxford: Oxford University Press, 2009.

McCall, Thomas H. and Michael C. Rea, eds. "Introduction." In *Philosophical and Theological Essays on the Trinity*. Oxford: Oxford University Press, 2009.

McGuckin, J. "The Paradox of the Virgin-Theotokos: Evangelism and Imperial Politics in the 5th-Century Byzantine World." *Maria, A Journal of Marian Theology* 2, no. 1 (2001): 8-25.

Meyerhof, Max. "'Alī al-Bayhaqī's Tatimmat Siwān al-Hikma: A Biographical Work on Learned Men of the Islam." *The University of Chicago Press on behalf of The History of Science Society* 8 (1948): 122-217.

Mihoc, Vasile-Octavian. "Aesthetics as Shared Interfaith Space between Christianity and Islam." *Ecumenical Review* 71, no. 5 (2019): 674-92.

Miron, Patrick. *Catholic & Christian: A Book of Essential Catholic Catechesis*. UK: Trafford Publishing, 2016.

Molnar, Paul. "The Function of the Immanent Trinity in the Theology of Karl Barth: Implications for Today." *Scottish Journal of Theology* 42 (1989): 367-99.

Moltmann, Jürgen. *The Trinity and the Kingdom: The Doctrine of God*. Translated by Margaret Kohl. London: SCM Press, 1981.

Muehlberger, Ellen, trans. "John Philoponus, Fragments on the Trinity." In *The Cambridge Edition of Early Christian Writings*. Edited by Andrew Radde-Gallwitz. Cambridge: Cambridge University Press, 2017.

Nasr, Seyyed Hossein. *Islam: Religion, History, and Civilization*. New York: HarperOne, 2002.

Nasrallah, Joseph. *Mansoor ben Sarjon al-Ma'roof bil Qidiis Youhana al-Dimashqi: 'Asroh, Hayatoh, Mo'alfatoh* [Mansoor the Son of Sarjon the Damascene: His Time, Life, and Writings], translated by Antoin Wehbi. Lebanon, Beirut: Al-Maktaba al-Boulisya, 1991.

Nasry, Wafik. *The Caliph and the Bishop: A 9th Century Muslim-Christian Debate: Al-Ma'mūn and Abū Qurrah*. Beirut: CEDRAC Université Saint Joseph, 2008.

Nawas, John Abdallah. *Al-Ma'mun, the Inquisition, and the Quest for Caliphal Authority*. GA: Lockwood Press, 2015.

O'Connor, J. B. "St. John Damascene." *The Catholic Encyclopedia: New Advent*. Accessed April 27, 2021. www.newadvent.org/cathen/08459b.htm.

Omar, Mohd. Nasir. "The Life of Yahya Ibn 'Adi: A Famous Christian Philosopher of Baghdad." *Mediterranean Journal of Social Sciences MCSER* 6. No. 2 S5 (2015): 308-14.

Otto, Randall E. "The Use and Abuse of Perichoresis in Recent Theology." *Scottish Journal of Theology* 54. No. 3 (2001): 366–84.

Paasch, J. T. *Divine Production in Late Medieval Trinitarian Theology: Henry of Ghent, Duns Scotus, and William Ockham*. Oxford: Oxford University Press, 2012.

Paavola, Sami. "Abduction through Grammar, Critic, and Methodeutic." *Transactions of the Charles S. Peirce Society* 40. No. 2 (2004): 261-62.

Parrinder, Geoffrey. *Jesus in the Qur'an*. London: Oneworld Publications, 2013.

Patricios, Nicholas N. *The Sacred Architecture of Byzantium: Art, Liturgy, and Symbolism in Early Christian Churches*. New York: I.B. Tauris, 2014.

Pelikan, Jaroslav. "The Theotokos, the Mother of God." In *Mary Through the Centuries*. New Haven, CT: Yale University Press, 1996.

Renard, John. *Islam and Christianity: Theological Themes in Comparative Perspective*. Berkeley: University of California Press, 2011.

Rescher, Nicholas. *Tatawer al-Mantiq al-'Arabi* [*The Development of Arabic Logic*],. Translated by Mohammad Mahran. Pittsburgh: University of Pittsburgh Press, 1964.

Reynolds, Gabriel Said. "On the Presentation of Christianity in the Qur'an and the Many Aspects of Qur'anic Rhetoric." *Al-Bayan—Journal Of Qur'ān And Hadîth Studies* 12 (2014): 42-54.

Roey, A. Van, ed & trans., *Nonnus de Nisibe, Traiti Apologltique, Etude, Texte et Traduction*. Louvain, Belgium: Bibliotheque du Museon. Bureaux du Muséon, 1948.

Rudvin, Arne. "Islam: An Absolutely Different Ethos?" *International Review of Mission* 71 (1982).

S. Thomae de Aquino. *Summa Theologiae*. Ottawa: Studii Generalis, 1941.

Saeed, Abdullah. *Islamic Thought: An Introduction*. Florence: Taylor & Francis Group, 2006.

Sahas, Daniel J. *John of Damascus on Islam: The Heresy of the Ishmaelites*. Leiden, Netherlands: E. J. Brill, 1972.

Sahner, Christian C. *Christian Martyrs under Islam: Religious Violence and the Making of the Muslim World*. Princeton, NJ: Princeton University Press, 2018.

Saritopark, Zaki. "Allah." In *The Qur'an: An Encyclopedia*, Edited by Oliver Leaman. London: Taylor & Francis Group, 2005.

Schleiermacher, Friedrich. *The Christian Faith*. Translated by H. R. Mackintosh and J. S. Stewart. Edinburgh: T&T Clark, 1989.

Senturk, Recep. *Medieval Islamic Civilization: An Encyclopedia*. Vol. 1. Edited by Joseph Meri. New York: Taylor & Francis, 2006.

Shahid, Irfan. *Byzantine and the Arabs in the Fourth Century*, Washington, DC: Dumbarton Oaks Research Library and Collection, 1984.

———. *Byzantine and the Arabs in the Sixth Century*. Vol. 1. Washington, DC: Dumbarton Oaks Research Library and Collection, 1995.

———. *The Martyrs of Najran: New Documents*. Bruxelle, Belgique: Société des Bollandistes, 1971.

Shakir, M. H., ed. *The Quran*. Medford, MA: Perseus Digital Library, 2016.

Shehadeh, Imad N. *al-Aab wa al-Ibn was al-Roḥ al-Qudus ilah waḥid, amin: Daroret al-Ta'adudiya fi al-Wiḥdaniya al-ilahiya* [The Father and the Son and the Holy Spirit On God Amin: the Necessity of the Multiplicity in the Divine Oneness]. Al-Matin, Lebanon: Dar al-Manhal, 2009.

———. *God With Us and Without Us, Volume One: Oneness in Trinity versus Absolute Oneness*. Carlisle, UK: Langham, 2018.

———. *God With Us and Without Us, Volume Two: The Beauty and Power of Oneness in Trinity*. Carlisle, UK: Langham, 2019.

———. *God With Us and Without Us, Volumes One and Two: The Beauty and Power of Oneness in Trinity versus Absolute Oneness*. Carlisle, UK: Langham Creative Projects, 2020.

Sim'an, Awad. *Allah fi al-* [God in Christianity].*Cairo: Qassir Ad-Dubara Church, 2004,.*

Sirry, Mun'im. "Other Religions." In *The Wiley Blackwell Companion to the Qur'an*. Edited by Andrew Rippin and Jawid Mojaddedi. Hoboken, NJ: Wiley Blackwell, 2017.

———. "The public role of Dhimmīs during 'Abbāsid times." *Bulletin of SOAS* 74 (2011):187-204.

Slotemaker, John T. *Trinitarian Theology in Medieval and Reformation Thought*. Switzerland: Palgrave Macmillan, 2020.

Society of Biblical Literature. *The SBL Handbook of Style for Biblical Studies and Related Disciplines*. 2nd ed. Atlanta: SBL Press, 2014.

St. Basil of Caesarea. *Letters* 38, 8. Accessed January 21, 2022. www.newadvent.org/fathers/3202038.htm.

St. Cyril of Alexandria. "The Epistle of Cyril to Nestorius with the XII Anathematisms." In *The Seven Ecumenical Councils*. Edited by Philip Schaff and Henry Wace. Translated by Henry R. Percival. Vol. 14. New York: Charles Scribner's Sons, 1900.

St. Cyril of Alexandria. *Festal Letters 8*. Edited by John J. O'Keefe. Washington, DC: Catholic University of America Press, 2009.

St. Gregory Nazianzen. *The Sacred Writings of Gregory Nazianzen*. Translated by Charles Gordon Browne. Altenmunster, Germany: Jazzybee Verlag, 2017.

St. Gregory Nyssen. *The Sacred Writings of Gregory of Nyssa*. Translated by Henry Austin Wilson. Altenmunster, Germany: Jazzybee Verlag, 2017.

Stillman, Norman A. "Dhimma." In *Medieval Islamic Civilization*. Edited by Joseph Meri. Vol 1. New York: Taylor and Francis, 2016.

Sullivan, James. "The Athanasian Creed." *The Catholic Encyclopedia: New Advent*, accessed July 4, 2023. www.newadvent.org/cathen/02033b.htm.

Swanson, Mark N. "Saints and Sainthood, Christian." In *Medieval Islamic Civilization*. Edited by Joseph Meri. Vol 2. New York: Taylor and Francis, 2016.

———. "The Cross of Christ in the Earliest Arabic Melkite Apologies." In *Christian Arabic Apologetics during the Abbasid Period (750-1258)*. Edited by Samir Khalil Samir and Joren S. Nielsen. Vol. 63. New York: Brill, 1993.

Sweetman, James W. *Islam and Christian Theology: A Study of the Interpretation of Theological Ideas in the Two Religions*. Vol. 2. London: Lutterworth Press, 1945.

Swinburne, Richard. *The Christian God*. New York: Oxford University Press, 1994.

———. "Richard Swinburne—Short Intellectual Autobiography." *Faculty of Philosophy: University of Oxford*. Accessed June 24, 2023. https://users.ox.ac.uk/~orie0087/.

———. "The Trinity." In *Philosophical and Theological Essays on the Trinity*. Edited by Thomas H. McCall and Michael C. Rea. Oxford: Oxford University Press, 2009.

Thomas, David. "Abū 'īsā Al-Warrāq and the History of Religions." *Journal of Semitic Studies* 41, no. 2 (1996): 275–90.

———. *Christians at the Heart of Islamic Rule: Church Life and Scholarship in 'Abbasid Iraq*. Leiden, Netherlands: Brill, 2003.

———. ed. *Routledge Handbook on Christian-Muslim Relations*. New York: Routledge, Taylor & Francis Group, 2018.

Thompson, Thomas R. "Trinitarianism Today: Doctrinal Renaissance, Ethical Relevance, Social Redolence." *Calvin Theological Journal* 32 (1997): 9-42.

Thomson, William. "Al-Ashᶜari and His Al-Ibanah." *The Muslim World: A Quarterly Review of History, Culture, Religions & The Christian Mission in Islamdom* 32, no. 3 (1942): 253.

Tillich, Paul. *Systematic Theology*. Vol. 1. Chicago: University of Chicago Press, 1967.

Tirmidhī, Muḥammad Ibn. *'Īsá*, "Jami' at-Tirmidhi." Book 7. Ḥadīth no. 634. Accessed December 14, 2020. https://sunnah.com/tirmidhi/7.

Torrance, Thomas. "Predestination in Christ." *Evangelical Quarterly* 13 (1941): 108-41.
Tradigo, Alfredo. *Icons and Saints of the Eastern Orthodox Church*. Translated by Stephen Sartarelli. Los Angeles: The J. Paul Getty Museum, 2004.
Trueman, Carl R. *Histories and Fallacies: Problems Faced in the Writing of History*. Wheaton, IL: Crossway, 2010.
Tschaepe, Mark. "Guessing and Abduction." *Transactions of The Charles S. Peirce Society* 50. No. 1 (2014): 115-38.
Twombly, Charles C., and Myk. Habets. *Perichoresis and Personhood: God, Christ, and Salvation in John of Damascus*. Eugene: Wipf and Stock Publishers, 2015.
Valčo, Michal, Marek Petro, Mária Kardis, Rozalina V. Shagieva, Maria A. Kuznetsova, and Nina I. Kryukova. "Ecumenical Trinitarian Reflections and the 'De Régnon Paradigm': A Probe into Recovering the Social-Trinitarian Emphases of the Cappadocian Fathers." *Constantine's Letters / Konštantínove Listy* 12, no. 1 (2019): 76–89.
Van Inwagen, Peter. "And Yet They are Not Three Gods but One God." In *Philosophical and Theological Essays on the Trinity*. Edited by Thomas McCall and Michael Rea. Oxford: Oxford University Press, 2009.
———. "Biography" *University of Notre Dame*. Accessed July 14, 2023. https://philosophy.nd.edu/people/emeritus/peter-van-inwagen/.
Van Nieuwenhove, Rik. *An Introduction to Medieval Theology*. Cambridge: Cambridge University Press, 2012.
Volf, Miroslav. *After Our Likeness: The Church as the Image of the Trinity*. Grand Rapids, MI: Eerdmans, 1998.
———. *Allah: A Christian Response*. New York: HarperCollins, 2011.
Winkler, Dietmar W. "Monophysites." In *Late Antiquity: A Guide to the Postclassical World*. Edited by G. W. Bowersock, Peter Robert Lamont Brown, and Oleg Grabar. Cambridge, MA: Harvard University Press, 1999.
Waines, David. *An Introduction to Islam*, 2nd ed. Cambridge: Cambridge University Press, 2014.
Walzer, Richard. "New Light on the Arabic Translation of Aristotle." In *Greek into Arabic: Essays on Islamic Philosophy*. Cambridge: Cambridge University Press, 1962.
Ward, W. E., s.v. "Hypostasis." In *Evangelical Dictionary of Theology*, edited by Walter A. Elwell. Grand Rapids, MI: Baker Books, 2013.
Ware, Bruce A. *Father, Son, and Holy Spirit: Relationship, Roles, and Relevance*. Wheaton, IL: Crossway, 2005.
Ware, Kallistos. "The Holy Trinity: Model for Personhood-in-Relation." In *The Trinity and an Entangled World: Relationality in Physical Science and Theology*. Edited by John Polkinghorne. Grand Rapids, MI: Eerdmans, 2010.
Watt, W. Montgomery. *Islam and Christianity Today: A Contribution to Dialogue*. London: Routledge & Kegan Paul, 1983.
———. *Muslim-Christian Encounters: Perceptions and Misperceptions*. New York: Routledge, Taylor & Francis Group, 1991.
White, James. *The Forgotten Trinity*. Grand Rapids, MI: Bethany House Publishers, 1998.
———. *What Every Christian Needs to Know about the Qur'an*. Grand Rapids, MI: Bethany House Publishers, 2013.
Winkler, Dietmar W. "The Age of the Sassanians." In *The Church of the East: A Concise History*. Edited by Wilhelm Baum and Dietmar W. Winkler. New York: Routledge, Taylor & Francis Group, 2003.
Winter, Tim, ed. "Introduction." In *The Cambridge Companion to Classical Islamic Theology*. Cambridge: Cambridge University Press, 2008.

Wolfson, Harry Austryn. *The Philosophy of the Kalam*. London: Harvard University Press, 1976.

Wood, Philip. "Christians in the Middle East, 600–1000: Conquest, Competition and Conversion." In *Islam and Christianity in Medieval Anatolia*. Edited by A. C. S. Peacock et al. New York: Taylor & Francis Group, 2015.

Woorhis, John, trans. "The Discussion of a Christian and a Saracen by John of Damascus." *The Moslem World* 25 (1935): 266-73.

Yaᶜqūb, Ignatious. *Al-Shuhada' al-ḥamiriyoon al-'Arab fi al-Watha'iq al-Syrianiya* [the Arab Himyarites Martyrs in Syriac Manuscript]. Damascus: Syrian Patriarchate of Antioch, 1966.

"Yaḥya ibn ᶜAdi." In *Encyclopedia of World Biography Online*. Vol. 37. Detroit: Gale, 2017. Accessed December 7, 2020. https://link.gale.com/apps/doc/K1631010726/BIC?u=vic_liberty&sid=BIC&xid=c5dd4b6a.

Zizioulas, John D. *Communion and Otherness: Further Studies in Personhood and the Church*. London: Bloomsbury Publishing, 2007.

Zwemer, Samuel M. *Arabia: The Cradle of Islam*. New York: The Caxton Press, 1900.

General Index

Abbasid, 2-3, 12, 14, 18, 22, 25-27, 29, 30, 32, 34-38, 43-44, 49, 51, 97, 181
ahl al-dhimma or *dhimmis*, 30, 33
ahl-al-ḥādīth, 84
al-Ka[c]aba, 72-73, 182
al-Azraqī, 73, 79
al-Inṣāf, 50
al-Ma'mūn, 27, 28, 37, 38, 49, 51, 96-97, 181
Al-Qurṭubi, 32, 40-41
Al-sifat al-dhatīya (attributes in essence), 163
Al-sifat al-fi[c]lya (attributes in actions), 163
al-Tabarī, 29, 32, 40-41, 43-46, 106
al-wāḥid or *wāḥid*, 108-13, 116, 151, 171, 184, 191
Anselm, 21, 23, 134
Ash[c]arism, 84, 94, 161-65, 181
Bayt al-Ḥikma (The House of Wisdom), 26-27, 51
Byzantine, 12, 14, 27, 30, 58, 62-63, 72, 79, 83
Christotokos, 59, 78
da[c]wa, 49, 73
economic Trinity, 124, 143-45
equivalence view, 146-48
fiqh, 37
ghazawat, 31
gradational view, 146, 150
Ḥadīth, 31-32, 37, 42-43, 54, 72-75, 79, 84, 86, 166
iconoclasm, 10, 18, 62-63, 75, 79, 190
iconophile, 63, 96
immanent Trinity, 143-45
immutability, 88, 118, 172-73
inter, 160, 167, 187
intrarelationality, 160, 164, 173-74
intrarelationship, 1, 115
Jacobites, 9, 11, 28-29, 36, 40, 47, 105, 107, 115, 181
Jahmites, 36
jizya, 31-34, 71-72, 85
John of Damascus, 2-5, 7, 10, 18, 28, 37, 81, 86, 95, 97, 105, 153, 173, 184
kalām, 97, 107, 131-32, 154-55, 161, 166, 167, 181
Kharaj, 32
Latin Trinity, 123, 125-26, 134-39, 185
Levant, 1, 3, 9, 25, 27, 29, 30, 57, 64, 72, 76, 78, 85, 96, 182, 190-91
maximally good, 117-18, 155-56, 170, 172
maximally great, 98, 155
maximally perfect, 155-56, 170-71
Melkites, 9-11, 27, 29, 36-37, 40, 47-48, 94-97, 107
Mesopotamia, 9, 25, 28-30, 95-96
miḥna, 37-38
Monophysites, 9, 28-29, 66-68, 77-78, 80, 94, 105, 115
Mubāhaleh, 71
Mu[c]tazilites, 37-38, 46, 49, 84-85, 92, 94, 161-62, 164-65, 181
Najrān, 66-72, 77, 79, 190
Naṣārā, 46, 49, 63, 65
omnibenevolence, 89, 117-18, 172-73
omnipotence, 84, 112, 18, 128-29, 131, 164, 171-73
ousia, 6-7, 36, 41, 182
perichoresis, 6-7, 10, 173-76
Qadarites, 35, 181
Qalis, 66
relationality, 17, 20, 151-61, 165, 167, 169-80, 186-88, 192
relative identity theory, 3, 23, 126-27, 140, 142-43
Shi[c]ites, 49, 181
shirk, 38, 40, 85, 91, 192
sifat Allah, 3, 185

social Trinity, 123, 125, 135, 138
tawḥid, 1, 5-6, 15, 17, 21, 38, 92, 105, 107-14, 153, 156, 165, 167, 171, 178, 180, 191
Theodore Abū Qurrah, 2-5, 10-12, 18, 23, 28, 81, 94, 97-105, 153, 183, 190
Theotokos, 4, 6, 18, 23, 53, 57-63, 72-73, 77-80, 182-83
Umayyad, 2, 3, 25-26, 30, 34, 51, 62, 75-76, 82-83, 92, 190
Uqnūm/Aqanīm, 6-9, 22, 39, 89, 101, 103, 108, 114-16, 118, 172-76, 179, 183, 187
Yaḥyā Ibn ᶜAdī, 2-4, 10-13, 18, 23, 28, 46, 81, 105-8, 112, 149, 153, 190-91
zakat, 30, 32

Scripture Index

Old Testament

Exodus
3:14, *7*
6:7, *177*
31:18, *157*

Deuteronomy
6:4, *138*

Psalms
4:3, *157*
45:6-7, *100*
110:1, *100*
110:3, *100*

Ecclesiastes
5:2, *159*

Isaiah
6:1, *159*

Jeremiah
7:23, *177*
11:4, *177*

Ezekiel
43:7, *177*
43:9, *177*

Daniel
5:25, *157*

Joel
2:28, *178*

Zechariah
2:10-13, *177*
2:11, *177*

New Testament

Matthew
1:1, *50*
5:48, *50*
16:13-16, *50*
28:18-20, *1*

Mark
8:27-29, *50*
14:62, *1*

John
1:1, *1*
1:1-2, *177*
1:14, *177*
3:3-7, *56*
4:39, *177*
5:26, *8*
6:38, *44*
8:37, *177*
9:31, *157*
14:11, *174*
14:16, *178*
14:26, *178*
15:26, *178*
16:13, *178*
20:17, *44*
20:28, *1*

Acts
2, *178*
5:1-16, *145*
11:26, *63*

Romans
1:20, *160*
4:21, *159*
6:4-6, *56*
9:5, *1*
16:26, *160*

1 Corinthians
8:6, *1*

2 Corinthians
9:8, *159*

Galatians
4:8, *7*

Philippians
2:6-9, *1*
2:6-11, *187*
2:9, *146*

Colossians
2:9, *7*

1 Timothy
1:17, *160*

2 Timothy
1:12, *159*

Titus
2:13, *1*

Hebrews
1:1-3, *1*
1:3, *177*

2 Peter
1:4, *7*

1 John
1:1, *177*
3:24, *178*
5:14, *157*

Revelation
1:4, *7*
1:5-9, *1*
19:13, *177*
22:13, *1*

New Explorations in Theology Series

The Reality of God and Historical Method

A Shared Mercy

Karl Barth's Infralapsarian Theology

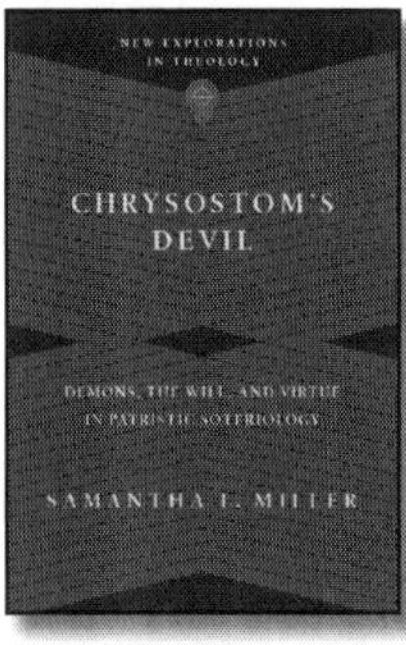

Chrysostom's Devil

The Making of Stanley Hauerwas

Reading Scripture as the Church

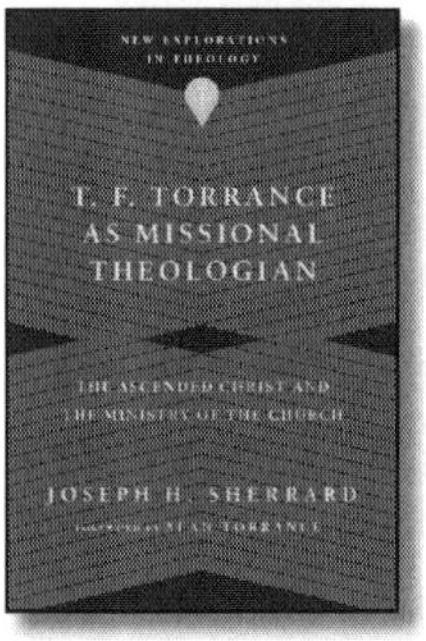

T. F. Torrance as Missional Theologian

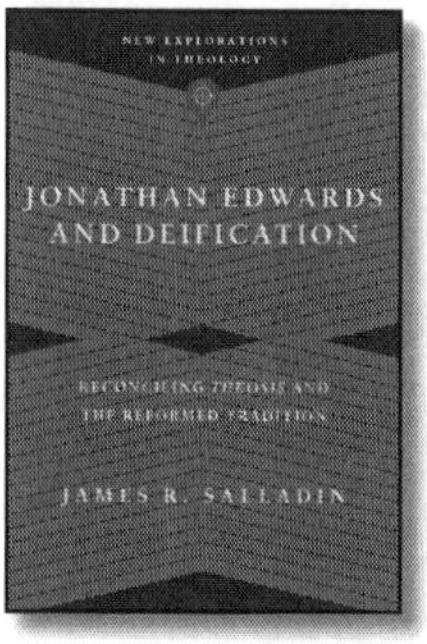

Jonathan Edwards and Deification

Martin Luther and the Rule of Faith

Kierkegaard and the Changelessness of God